INDIA FILE

Inside the Subcontinent

India File is a vivid, candid and moving picture of modern India – a journey through an astonishing land. 'India is a fabulous estate,' Trevor Fishlock writes, 'intricate, subtle, ancient and worn. It is also one of the world's great dramas: a vast and crowded land committed to the most formidably challenging exercise in mass democracy.'

Here is a society of more than 700 million people, growing by a million a month, divided and united by language, caste, religion and regional loyalty. It has been called a functioning anarchy; and it is in many respects an amiable one, of marvellous fluidity and tolerance. But there is also a sombre side, prejudices and heartlessness that lead to cruelty and horror. For westerners, and for Indians themselves, the contradictions can be painful and confusing.

In this detailed portrayal Trevor Fishlock explores these contradictions and much else. He has travelled widely in the Subcontinent, talking not only to the administrators, politicians, police officers, doctors, businessmen and educationists in the mainstream; but also to those on the fringes, the astrologers, bandits and godmen who play their supporting roles on this extraordinary stage.

He examines life, death, love and marriage, crime, religion, corruption, politics, the everyday struggle for survival in the cities and the countryside. He considers how the Indians look at themselves in the media and treat their neighbours throughout the Subcontinent, and ends with the love-hate relationship between Indians and the British. It is a book of strong contrasts, written with compassion and insight, humour and frankness. As the 1983 British Press Award citation said of Trevor Fishlock's reports in *The Times*, his writing reflects 'a deep understanding of the country combined with descriptive powers of a high order.'

OTHER BOOKS BY TREVOR FISHLOCK

Wales and the Welsh (*Cassell*)

Talking of Wales (*Cassell*)

Americans and Nothing Else (*Cassell*)

The State of America (*Murray*)

Trevor Fishlock is a foreign correspondent. He has been a journalist since he joined an evening newspaper in Portsmouth at the age of sixteen and worked as a newsagency reporter before going to *The Times* at the end of 1968. He was based in Wales for several years and became a frequent contributor to radio and television programmes, and a writer and narrator of documentaries. He took up a fellowship in the United States in 1977–78 and worked in London before going to Delhi in 1980 with responsibility for coverage of India, Pakistan, Nepal, Sri Lanka, Bangladesh, Burma and Afghanistan (which he visited clandestinely). In 1983 he won a British Press Award for his outstanding reports from India. He was *The Times* Correspondent in New York for three years from 1983 and in 1986 joined *The Daily Telegraph* as a roving foreign correspondent. His first assignment for the *Telegraph* was to return to India.

INDIA FILE

Trevor Fishlock

JOHN MURRAY

© Trevor Fishlock 1983

First published 1983
by John Murray (Publishers) Ltd
50 Albemarle Street, London W1X 4BD

Paperback edition 1984
New edition 1987

Typeset by Inforum Ltd, Portsmouth
Printed and bound in Great Britain
at The Bath Press, Avon

British Library Cataloguing in Publication Data

Fishlock, Trevor
    India file.
    1. India — Social conditions — 1947–
    I. Title
    954.05'2   HN683.5

    ISBN 0–7195–4389–4

Contents

Illustrations

All photographs were taken by Trevor Fishlock

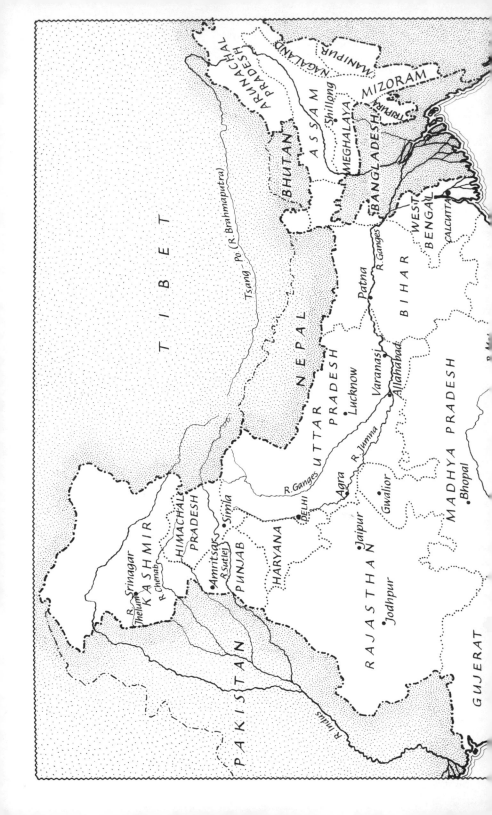

For Penny

Preface

A foreign correspondent in India experiences an authentic adventure – stimulating, absorbing, daunting, sometimes moving and shocking. Here is one of the world's great dramas: an ancient, vast and crowded land committed to the most formidably challenging exercise in mass democracy. It is a spectacle in which hope, pride, paradox and uncertainty mingle and struggle; it is conducted, on the whole, and to India's credit, in the open. It has been fascinating to be a close witness. I cannot recall that the sun has ever set on a dull day.

Correspondents are not always the most welcome of people, but my strong memory is of the hospitality, kindness, good humour and generosity I have been shown everywhere. Indians love to talk about India and each of the hundreds of people I have talked to has revealed something of his country to me. Some of those on whose knowledge I have drawn have become friends as well as teachers, and I am lucky to have had the pleasure of their company.

I wish to thank Kuldip Nayar, Tyler Marshall and Bruce Cleghorn who read parts of the manuscript and made helpful suggestions; and Roger Hudson for his meticulous editing. My wife, Penny, who shared many Indian experiences with me, was my co-worker, rendering scribble into typescript, unflagging even when the fans sighed to a stop in the monsoon.

Delhi   *Trevor Fishlock*
January 1983

A Note on the Second Edition

Much of India is unchanging, or changes only slowly, so that the essential structure of this book remains the same. But there have, in the meantime, been significant changes and I have reworked and extended certain sections to keep pace. Principally, the changes concern the Sikh question, the murder of Mrs Gandhi, and her son's arrival in power.

London
January 1987

Glossary

ADIVASI	a tribal or aboriginal person
AHIMSA	non-violence
ASHRAM	a retreat for study or worship
BABU	rather disparaging term for a clerk or official
BANDH	a general strike
BANYAN	Indian fig tree
BEGUM	courtesy title for married women in Pakistan
CHOWKIDAR	nightwatchman
CRORE	ten million
DACOIT	bandit
DARSHAN	an interview or audience
DERZI	tailor
DHOBI	washerman
DHOTI	white garment wound around the waist and drawn up between the legs
FLEETFOOTS	canvas shoes
GHATS	riverside steps
GHEE	clarified butter used in cooking
GHERAO	to surround a building so that no-one can leave or enter; a form of protest
GURU	spiritual adviser
HARIJAN	child of God, Mahatma Gandhi's word for an untouchable
HARTAL	a local or restricted strike
KHADDI	homespun cloth
KIRPAN	the Sikh's dagger
KOTWALI	police station
KURTA	long shirt, usually worn with pyjama trousers
LATHI	a stave, three or four feet long, carried by police
MORCHA	defiance or a restriction, a form of protest
PAN	betel leaf, sold with a variety of fillings, like areca nut or tobacco, mild stimulant and very popular as a digestive

PEON	messenger
PUJA	worship, prayer, offering to a god
PUKKA	good, genuine; made of brick; real McCoy
SADHU	sometimes a genuine holy man, sometimes a wandering beggar
SHIKAR	hunting, shooting
SWAMI	leader of a caste or religious group
TAMASHA	fuss, disturbance, spectacle
TIFFIN	lunch
TIKKA	dot of paste worn on the forehead by married Hindu women
TONGA	two-wheeled pony cart

1

Inheritance

The new Indian takes up his birthright

> If you wish to know something about India you must empty your
> mind of all preconceived notions. Why be imprisoned by the
> limited vision of the prejudiced? Don't try to compare. India is
> different and, exasperating as it may seem, would like to remain so
> ... This is the secret of India, the acceptance of life in all its
> fullness, the good and the evil.
>
> INDIRA GANDHI

AT LAST the gasping newcomer floats free to take up his inheritance of India. If it is a son there are murmurs and grins
of pleasure. A conch may blare and the midwife's fingers close
over a large reward. If it is a daughter there is neither tip nor
fanfare. Birth is the beginning of what Hindus believe is the soul's
adventure on earth and one of the tutting women around the
nativity notes the time of day, for the family starmonger will want
to know what planetary and stellar forces were tugging when the
cord was severed. This sage will consult his charts and draw up a
horoscopic identity card which will have to be produced by its
owner at life's checkpoints: before his ritual toddler's tonsure,
before marriage, examinations, journeys, a new job, elections,
war, ceremonies, crop sowing, business transactions and other
gambles. Indians embrace the universe and their fated imperish-
able souls move to its mysterious awesome rhythms, out of one life
and into the next, sins and atonements inked in heavenly ledgers.

The astrologers are therefore at hand, like discreet, wise and
reassuring valets, with star charts rather than freshly pressed
trousers. As nothing is accidental, as the universe and all its living
components have a fundamental order, the horoscope is a chart
showing an individual's way to his future and to his past. The
astrologers have their part to play in deciding the auspicious time
for sinking wells, erecting buildings, consummating a marriage,
launching a ship, swearing in prime ministers, calling an election.
They perform tasks large and small. They chose the date of

India's independence. They comfort parents whose sulking sons
have left home by predicting the 'when returning of gone person'.
They suit all pockets and may be found in luxurious suites or
squatting on the spittled pavements. They are there in cities,
towns and hamlets, and in the splendid hotels, along with the
travel agent, bookstall and florist: a service and a crutch, to
help the Indian cope with the labyrinth and uncertainties of his
inheritance.

What a panoply of astonishments his inheritance is: fabulous
estate, intricate, subtle, ancient and worn. It unrolls for 2,000
miles from the ramparts of the Himalaya to the doffing palms of
Comorin. It spreads its broad shoulders 1,700 miles from the
steamy spinach-green edges of China and Burma in the east,
across the burning pan of Rajasthan to the black naked mudflats
of Kutch.

India, said Mrs Gandhi, who travelled it more widely and
more assiduously than any other person, is large, very large, and
not at all easy to understand. She seemed to be saying, as she
inspected me across her teak desk in the parliament building in
Delhi, that the vastness and complexity could only be compre-
hended with the aid of compassion and some humour and much
patience. She smiled, but it was in part a gentle admonition,
formed from the pride that Indians possess, their sensitivity about
their country's portrayal and their recognition of its stark contradictions, the abysses counterbalancing the pinnacles.

Although in sheer size the inheritance is mighty, there is, as
time unreels, less for all. The pie must be tranched into smaller
wedges. When midnight's children were born at the hour of
independence in August 1947, there were 350 million Indians.
Today there are more than twice that number, a sixth of mankind
on a fortieth of the planet's land. There is much labour for
astrologers and midwives as India swells inexorably towards a
billion and beyond, its strength increasing by more than a million
a month. Agricultural fertility has been more than matched by
human fecundity. India also has, incidentally, 176 million cattle, a
quarter of the world's cattle population, and in parts of the
country it is much easier to get medical help for a cow than for a
child.

A generation after midnight, in the fourth decade of independence, numbers alone ensure that the new child will not know
much of the wilderness and unpeopled places. At times he might

imagine that he prizes solitude, but if there were a real prospect of it he would probably avoid it. Numbers apart, his skein of roots, the banyan of extended family, caste, and secretless communal living, will ensure that he does little in isolation. Perhaps the first act for which a young man is entirely and privately responsible is to play the sturdy husband to his nervous wife on their star-ordered marriage night.

The constant rubbing of shoulders, in the home, streets and fields, gives India its distinctive patina. All its joints are worn and its edges smoothed, honed by feet and hands like pilgrims' stairs. Indeed, the true Indian motif is not the Taj Mahal, the elephant or the patient peasant behind the ox-drawn plough. It is the crowd, the ocean of faces in the land of multitudes, endlessly stirring, pushing, moving: as teeming and vigorous and urgent as spermatozoa. It is in this human circulation that one sees India's colour, variety, and hive-like busyness, and senses also its power, vitality and grandeur, its near-inertia, its remorseless glacial movement, as imperceptible and irrevocable as continental drift.

Indians are a tactile people, living thigh by thigh, jostling, rubbing, holding hands and embracing, close to each other's breath and borborgymi, the bubble of each other's pots. They have learned to cram, to take a deep communal breath to admit just one more, to fill every crevice, to hang by their nails, to sit on one buttock, to stretch the seams of their streets, houses and vehicles.

There is no Plimsoll line in India and House Full is a negotiable and elastic term carrying no idea of finality. Like the ferry boats on the Ganges, the country is almost everywhere gunwales down. I have felt myself squeezed like warm wax at religious rites and political festivals.

Safety laws and ideas of danger are bulldozed by the weight of people. Two-wheeled tonga carts, drawn by desperate horses with toast-rack ribs, are piled high with swaying people and lolling babies. Bicycles often carry three. Motor scooters are often seen captained by father, with the eldest son standing in front of him, mother elegantly sidesaddle behind, a daughter clinging to her waist and a baby on her knee. Three pot-bellied men, comical in their gravity, ride by astride a motorcycle. Lorry drivers have three or four companions in the cab and knots of labourers on the back. Cage-carts, drawn by bicycles, are stuffed with little school-children on their way to lessons. If mother, uncle and brother-in-law are not too fat, a car may be able to carry seven or ten. In the cities pedestrians walk in the roads because they are often forced off the pavements by the communities living, sleeping and trading on them. The popular letter-drafting books, which contain specimen letters covering myriad circumstances and predicaments, have letters you can copy to complain of overcrowding on the pavements and in offices.

Buses are jammed, their proprietors packing them like the ruthless masters of slaving ships. At bus stops young men are disgorged from the windows of these ramshackle stinking monsters like weevils abandoning a tapped biscuit. Others scramble in to replace them. Women and children get little quarter. People wait in a mob on the road, eyeing the middle distance like anxious rugby fullbacks awaiting kick-off. Those who cannot get in cling to the outside and perhaps fall off, or are wiped off by other buses. When buses fall into rivers or canals, as they frequently do, the squirming passengers are too tightly jammed to extricate themselves, and the papers publish pictures showing corpses among the melting ice blocks of the morgue, cheek by jowl in death as they were in life.

From the earliest days of railways Indians have ridden on the roofs of packed carriages, free travel of this kind being part of the calculation of cost and mobility among poorer people. Wedding parties ride rooftop, complete with tearful brides, their teeth gritting in the coal smoke. When a train fell off a bridge in Bihar in 1981 hundreds drowned, the carriages swept away like logs, but there could be no accurate death toll because no-one knew how many people had been on the carriage roofs.

In 1982 there was a row in parliament when it was revealed that extra passengers had been squeezed into a full airliner, some having been compressed two to a seat and a brace inserted in the lavatory. 'Indian Airlines Toilet Class', sniggered a newspaper headline.

If you drive through India, or observe it from a train, you will see few parts of it unpeopled. You may stop the car in a seemingly empty space, to drink some water and sleeve the brow, only to find that people emerge, as if from the soil, to watch with curiosity. Once I saw a woman carrying a water jug on her head and, attracted by the grace and symmetry of this solitary figure in a burnt landscape, stopped to photograph her. Within moments the car was encircled by similar graceful figures who arrived like genies, demanded to be photographed and paid, and allowed me to escape only with difficulty. Satyajit Ray, the film maker, recalls that he once began shooting a film in a quiet country location fifty miles from Calcutta. After three days, however, a large and curious crowd arrived by rail from Calcutta and climbed trees to watch the filming. The shooting plan had to be changed, and six spectators were hurt when the branch on which they perched suddenly snapped.

The great Indian crowd the newcomer joins is the second largest in the world and the largest of the democracies, with thrice the population of the United States. On its headed notepaper it describes itself officially as a sovereign democratic socialist secular republic, a union of twenty-three states and eight territories. The democracy is lively, in spite of having had its air supply interrupted for two years from mid-1975. Socialism can hardly be said to have been practised with any determination, and the secular state is profoundly religious. The noble goals and rights of equality, liberation and justice set out in the constitution are cynically ignored by many in the ruling classes and for millions of people will remain unfulfilled.

India has been from ancient times a geographical billiard pocket, a destination and a place of settlement rather than a staging post. Religious as well as physical constraints kept its people inside its boundaries and prevented migration until recent times. Hindus were forbidden to cross the sea, the black water as it was called, the penalty being loss of caste. Mahatma Gandhi boldly defied it when he sailed for England to study law and was ostracized by his caste. This constraint on foreign travel however, could be lifted through rites of purification; and the performance of them enabled Indian soldiers to ship to Europe, and the trenches, in the First World War: the names of thousands who never returned are carved on India Gate in Delhi where people gather to eat ice cream on hot summer nights. The taboo of the black water was smashed long ago and Indians have taken their trading, doctoring, engineering and cooking talents to the world.

In the Indian net there exists an extraordinary heterogeneity, greater than that of Europe, a tapestry of cultures, tongues, diets, deities and dress. And of colours, too. The physical appearance of the people presents a vertical spectrum of shades, Aryan milk poured onto Dravidian chocolate, making India darker in the south, lighter in the north, where paleness is prized.

The state recognizes fifteen major languages; and there are altogether 1,652 mother tongues, so that every state in the union is multilingual. Even Hindi, the official language, the fifth major language of the world after Chinese, English, Russian and Spanish, is not spoken by the majority in the country. English, the most notable legacy of British management, is the common linguistic currency, but it is spoken by only two or three in every hundred and these people have the lion's share in running the country, the greatest influence in politics, culture, administration, industry and education. Along with religion and caste, land and deprivation, language is one of the ingredients of India which is an abrasive, and over which people fight and die.

There are, however, remarkable binding cords, resisting India's numerous centrifugal forces. They are tugged and gnawed but somehow they hold. There is, pre-eminently, the central dynamic of Hinduism, its pervasive religious power and code for living, and the mesh of caste. These forces are inseparable. Caste and religion grind together like gears and their fundamental place and influence in Indian life are not always easy to comprehend.

The framework of caste has existed for more than three thousand years and evolved under the racial, social, occupational and religious pressures of ancient peoples developing their civilization in isolation. For the majority, caste is a watermark, the determining factor in their place in society, providing a matrix of rituals and rules, and in many cases preordaining occupation, political allegiance, choice of bride, dietary habits and social relationships in respect of other castes. There are taboos on mixing and feeding, designed to prevent cross-caste pollution, and a widespread insistence on endogamy, marriage with the caste.

A caste is a complete community, a firm identity, a defence against enemies and difficulties, conferring the benefits of stability and certainty. Caste is so strong that it has seeped into Christian and Muslim communities. A study conducted after a cyclone in 1977 showed that survivors searched first and foremost for their caste-fellows.

The black side of caste is its institutionalizing of prejudice. It has generated a maze of rules and apartheids, plumbing the depths of absurdity and cruelty. Caste overturns reason and justice in a society which often strikes visitors as being long on ruthlessness and callousness and short on compassion. Caste demarcation frequently seems to demand that men humiliate others; and the violence and heaped indignities of caste practices often outrage the sensibilities of westerners and Indians alike. Letters in western newspapers say that India will be justified in criticising South African apartheid when it demolishes the pernicious caste system. And in some respects, of course, India does throw stones from its crystal house, a certain sanctimoniousness being part of the political character. But caste is in India's fibre, inextricably bound up with Hindu ideas of life, rebirth and predestination. Its strength and conservative character are features of Indian endurance, an evolved ordering of a complex society that might otherwise be ungovernable; and perhaps a defence against revolution. It survives partly because it adapts. It is strong and accomodating, yew rather than iron.

There are other unifiers in India, like parliament, the courts, the civil service, railways, the airline, All India Radio, newspapers, the cinema and cricket. There is also an idea of India as an entity. It was a glimmer in the last century, a force in this one, and has developed strongly since independence during which time the country has been mostly under the leadership of the house of Nehru.

There is also, however battered and imperfect, an Indian idea of democracy which is likely to persist, in spite of erosions and shameful assaults, because enough of the people like it and care for it. It enables the ordinary man to feel, on polling day at least, that he is part of some great enterprise and drama. It has become sacred, like the cow, an integral part of the structure. It enhances Indian self-respect, in part because India has retained it while its Muslim neighbours have been unable to sustain it. They envy India for it, and India knows it, hence the loss of face when Mrs Gandhi shelved democracy during the emergency: she took something from the people they valued (to defend it, she said), and when she gave it back they punished her at the polls.

Indians often feel their country is severely rather than generously judged by the western democracies and press. They are proud and sensitive and as far as criticism is concerned are often inordinately touchy, seeming to find offence where none is intended. As a people they take themselves seriously and their sense of humour remains as yet an undeveloped region. They are, however, enthusiastic analysts of their society, bitter and persistent critics of their politics, institutions and each other, as disputatious as starlings.

If India is judged by stringent standards it is because it is large, powerful and a pace setter; and also a repository of hopes. India is a democracy in a developing world which has few of them, and, democracy being a club with strict rules, India is expected to live up to them, to do better than countries with other systems. As a democracy, it is open to inspection; and if that is sometimes painful India should nevertheless be proud of it. Indians feel they do not get enough credit for what they have achieved, and only time and growing confidence will reduce this sense of grievance.

The unifying forces of India show weakness and contradictions. India has always baffled and affronted as well as delighted, and time and modernity have not lessened its paradoxes. Its marvels and achievements stand side by side with its outrages and horrors. All societies exhibit painful contrasts between obverse and reverse, but in India these so often challenge western comprehension and seem to be on a stupendous and dumbfounding scale. On the whole they are not hidden, but are there in full public view.

It is simply that India occupies several centuries at once. Here is a country whose scientific and industrial skills, along with the living standards and styles and manners of some of its people, place it firmly in the 20th century. It can be very exciting, for example, to be a young woman – with good looks, a degree, a doting daddy, parental wealth, blue jeans and a wide horizon. But it is also a society where millions of women are oppressed and, like their men, pass their lives in versions of slavery. That five star hotel through whose marble halls the Delhi or Bombay heiress clicks on Gucci heels en route for the disco or the coffee shop for a creamy cake, is built by her exploited sisters who live under sacks, wash in muddy water, and somehow find time to scoop up their babies and fasten them to their breasts. There are multitudes existing in the sort of wretchedness that made Wat Tyler angry. There are some men who live in splendour, some who exist by raiding the food stores of rats.

Critics in India say the country should not spend huge sums bolstering its self-esteem with space-satellite programmes, Antarctic exploration and huge prestigious public works projects like the Asian Games. 'That's rubbish', a businessman said. 'We will get nowhere if we stop to consider the poor all the time. The Americans did not wait for the poor to catch up when their country was developing, nor should we. India will only improve if we forge ahead on all fronts.'

In the palaces of progress scientists confer in computer jargon. The expended computer tape is borne away on an ox cart. In 1981 bullock carts were used to transport Mig 21 fighters to the Republic Day parade in Delhi.

Air travel is in the 1980s, most cars are in the 1950s and the telephone is in the 1930s. Communications in India could be symbolized by a rocket crossed with a cleft stick. In one of the world's industrial giants, possessing atomic power, the generation of electricity is stuck somewhere in the 1920s, in a bog of corruption, overmanning and inefficiency, and industry and commerce are often illuminated by candles.

The agricultural revolution has been a notable achievement: India feeds a population doubled since 1947. But the ordinary man gets no more to eat now than he did then. Half the people live below the poverty line, defined as a monthly expenditure on food of £3.80 per head in the country, and of £4.40 in urban areas. Much more of the land is under the plough, but the destruction of forests is creating the conditions for a crisis. India is being stripped bare. The country has become an industrial giant on a world scale, and the slums have grown apace. The pool of educated has increased and the number of unemployed has increased faster. But public health has improved. Malaria and the great plagues like cholera no longer devastate, and the mitigation of them is a prime factor in the rapid growth of the population.

While the urban educated raise points of order about democracy, the landlords' thugs and policemen in the countryside thrash those among the poor who dare to talk of rights. Troublesome crowds are dealt with by the application of a Napoleonic whiff of grapeshot, a few bullets from police rifles. 'Two dead in police firing' is a commonplace headline, downcolumn in Indian newspapers.

In the courts of law advocates wear striped trousers, waistcoats, neckbands and gowns, their arguments backed by Halsbury, uttered in the cadences of Gray's Inn. In the cells of the country's awful prisons lie tens of thousands of men, women and children who have been waiting years to come to trial while lawyers spout. There are people fettered and forgotten under a tottering system of justice, an enduring indictment.

The new Indian today takes up his inheritance of a country where dreams that bubbled in the wake of independence have remained to a large extent unfulfilled. The unity and sense of purpose that fuelled the push for freedom, and made the years of struggle and transition seem a golden age (as it was), have faded. The fizz has flattened. All of the good intentions of Nehru's 'tryst with destiny', of making the people literate, better housed, bigger consumers, better fed and watered, less the victims of their own fecundity, of mitigating the cruelties so many endure, have been corroded.

More than three-quarters of the people have been born since independence. 'Freedom fighter dies' is a headline frequently in the newspapers, recording the passing of those jailed by the British in the struggle for a free India. Nevertheless there are still millions of Indians who remember independence as a new dawn, when Mahatma Gandhi's moral force and Nehru's ambition for his country combined in what seemed an unquenchable flame. Nehru suffered setbacks, but did not live to see widespread disillusion. Since his death Indians have been ambushed by shadows, confronting with increasing dismay the realities and harsh paradoxes of their land, the sordidness of politics, the rule of greedy and endomorphic satraps, the spreading fungus of corruption, and inherent cruelty and brutality which persist unabated. The hopes of Gandhi and Nehru have been swiftly overwhelmed and a generation after midnight there is profound disappointment that so much seems ill-ordered: politics, policing, poverty and population. Breasts are beaten, hands wrung, the nation's chiefs call futilely for discipline and neither they nor the people know what they mean.

Most of the inheritors of India are likely to live their lives in a manner that would be familiar to their distant ancestors, yoked to the land as labourers and share croppers and farmers, their existence governed by the rhythms of monsoons and the planting and harvesting of crops, their speed paced to that of oxen. These people are India's constant, her human bedrock, who have, for thousands of years lived the same lives, worn the same clothes, steered the same ploughs, fought the same feuds, lived in the same dwellings, bowed their heads to the same oppressions and the same jobs. India has been conquered and reconquered, ruled by moghuls, rajahs, Britons and modern politicians, fought over and fought for, while the vast mass of people have endured, almost unchanging, and for the most part uninvolved, unconsidered, unrevolutionary, unschooled, passive and almost mute.

More than seven-tenths of the people depend on farming for their living. Only in recent times have the towns and cities swelled to create a significantly large industrial and commercial urban population. The villages remain the root, and there are 576,000 of them, less than half with electric light and many without road access. The steady seeping of education, of health measures, of power and communications have brought improvement to the lives of many of them, but better health care, population control and decent drinking water are needs that remain pressing and in some places desperate.

Literacy is low, especially in village India. Only one woman in four and less than half the men can read. In spite of enormous strides made in education, the number of illiterates has increased, there being 130 million more than at the time of independence, with women trailing far behind men. More than a third of the world's illiterates live in India, so that a goal enshrined in the constitution, of free and compulsory education for all up to the age of fourteen, remains distant. It is a common sight in town and country to see a boy or young man who can read, surrounded by a small group as he quotes from a newspaper.

The infant mortality rate of 129 per 1,000 is one of the highest in the world and compares with 56 in China, 92 in Brazil, 28 in Russia and 14 in Britain and the United States. Life expectancy is officially put at 54 years, but is probably lower than that. It is one of the lowest in the world, about the same as in the United States at the turn of the century.

The fact that women may expect shorter lives than men says something about the treatment of girls and women in a society where custom, religion and economic demands place strong emphasis on the male. There are 24 million fewer females than males largely because of the tradition of discrimination against women and girls, who are seen as a burden and a future debt.

To a man on the land sons are workers as well as inheritors

and strengtheners of the all-important family. A son also has a religious function, for he is required to light his father's funeral pyre to ensure the best send-off for the soul. A son will grow up in awe of his sire, for the father in India is a powerful figure, chief of the joint family, and respect for him is often strongly accentuated. Sometimes pater-worship becomes an almost grovelling deference.

The new Indian is more likely than not to be a Hindu, one of the 582 million and 83 per cent majority. He might also be one of the substantial Muslim minority of 77 million; or one of 14 million Sikhs, so busy and distinctive that there seems to be more of them than that; 18 million Christians, who will cook both beef and bacon; 3.5 million Jains who would not hurt a fly; or 5 million tolerant Buddhists, a mere splinter of the great faith in the land of its birth. He stands a one in twelve chance of being born into one of the aboriginal tribes which inhabit forests and remote regions, and which are gradually being drawn into the mainstream; and a one in ten chance of being a Brahmin, the upper crust of society; and a one in seven chance of being born into the community of those Hindus whose place is, strictly speaking, outside the caste structure and who are graded as untouchables, also known as harijans, Mahatma Gandhi's appellation, meaning god's children, which has done nothing to improve their treatment.

There are 100 million of them, and it is in their ranks that one finds many of India's poor, maltreated, bullied, enslaved and deprived. It is they who feature in the routine small change of brutality recorded in the daily newspapers . . . 'Harijan beheaded' – 'Two harijan women raped' – 'Harijan village burned: seven dead' . . . small items easy to miss if you read the papers in a hurry. These are the people who sell themselves into bonded labour, in their ignorance and desperation, who work without pay, or for a pittance, for the farmers, landlords, construction bosses and the coalfield mafia.

The rights of the harijans and so-called backward classes are stated in the constitution and the law, their protection and advancement are among the most noble of India's ideals. Their long slow march is part of the dynamic of developing India and one of the areas in which the country smoulders and occasionally blazes. Untouchables are both the beneficiaries and the victims of the spread of enlightenment and democracy, for their assertion of rights and their accretion of knowledge disturbs an old order; and the prospect of change is regarded with resentment and resisted with violence.

The question of the poor is sensitive, for Indians believe, and rightly, that life has steadily improved for many millions and will continue to do so. They object to western representations of their home as a land of abject poverty and resent the cameras' lingering on the hopeless rock-bottom poor with the suggestion that this is all of India and that India does not care. They do not mind examinations and representations *of* poverty, but they bristle when their country is represented *by* it.

They point to other Indias: the colleges, steel mills, factories, chemical plants, mines, towers of commerce, nuclear power, science establishments and the space programme, the nuts and bolts of a major industrial and business country. They feel that the west does not give India enough credit for its achievements.

Although, statistically speaking, the new Indian is likely to be born into a poor farming family, the growth of education and economic opportunity provides an increasing possibility of improvement. He can aspire to be a commerce rajah, founding a new dynasty like the Birlas and Tatas, the great business families of India. He can hope to run an hotel empire, or prosper as a merchant or factory owner; or be a well-off farmer, perhaps in Punjab, with tractors and other machines, and a twice-a-year trip from Amritsar to Birmingham to see how his relations are doing. He might be a doctor with British and American degrees on his surgery wall, and the status symbol of an imported car; or a professor, an engineer or a high flier in the civil service, with Scotch whisky in his cupboard (preferably Johnny Walker and Chivas Regal, for these have cachet, and Indian drinkers are label conscious).

He might have a position in a firm, or be one of those tireless and patient businessmen with glass fibre briefcases to be found beginning their migrations early in the morning at the dismal airports in Delhi, Bombay, Calcutta or Madras, enduring waiting room seating made of unyielding plastic (instead of cheap, indigenous, comfortable cane), apparently designed by an ergonomist with a grudge against humanity; and lighting that might have been installed by a conspiracy of opticians wanting business.

In pursuit of fortune or fame the new Indian might enter the film industry, the largest in the world. If a man aspiring to stardom he will have a rather overfed handsomeness like that of a spoilt only son; if a woman, she will tend to the Rubensesque voluptuous and will spend much of her career getting wet, the soaked sari being the acme of modern Indian eroticism.

The newcomer might also join the million who make up the largest standing army in the world. India is proud of its might and there is no cavilling at the cost of maintaining it. The profession of arms is admired and respected in a country that once made a reputation for non-violent protest. The martial strain is vigorous, and the traditional fighting peoples from the warring north, the Rajputs, Punjabis and Sikhs, are well represented in the forces. So are Gurkhas from Nepal.

Mahatma Gandhi wanted the Indian national flag to bear the device of a spinning wheel, with its connotation of humility, the development of spiritual resources and self-sufficiency, the symbol of his philosophy and campaign of non-violence. But such a symbol was hardly likely to appeal in a country of ancient martial tradition and great size and power, with neighbours to consider, and its assertive way to make in the world. Instead India chose Ashoka's wheel for its tricolour, badge of a warrior emperor's might. For its national emblem it took the leoglyph of Ashoka, a fist made from four lions sitting back to back.

Whatever he chooses, an Indian with even a little education will hope to occupy a 'position'. India is a community of hierarchies, rigidly stratified, and a position is of great importance. It is more than a question of social standing: it is a matter of living up to family expectations and of falling in with one's dharma, the way of life ordered by the fates. That is why there is so much cheating in examinations: failure cannot be afforded. There is no alternative to success. Examinations are a way of reaching a position, of satisfying economic, social and dharma demands, and are not seen as a process of sieving. Students and their parents therefore pay large sums to secure previews of examination questions, or 'help' with having the final papers marked.

Position enables a man to wield power and to assert his place in a hierarchy. Any progress in India involves treating with people in positions.

Their work may be irrelevant but their mark has to be made during a transaction before one can proceed to the next stage. A man's lot in life may be to rubber stamp a document or chit: he does not need to read it, he merely has to stamp it. By stopping in front of him you recognize his existence and position. His power is that of a tripwire or a pin on a bagatelle board.

When you cross the frontier between Pakistan and India you have to show your passport eight times on the Indian side, and often you have to queue to be examined by a single harassed customs officer while his colleagues smoke and do nothing. At Bombay airport you present your boarding pass to a young woman at a table and she stamps it. This serves no purpose. There are two other young women alongside her doing nothing. It is the same throughout the subcontinent: the bureaucratic warrens are overrun by clerks with little or nothing to do. Americans tell me it is all the fault of the British. But if the British gave it the Indians embraced it.

'Please sit down. What is your good name. This will take some time. You will have tea? There is no problem. We will expedite. Please be comfortable. There is no problem at all. Mr Bannerji? He is not in his seat. He is out of station. He is on tour. The first money has been consumed, so you must pay again. This will take some time. But there is no problem.'

A public servant does not necessarily think his position involves service to the public. The superciliousness of a clerk, the arrogance of an official, the way that deskmen push citizens around are the underlining of hierarchical position. Position is often looked on as a lever for making money in corrupt ways, which is one reason it is sought. A uniform does not necessarily remind its wearer of his obligations or convey an idea of service. It often seems to serve as a licence for rudeness, persecution and extortion, so that uniformed public servants are often not the object of respect, but of contempt and fear.

Humanity, however, can shine through. I once had to leave India in a hurry after receiving a message about my father's serious illness. As luck would have it I was carrying a newly-issued passport which did not contain the stamp attesting to my earlier arrival in India. The airport official gave a withering look.

'You cannot leave the country. There is no entry stamp in your passport. Therefore you have not arrived. As you have not arrived you cannot be permitted to leave.'

He pushed the passport back at me. It was a bad moment in the sweaty small hours at Delhi airport. I showed him the cable with the message about my father's illness. He changed from a bloody-minded functionary into a human. He opened my passport and applied the appropriate exit stamp.

'There is no problem. At such a time a son's place is with his father.'

The bureaucracy in India is exalted and wondrous to behold. There is a monstrous surfeit of cheap labour and jobs have to be halved and quartered. If you buy a shirt there will be one man to sell it, another to wrap it, another to take the money, another to give the change and receipt and perhaps another to bang the stamp at the end of the process. In commerce it is probably harmless, but in administration the bureaucracy is a sargasso. For a vision of a kind of hell I can think of nothing better than the Writers' Building in Calcutta, with its vast gloomy halls of serried desks whose occupants look up, blinking, like disturbed moles; its carrels of clerkery and great mouldering mounds and stacks of files all crumbled at the edges, charred looking, as if rescued from a fire long ago; and, withal, the smell of ink, dust and old, old paper.

Bureaucratic inertia is a way of life as well as a national problem. Plans and people get lost in the morass. Prisoners decay without hope in jail because the machinery has rusted and few are much inclined to do anything about it. The mentally sick lie forgotten for years.

At higher levels too the decision makers are left feeling they are swimming in custard. Even the Hindi phrase books have all the required sentences:

'Unnecessary procrastinated correspondence has wasted so much time.'

'Those who are conversant with the difficulties of the matter would never press for hustling it.'

'There has been unusual delay.'

'This is not under us.'

Over the years India has been unable to make use of all the money it has been offered in aid simply because some of the plans for spending it have been left hanging on bureaucracy's barbed

wire. Indecision runs as a distinctive thread in India's independent history, and it has always started at the top. Indians recognize
the failure all too acutely. That is why the emergency was
welcomed by some, as a way of knifing through the knot: the
seductive and facile course which has always appealed to impatient authoritarians.

Everyone knows that when the right people give the right
orders India can move quickly. Many foreign businessmen have
been impressed by the shrewdness and knowledge of Indian
negotiators, the imagination of designers and planners and the
inventiveness of engineers.

I spent weeks dealing with the bureaucracy when I first arrived
in India, attempting to get a document which had some relevance
to my work. I dealt with a courteous official who played me along,
wasting his time and mine, until at last I mentioned the matter to
his superior. In my presence the wretched official was called in,
asked to explain and when he could not he was admonished. His
superior uttered the dreadful and wonderful word of Indian
executive action: 'Expedite!'

The document was in my hands in half an hour.

By shouting 'Expedite!' Indian leaders can achieve much. As I
write, builders and engineers and designers are creating records
in building stadiums, hotels, roads and bridges for the Asian
Games in Delhi. Four or five years' work is being compressed
into two. It is a feat by any standard. (Why it all had to be done in
such a rush is another matter.) In India the eleventh hour often
seems to be soon enough. I remember that when the Prince of
Wales arrived at a sports ground in Delhi, to play polo, a huge
hoarding offering him a welcome was still being hammered into
place. The first time I went to a wedding I arrived on time and was
the only person there: the other guests arrived an hour later and
the event began an hour after that. Cinemagoers often arrive as
late as halfway through the film. Sometimes, of course, the
eleventh hour is too late. Mrs Gandhi was called to open a bridge
across the Ganges in 1982 and the event was advertised in the
newspapers as a triumph, complete with tributes to the gallant
workers who had been killed, sacrifices to the god-river. Unfortunately the structure was incomplete, there being a large gap in

the middle that would have tested Evel Knievel. Mrs Gandhi was photographed looking unamused.

Foreigners can find such episodes exasperating, along with other aspects of Indian performance and character. A few years ago a British diplomat wrote a paper for private circulation in which he concluded that dishonesty and incompetence were a product of Hinduism. It leaked out and was published. It was of no importance and expressed a personal opinion, but it generated furious letters in the press. I do not think Hinduism has much or anything to do with dishonesty. Hindus want to prosper, and are enjoined to, but that does not have to involve dishonesty. Such things cannot be measured, but I would suppose that Indians are as greedy, venal, and fish-hook-fingered as most other people; they are also as fair and honest, as competent and incompetent. We judge them by our own standards, not theirs. They give priority to family or group over the broader interests of society; and while this is merely human, rather than Indian, it does water the ground for corruption in the Indian context.

Enforcement of laws and regulations is less efficient than in many other societies; and society is less well ordered so that those who should be above reproach, civil servants, policemen and others, are badly paid and badly supervised, and encouraged to rely on graft. Corruption has many roots – greed, need and cynicism among them – but Hinduism is not one of them.

Nor do I believe that Hinduism is a magic well, a source of knowledge or enlightenment unavailable elsewhere. Those skinny, scabby westerners in pink gowns, looking like prawns drifting through India in search of rainbows' ends, are unlikely to find anything they could not discover at home. India is material-istic rather than mystical, as the bank managers of gurus will testify.

There is much about India, however, that a westerner cannot know and cannot see.

He may get a distorted view in brief visits in which he is charmed by the colour, variety and drama, and by generous and hospitable people. But he can have only an inkling of the dimen-sions of the problems and no way of measuring the achievements.

For his part, the Indian taking up his inheritance in the last fifth of the 20th century arrives at a time when much has been accom-plished, but when there is disappointment that there has not been more. History may show that advantage was not taken of the many years of post-independence political stability. The green revolution can produce more grain to feed more people, but it cannot build the schools, hospitals and roads and create the jobs that the new millions will need. Such failings as there have been in, for example, industrialization, production, communications and power supply, might not be the basis of grave threats in ordinary circumstances. But India lies under the shadow of a phenomenal population growth, about which little has been done. This will increase economic pressures and intensify social rivalries and antagonisms in a future time when political authority may not be as complete and unchallenged as it is now. No-one can be certain that the swelling multitude of the poor and passive will always be uncomplaining. The signs of restlessness are there. The people behind the dam are being enlightened by education and politics and acquaintance with urban living. They are stirring. But the political structure has been changed and weakened and there must be doubts about its ability to accommodate new pressures.

Although much of the idealism of the post-independence years has withered, India remains united and a democracy, shaping democracy to its own unique circumstances. These are good reasons for optimism. But in the fourth decade after midnight India is aware that it has not made the best use of the foundation-digging years. There is a sense of future ambush. The shadows seem somehow inkier.

2

Girl for ardent boy

Marriage, money, love and sex

Woman, you are blest!

RABINDRANATH TAGORE

THERE WAS a story in the morning newspaper about a drunken bridegroom in Delhi. He and his friends had fortified themselves before the ceremony and arrived in an excited condition. The bride's family was furious and its senior male representatives went to their counterparts in the bridegroom's family to remonstrate. The wretched bridegroom was sacked on the spot. But both sides needed to save family honour. Fortunately there were several young single men at the wedding and a likely bachelor on the bridegroom's side was selected. His income, family background and prospects were swiftly vetted and, it may be assumed, his horoscope was also checked. He fitted the bill and was, moreover, sober. The marriage went ahead with the reserve, and one can only guess at the feelings of the bride.

I was reading this on the plane heading south over the brilliant beaches of the Malabar coast to Mangalore. The Boeing swooped in over lush green and hilly country, dotted with pastel-coloured houses with red tiled roofs, and landed on a flattened hilltop rather as if on an aircraft carrier. The landscape in this part of India is attractive and ordered: paddy fields with low mud walls and terracing dictate neatness. The air has the distinctive southern smell of coconut and blossom, and the wooded hills and palm groves of the region contribute to a softness which is in contrast to the flat, blasted and harsher northern plains.

On the way out of Mangalore I stopped to watch a woman making bidis as she sat on the steps of her cottage. Bidis are thin cigarettes, made from a rolled green leaf enclosing a sprinkle of tobacco inside, and their pungent smell is part of India's array of odours. They are sold in bundles of twenty-five for about five pence. The woman worked with a basket of leaves sent from Madhya Pradesh and a tin of tobacco, deftly rolling each leaf and sealing both ends with a sort of marlinspike, tying the bidi with a piece of pink cotton. From time to time she looked up to keep an eye on her children and to watch her husband working with two glistening buffalo, knee deep in a paddy field. She said she could make 1,000 bidis a day and supplement the family's daily income by seven rupees. She smiled. 'We can have better clothes.' In many families bidi manufacture is the main source of income.

I drove on to Dharmastala, forty miles from Mangalore, in the hills of the Western Ghats. There was a large, buzzing, good tempered crowd gathered outside the temple. It was very hot and the bare-armed people felt like warm toffee.

'There is very much of marriaging here today', a man said, by way of explanation. 'This is our famous day of mass marriage, of which you must have heard. Today more than 600 will be turned into husbands and wives.'

Marriage for millions of Indian families is a dreaded financial burden, a cause of debt and debt bondage and a contributor to misery. In some regions and among some classes the marriage of a daughter is the loss of a pair of working hands and parents demand a bride-price in compensation from the bridegroom's family; but more usually a bride is expected to bring a dowry. On top of this expense, parents try as a matter of honour to stage weddings on a lavish scale. The wealthy can meet such expense, and rich men will welcome the opportunity to dazzle their friends and pour away some black money, the money they do not declare to the taxman. But poor men marrying their children may have to borrow and take on debts that will shadow their lives, forcing some to become bonded labourers, a species of slave.

The temple at Dharmastala has an 800-year tradition of charity and social service, and mass marriage was started here in 1972 as a way of ending the financial burden of marriage ritual while providing the dignity and sanction of a 'proper' wedding to enable the participants and their families to keep face. Indeed the marriages cost the participants nothing. The temple provides all: a sari and blouse for each bride, a dhoti and shirt for each groom, the music, the paraphernalia of ritual, dinner for twenty guests per couple, and the silver and gold necklace which, in southern India, is the equivalent of a wedding ring. When I arrived the couples were queueing to receive their wedding clothes from the leader of the temple, known as Heggade, or chieftain.

Stewardship of the temple has been passed through one family, from father to son, for 600 years, and the present leader is Veerendra Heggade, an amiable economics and politics graduate, who was twenty when he succeeded his father in 1968. He is regarded as the voice and representative of the god Manjunatheswara. When he had finished distributing the wedding clothes, he came over to talk.

'I started mass marriages because people were coming to the temple asking for loans to pay bride-price or wedding costs, and being poor they had no hope of re-paying the money. It was wrong that the temple should be a money lender when its tradition is charity. Mass marriage is a way of freeing people from debt and unhappiness, but it would not work if it had no status. Marriage is so important that it must have a sense of occasion: it may be free but it must never appear cheap. The temple bestows the status.'

Out in the gardens brides and grooms were putting on their wedding clothes with the help of friends. It was like a scene backstage, before curtain-up. The men crowned themselves with large pink turbans, and the girls pinned flowers into their hair, eyeing themselves seriously in little mirrors. When they were ready they gathered in a square and a band played raucously, with curly sousaphones and trumpets blaring and drums thundering. Two temple elephants with red painted brows and bells on their feet were prodded by mahouts into a ponderous avuncular dance. The brides and grooms watched gravely. They were very young, early marriage being both a tradition and the desire of parents. The girls were shy and looked down, and seemed to wish they could hide. The young men looked nervous.

After the elephants had curtseyed the couples set off in procession to get married. Caste considerations were set aside as brahmins and untouchables, along with more than sixty castes in between, walked together. But they settled down under awnings in caste groups, so that the differences in caste rituals could be more easily observed. Small variations in the composition of the material in the wedding fires, for example, had to be respected. The air was filled with the scent of blossoms and the smell of burning sandalwood. Heggade, clad in white dhoti and shirt gave each bridegroom a mangalsutra, the wedding necklace a woman wears while her husband lives; and precisely at 6.46 pm, the time chosen by the temple astrologers as the most auspicious for the joining of fortunes, 323 grooms placed the necklaces around the bowed bare necks of the girls.

There was a sudden sense of relief. The trumpets blared and the couples and their thousands of relatives and friends surged away in a rush of noise for a wedding feast in the temple halls. The wedding guests squatted in long lines, with fresh leaves on the floor in front of them and servers scuttled up and down doling out rice and curry from steel buckets onto their leaf-plates. In the kitchens women with wooden shovels bent like stokers over bunkers of rice, and men ladled curry from huge copper vats.

It was the height of the wedding season, the moon and stars in happy agreement, and it was impossible to travel anywhere without encountering noisy bands, gangs of boys earning a few rupees for holding flaring oil lamps aloft, grooms astride white horses while around them their friends danced in the streets. I reached Jaipur one evening to find the main streets full of wedding parties in procession, decorated elephants, bobbing lights, excited people moving to the thud of drums while pop-cheeked trumpeters tried their best to make the city's pink walls go the way of Jericho's.

In Delhi I attended a Sikh wedding, removing my shoes and covering my head with a white cloth. The groom sat on the floor waiting for his bride. He was straight-backed and handsome. His saffron turban was decorated with gold thread, he wore a long ivory silk coat and clutched a curved sword, symbol of his determination to protect his wife, and a reminder of the fighting traditions of the Sikhs.

The bride was a Hindu, but her family agreed that the wedding should be in accordance with Sikh rites. The focus of a Hindu wedding is a fire, symbolic of the god of truthfulness, but the centre of a Sikh marriage is a flowered canopy under which reposes the Guru Granth Sahib, the holy book of the Sikhs. A priest in white sat behind the book and three men in black turbans played squeezebox organs and gently chanted hymns. This went on for an hour, and then the bride appeared. She looked as fragile as she was beautiful, hung about with jewelry and wrapped in silk, so that as she walked she tinkled and rustled like a Christmas tree. She wore a pink dress over pink pantaloons. On her forehead was a gold disc and her nose was pierced by a gold ring, as fine as a hair, with a small jewel suspended from it. There were heavy necklaces at her throat and her wrists were laden with bangles.

Her hands and feet were decorated with painted designs, and silver rings gleamed on her toes.

A saffron scarf was placed around the groom's shoulders and one end was given to the bride. The priest began to read from the holy book and after a while the couple rose and walked slowly around the canopy, the bridegroom bearing his sword, the bride walking behind clutching the saffron scarf. They made three circuits of the book and exchanged rings: now they were married. (Hindus make circuits of a fire.) They ate a handful of ritual food, which tasted like marzipan, and people pressed forward to shower them with rose petals. They sat on a carpet of petals and their parents placed garlands around them and kissed their heads. More people arrived with garlands and soon the pair were swamped with flowers. The bride's nervousness evaporated and she began to laugh. Her friends began to cry, their tears falling onto the rose petals.

The couple had known each other as children. He had gone abroad to study and to work and returned to India, a qualified doctor, seeking a wife. He was delighted to find that his childhood friend was free, now 19 and pretty. She was his choice, but the formalities of the union and the question of suitability were left to the parents.

Most marriages in India are arranged by parents, and in general young men and women do not have to concern themselves with finding a mate, a burden they are quite happy to be relieved of. It is much as Lady Bracknell said, in *The Importance of Being Earnest*: 'When you do become engaged to someone, I, or your father, should his health permit him, will inform you of the fact. An engagement should come on a young girl as a surprise, pleasant or unpleasant, as the case may be. It is hardly a matter that she could be allowed to arrange for herself . . .'

Courtship and dating are practised only by a very small, although increasing, middle-class minority. Many men and women meet for the first time on their wedding day, but in the middle and educated class there is a tendency for a young man and his intended bride to meet on several occasions beforehand. The great majority of Indian brides are virgins on their wedding day, a most important attribute, and parents seeking a husband for their daughter will often advertise her mint condition in the newspapers.

Westerners raised in societies where love marriage is the rule are intrigued by arranged marriage, although arranged marriage, in some form or other, has been common even in societies where free choice is now practised, to create alliances between families royal, political and commercial.

The marriage of the Prince of Wales in 1981 had elements familiar to Indians. He had, quite properly, to accept the constraints of his position and marry in accordance with his dharma, his responsibility and role in life. He could not permit himself to fall cap over spurs for just anyone: his great-uncle, Edward VIII, strayed from his dharma and inevitably lost his throne. The Prince of Wales's marriage had to a large extent to be an arranged one. His bride had to be a virgin, and capable of bearing children, facts announced in the newspapers. She also had to be attractive, and of the prince's caste, the landed gentry. (Out-of-caste marriages still make news in Britain. The union of an earl's daughter with a lorry driver will always provide newspapers with a story.)

As a rule Indian marriages are not merely the union of two people, but a linking of families, clans and groups. Parents take pains to find compatible partners within the usual social requirements. They look for what any parent would look for, an attractive and decent character. Love is regarded as an unreliable basis on which to begin a marriage and is an emotion which is expected to develop. Perfect physical specimens are hoped for, but, as advertisements indicate, a flaw is often admitted. Parents ensure that the couple's stars are not at odds. An astrologer in Delhi told me that on several occasions he had observed that a couple's horoscopes had shown trouble ahead, and on his advice the proposed marriages had been abandoned.

Parents do their match-making through personal contacts, marriage agencies and newspaper advertisements. In the country the barber is the traditional match-maker, as well as confidant, and his equivalent in the town is the agency which advertises in the newspapers or employs people to daub its telephone number on suitable walls. The fashionable and expensive clubs, resorts of the cities' gentry, are places where nubile women and young men are taken by their parents to be discreetly paraded and considered.

Sunday editions of newspapers like the *Hindustan Times* and the *Times of India* are especially instructive:

WANTED: Girl for ardent boy, 28 years, 171cms, from middle class family, executive multinational company, caste no bar.

WANTED: Match for handsome teetotaller, 165cms, 54kg, executive in good company. Girl should be exceptionally beautiful, slim, homely, convent educated.

WANTED: Really beautiful virgin for handsome, good lecturer, only son, parents with high four-figure income.

WANTED: Match for beautiful 26 years, 160 cms divorcee girl (marriage dissolved due to impotence of husband and only lasted three months).

A WELL ESTABLISHED Gursikh family having flourishing property business wants a suitable bride for Gursikh boy, their only son, 29 years, running independent carpet business. Boy uses artificial limb for left hand but can do entire work.

WANTED: suitable match for Kapoor girl aged 25 from respectable family, girl a little bulky.

WANTED: Handsome Kerala Catholic Bodybuilder Boy of 27 drawing 6,000 rupees invites alliance from parents of Catholic working girls around 25. Young pretty Kerala Catholic BSc nurse with name Mary preferred.

WANTED: Matrimonial alliance for girl MA, 24 years, 161cms, slim, tall, wheatish, beautiful, homely, unnoticeably hard of hearing, otherwise normal, proposals from minor handicapped boys from decent families with details of shortcomings invited.

OPPORTUNITY to live princessly life that every girl dreams of and sees in movies. Details invited from young, cultured, beautiful, sincere, preferably doctor ladies for successful Bombayite US citizen . . .

Advertisements sometimes state that no dowry is being offered. But a phrase like 'decent marriage promised' will make it clear that a dowry will be negotiated. Originally a dowry was a woman's wealth, a gift from her parents; usually some gold, jewelry and clothing, a kind of trousseau, enabling a woman to have some wealth in her own right and to have something to pass on to her daughters.

But dowry has today become for many a matter of business. Wedding ceremonies enable men to display their wealth and standing in public, and dowries are part of the exhibition. A man might spend £15,000 or more on the wedding feast, and will boast about the expense, and spend as much again on the dowry.

While rich men order up lavish banquets in marble palace hotels, poorer men have to scrimp and borrow to raise the required dowry and to put on as handsome a show as possible. Giving and receiving of a dowry is forbidden under the Dowry Prohibition Act of 1961, but it is almost impossible to prove an offence in which giver and receiver conspire. The dowry flourishes because of its part in social and religious tradition, in family pride, and consciousness of social position. It is also sustained by greed. Although illegal it is hardly covert. No one openly encourages, but many connive, and it is as widely condoned as condemned. As the *Indian Express* commented in 1982: 'The law holds no terror for dowry vultures.'

Mahatma Gandhi once said that 'any man who makes dowry a condition for marriage discredits his education and his country and dishonours womanhood. Young men who soil their fingers with such ill-gotten greed should be excommunicated from society.'

Many Indians agree that dowry is deplorable because it can lead to impoverishment, humiliation, and, as we shall see, to violence, misery and murder. The tradition, however, is unlikely to be shaken quickly because enough people want to retain it or can see no way out of it.

A number of things dictate the dowry's size. The better a young man's education the larger the dowry that may be commanded. The spread of education has strengthened the hold of dowry. There is virtually a sliding scale: a graduate of a British or American university, a doctor, an engineer, a well-placed civil servant or professional man, can think of receiving a dowry of £30,000 or so. A man resident in Britain or the United States who returns to India to find a bride can also expect a handsome dowry. 'Green card holder' is a fly commonly played over the waters, a green card being the permit to settle in America. But the qualifications of bridegrooms and brides are not the only consideration. As the advertisements illustrate, match-making parents will want to know about the financial and business standing of other parents, and brothers and uncles, too.

An uneducated boy is obviously worth much less, but a bright office boy can trade on his position to call for a dowry of £1,000 or £2,000. In the middle reaches of society a young man might demand a car as part of the deal, or a television set, or a motor scooter. Lower down the scale a bicycle might be expected. For his part, a girl's father can talk of his daughter's comeliness,

homeliness, purity, educational qualifications and fair skin. A
light complexion is a most desirable quality in a colour conscious
society, and many girls are advertised as being of a 'wheatish'
colour. But a girl's pale beauty will never be enough on its own for
a father with an eligible son and an eye for a large dowry.

Defenders of dowry say it allows people to climb society's
ladders. A well-educated boy from a modest home can get a good
cash settlement with which to start his married life. A graceful
and beautiful girl can attract a captain of industry and move up a
rung, if her father can put together a large enough dowry.

'Look at it my way,' a businessman in Delhi said. 'It cost me a
lot to educate my son. Schooling is expensive and you have to lay
out some money to get your boy into a college. There are not
enough college places and you have to pull strings. Now that the
boy is qualified, and we are looking for a wife for him, I'll want a
dowry, not just because it's the custom, but because it will give me
some recompense for all I've spent. The father of the sort of girl
we have in mind will be able to afford it.'

In the ordinary course of events dowry is paid and the couple
live happily ever after. But for many people dowry is a poison in
their lives. Thousands go to moneylenders to raise cash for a
wedding and a dowry and their lives are never the same again.
Countless families are ruined. A man will feel himself cursed, and
certainly burdened, if he has too many daughters. An old poem
goes

> Let no one be born,
> But if one must,
> Let no one be a girl.

In the mainstream of Indian society girls are less highly
regarded. They are at the back of the queue for food and medical
help, so that there are fewer of them than men and their expectation of life is lower than men's.

The ability of doctors to determine the sex of a child in the
womb, a by-product of amniocentesis, was exploited by a clinic in
Amritsar in 1982 which offered its services to parents with too
many daughters. In a circular to doctors the clinic wrote: 'Most
prospective couples in quest of a male child, as the social set up in
India demands, keep on giving birth to a number of female
children, which not only enhances the population but also leads to
a chain reaction of many social, economic and mental stresses . . .
sex determination has come to our rescue and can help in keeping

some check over the accelerating population as well as giving relief to the couples requiring a male child . . . Assessment of the foetus sex has been made possible after completion of the 16th week and up to the 20th week of pregnancy when abortion is medically feasible and legally permissible.' The fee for sex determination was about £30. The clinic did not itself perform abortions; but abortion is, in any case, readily available in India.

Unfortunately, dowry agreements are not always neatly tied. Sometimes a girl's family does not, or cannot, pay all that is required; or the husband's family applies pressure so that a dowry becomes a drip-feed of money and goods rather than a once and for all payment. Dowry has become a form of extortion. A wedding ceremony in Delhi in 1982 was interrupted when the bridegroom's family heard that the bride's father had just made a large profit in a business deal. They asked for a share of it to be added to the dowry. The businessman agreed and the wedding was resumed. A cartoon in the *Hindustan Times* showed a bride entering her in-laws' home. She was depicted in their minds' eye as a parcel of rupees labelled dowry.

The exploitation and pressuring of young married women in respect of dowry is part of the phenomenon known as bride burning. An extraordinarily large number of young wives have ended their lives by immolating themselves with kitchen-stove paraffin, and a number have been murdered by their in-laws and their bodies burnt. In 1981, in Delhi alone, more than 500 women were burnt to death in their homes. Some were accidental deaths, but notes and other evidence have shown that many girls ended their lives because they could no longer endure the harassment of in-laws, the demands for more dowry. Others were murdered.

For newspapers it is a popular, if tidal, subject. A crop of suicides or mysterious deaths inspires a series of articles, investigations and angry editorials. A case came to light in 1982 of a businessman in Delhi who had three wives in seven years and they all died of burns. The *Hindustan Times* published a cartoon on its front page showing a heap of ashes, a tin of paraffin, and a mother and father looking through the matrimonial small-ads in a newspaper, and telling their boy: 'Don't be upset son, we'll find the right girl . . . even if it means burning a few more!'

When a girl marries and goes to live in her husband's joint family, she moves from one subordinate position to another. If she is unfortunate she will have to live closely quartered with a mother-in-law and other women with whom she may not get on and who might treat her badly. Mrs Gandhi observed how her own mother suffered at the hands of other women in her grandfather's home. The bride bullied by the mother-in-law is a well-worked theme in the Indian cinema; and a girl may suffer in a marriage and seek escape through desperate means for reasons unconnected with dowry. A harassed girl may also try to buy peace by persuading her parents to give something to her in-laws.

Divorce, rather than suicide, is a way out of an unhappy marriage for some, but it takes courage to seek one. An educated woman can support herself, but for a woman without much education and few or no friends, conditioned to a life in the cocoon of a joint family, life outside is a wretched and frightening prospect. Divorce is rare, but is becoming more frequent in cities.

An unhappy or abused girl might find it difficult to go home to mother for she might not be welcomed back. The girl's family could feel disgraced if such a thing happened, for marriage has to do with ambitions and with obligations to ancestors, future generations and the broader family. A woman is expected to stay with her husband's family, even when she is widowed. When Maneka, widow of Sanjay Gandhi, left the home of her mother-in-law, the prime minister, after a well publicised and unseemly row in 1982, she did not return to her parental home. For many Indians the incident seemed a variation on a familiar cinema theme, the saas-bahu (mother-in-law, daughter-in-law) conflict.

In places like Delhi, Bombay and Calcutta, India's international bridgeheads which have closer contact with western manners, there are some who reject traditional marriage and choose courtship, love marriages and the small, independent family: husband, wife and children. The way of life and work in cities makes this easier. Instead of being kept apart, as was traditional, young single men and women mix at universities, in research institutions, in the civil service, in banks and offices. In the same way that city life breaks down some of the caste barriers, because people mingle, it also breaches the sex barrier. In this respect urban India is going through a transition.

A western style courtship and marriage, however, leads to strains of a kind familiar in the west. Expectations are different and there is not the kind of support found in the best of joint families, where cares and chores are shared and children know the warmth and intimacy of many loving arms. In independent marriage husband and wife will be thrown together much more than in a traditional home, and for all his liberated outlook a new husband in a love marriage may expect his bride to be old-fashioned and subordinate. As it happens his wife may well be; but attitudes are bound to change.

In joint families strains may be imposed by the arrival of a bride who has been educated and had her horizons broadened. She arrives in the joint home with her character formed and ideas of her own, perhaps unwilling to accept domination. One of the advantages of a very early arranged marriage is that the girl exchanges one family for another while she is still growing up.

Western ideas about relationships between men and women are seeping, not flooding in. The liberated talk and activities of a minority do not represent a large-scale shift in attitudes. Adultery is an upper-middle-class activity. A Bombay film star or socialite may be interviewed about her way of life, and shockingly reveal she is living with a man, but such articles are not evidence of the tide turning. In marriage India remains traditional and cautious.

Virginity is prized, but for most girls virtue never becomes a pressing matter because they are married very young. The law forbidding girls to marry until they are 18 is everywhere ignored, India being a country of great freedoms because laws simply cannot be enforced.

Mahatma Gandhi, who married at 13, spoke against the cruel custom of child marriage but few listened. An analysis of 1971 census figures revealed that 5.4 million children aged 10-14 were married and that more than a third of people aged 15-19 were married. Child marriage is advocated in old Hindu teaching; and in the countryside in particular there are strong social pressures for parents to marry off girls at or before menarche. A girl still unmarried in her early teens is considered on the shelf. The custom is seen as a practical way of dealing with the onset of sexual maturity, especially in a society where virginity is important. In Uttar Pradesh, India's most populous state, half the girls married in a year are under 15. Many thousands of children are married at a tender age, boys of 10 to girls of 7, for example, and usually remain in their own homes after the ceremonies until they are old enough to live together: in many cases until the boy has grown a moustache.

During 1981, there was controversy in Rajasthan after the

13-year-old daughter of the state's minister for mines was married. Although many illiterate parents do not know there is a law against child marriage the minister had no such excuse and newspapers accused him of being yet another politician breaking laws with impunity. The minister said sulkily that his opponents were getting at him.

Child marriages are not secret and are often condoned by the authorities. A mass marriage in Madhya Pradesh, at which some of the couples were pre-pubescent, was attended by the state's chief minister. In Rajasthan there are thousands of such marriages during the auspicious time known as teej. Only one Indian state, Gujarat, has an official, the child marriage prevention officer, concerned with enforcing the law which seeks to prevent girls being exploited, burdened and damaged by too-early pregnancy.

In August of 1980, in the village of Jhadli, fifty miles south of Jaipur, chief city of Rajasthan, a girl called Om Kanwar, aged 16, climbed onto her husband's funeral pyre, placed his head in her lap and ordered the pyre to be soaked in ghee, clarified butter, and lit. She was dressed in the clothes she had worn at her wedding. A large crowd of men, women and children looked on as the fire started. The girl was consumed in the flames and made no cry of pain.

Word of the event flew round the region. The village became celebrated and twelve days later thousands of people jostled at the site of the sati to see the ashes ritually cooled with milk and heaped with coconuts, the commonly used offerings to the gods. It was a festival: local politicians attended and monkeys danced. The girl's memory was honoured and her family was elevated to a new status. The place where she died became a shrine.

Sati, or suttee, was outlawed by Lord William Bentinck, the governor general, in 1829, his action being a test of the principle of British interference in Indian rites. Although the British thought sati barbaric they were wary of doing anything about it and only did so when Indians, themselves, led by Raja Rammohan Roy, demanded its prohibition. Sati was idealized as an act of romance, sacrifice and devotion, and among many women it was regarded as virtuous. The word sati means 'a true wife'. Some months after the Rajasthan sati a group of women staged a procession in Delhi, not in protest, but in defence of what they called a sacred tradition. That sati persists, albeit in a very small way, is an indicator of the potency of tradition and ritual in some parts. Women used sometimes to burn themselves after their men were defeated in battle, for victors often used to take and enjoy the women of their foes.

Widowhood still stigmatizes many Indian women. Custom makes them feel outcasts, unwelcome burdens on their husbands' families. In traditional families, especially, a widow is still widely regarded as a person who may cast a shadow, her presence being considered inauspicious at events like marriages. Widowhood therefore brings a double pain and a widow may find herself excluded from normal social intercourse and may be happier, because she is accepted, in the company of foreigners. Because youthfulness and virginity are important, prospects of remarriage are poor, and special efforts are made by the few organizations concerned about the plight of widows to help them remarry. There are, for example, societies which arrange remarriage for the young widows of servicemen. A recent Hindi film which depicted a widow living in poor circumstances was not well received by the public. The widow met a man who, unusually, wanted to marry her, but her daughter put a stop to the idea – and won the sympathy of the audience.

After marriage there is sex.

In India it is usually in this order. Early marriage, parental discipline and custom are the pillars of the sexual status quo. There is also a lack of opportunity. A survey on premarital sex in India would be as thin as a book on Indian cars (although Bombay boasts that it is in this, as in many other endeavours, an exception). Those liberated young men and women who have dates and go to discos, the sophisticates Mrs Gandhi disparagingly labels the 'hotel culture', are a very small section of Indian society; and as psychiatrists testify, some of these young women find themselves in turmoil, caught between opposing mores and their own sexuality.

Single Indian girls are, on the whole, chaste and dutiful. This is only partly because they do not have much opportunity for pre-marital sexual activity even if they wanted it. They tend to be respectful to their parents, with a strong sense of family, and this applies throughout the social spectrum. In a joint family, a girl knows her place and is very much part of the female community within it, being the recipient of its comforts in an unequal world. She usually has a strong relationship with her mother, for her mother knows that she will soon leave home, and the bond is sympathetic because her mother is well aware of a woman's lot. Even when girls remain unmarried because they are at college or are working, they generally live at home and are under the control of their parents; and Indian girls tend to be obedient. The teen-ager with emotions complicated by boyfriend problems, well known to western parents, is largely unknown in India. A middle class mother recently told me that her daughter was dating, and said it in a way which indicated she thought it avant-garde. When I asked if she were anxious about this break with tradition, she said: 'No. The ayah is with her all the time. The girl and the boy talk and play records, and the ayah goes for tea in the servants' quarters, but she's never far away.'

An Indian acquaintance was walking home past the university in Delhi one evening when he saw a girl, a student, being molested by several young men. Delhi has a rather bad reputation for this kind of Eve-teasing, as it is known. The girl's clothing was being pulled and she was frightened. My friend drove her attackers off, being punched and injured for his pains. The incident had an interesting outcome. It was pursued with no vigour by the police because one of the attackers was a police officer's son; and it became clear that there was no chance of the girl giving evidence against the attackers if the matter had gone to court because a molested girl, however innocent, however good her background and family, becomes damaged goods, her chastity questioned. In short, her prospects of marriage might easily have been narrowed.

Few girls, it seems, learn anything about sex from their mothers, and there is very little literature of the kind available in the west. 'It is a subject that never comes up, a taboo', a bright and young middle-class woman said. 'I was given a rough idea by my ayah, but my mother never discussed it. Others might get a hint from their married friends, say, but many girls go into marriage without any idea of what happens.'

It is not surprising that initiation can be traumatic, for the husband as well as the wife. In rural society, girls are sometimes locked in a room with their husbands for consummation. A girl recalled for a researcher that she was locked in a dark room and, unknown to her, her husband was already hidden there. 'He came out and grabbed hold of me. I let him do whatever he wanted to do. I just clenched my sari between my teeth so I wouldn't cry out.'

Khushwant Singh, the distinguished journalist and acute observer of his countrymen, says that many young Indian boys get sexual knowledge from school chatter, occasionally from obliging female relatives in the joint family and also from prostitutes in the towns. To most Indian couples, he says, the concept of privacy is as alien as that of love, and they rarely get a room to themselves, the wife sleeping with women members of her husband's family, and the husband sleeping alongside the men.

'No Indian language has a word for orgasm. Frankly, most young men go into marriage for sex, children and companionship, in that order, and most Indian men are not even aware that women can also have orgasm.' Mr Singh regards this as 'a sad commentary on the people of a country which produced the most widely read treatise on the art of sex, *Kama Sutra*, and elevated the act of sex to spiritual sublimity by explicit depictions on its temples.'

The charming and comical *Kama Sutra* (comical, in part, because it takes itself so seriously: all that assiduous cataloguing) is better known in the west than in India where it belongs. The erotic has its place in Hindu mythology and this is all many westerners know of Hinduism. But the existence of such works does not mean that there is some vast store of knowledge, some Indian secret, passed down the generations. Sexual ignorance is considerable and the problems are familiar, hence the growth of the advice and treatment clinics which advertise in newspapers and garishly on hoardings.

'A large number of men know nothing of sex when they marry', said a doctor who runs one of these clinics in Delhi, and charges 20 rupees for a consultation. 'Sometimes they are informed by married friends, but many of those who come to see me want the basic facts of life, to know what to do.'

'My clients are of all ages. A few come because they think they have VD, but the majority, about 80 per cent, consult me because they are impotent. Of course, impotence is mostly in the mind, and so I talk to them and give them confidence. I explain the facts and you can say I wash their brains . . .'

This man treats patients with ayurvedic medicines, herbs and roots and minerals, for complaints which come under the general heading of lost vigour; and his treatments range from General, through Special, Super Special, Royal, Super Royal and Nawabi, from 225 rupees (£14) to more than 5,000 rupees (£300).

Judging by the literature they distribute to hopeful clients Indian sexicians are careful to instruct men to be considerate to their wives, to fulfil them sexually, to respond if there is 'a twinkle in their eyes', and to be especially thoughtful when on honeymoon. 'In case the man hurries to commence the job without first stirring the woman she remains dormant and the sport is only one-sided. The man is looked down upon as selfish.' This is an echo of the boudoir chivalry illustrated in the *Kama Sutra*, and in the carefully executed 18th- and 19th-century paintings of tubby noblemen and their voluptuous ladies enjoying their *parties de jambes en l'air*.

The health and vigour clinics no doubt perform a useful service if they can relieve anxiety, spread sexual courtesy and banish ignorance, but the opportunies for quackery are boundless and the literature reveals that the sex instructors themselves are often superstitious and saddled with old beliefs.

Above all, youngmen (it is almost always one word in India) are impressed with the importance of the old tradition of retaining their semen, the 'gem of life, the treasure of life' as it is called, and to avoid losing it through 'hand practice', too much love-making and what is picturesquely called 'nightfall'. Indeed, clinic literature warns of 'the horrors of the wastage of semen . . . the human machinery becomes defective; stomach, liver, heart and eyesight go weak. The very imagination of a woman causes waste of semen and youngmen look old at the age of 25. Many youngmen have sex many times at night and thus waste this essence of life recklessly. With small production and heavy drainage, supply will exhaust soon and critical consequences will have to be faced.'

To avoid nightfall, men are advised not to drink milk at bedtime, not to eat spicy food, to 'boycott love thoughts and avoid excess of cycling, fast running and horse riding.' Similar beliefs about nocturnal emission persisted in Victorian Britain. A patent electric alarm could be purchased for attachment to the member, whose swelling during slumber would ring the bell, warning the owner to take appropriate action.

There are strong lectures from the clinics about the perils of masturbation, said to cause headaches, backache and amnesia. 'The organ becomes small and thin, the man starts feeling giddy, weak and becomes impotent.' The literature often carries a cautionary tale, of which the following is a typical example. A weeping man tells the sex expert of his decline and fall.

'I am the only son of a rich family and my parents fulfilled my every desire. Unluckily I fell in bad company, due to which I started masturbation. After some time I felt myself very weak and decided to give up this bad habit, but when I supressed it I suffered from night discharges. It ruined me. Due to overthinking I had gone mentally weak. I have gone lazy. I am worried because my parents have settled my marriage with a beautiful girl, but I tremble because I know that I have lost the most important treasure of my life and I feel I am unable to satisfy my would-be wife.'

The sex expert then recounts: 'I told him to have faith in God and he would be all right. Then I examined him and his genitals in privacy. Indeed he had ruined his youth. My heart is filled with sympathy for these poor fellows . . .' Rather more luridly another expert writes: 'His organ had gone black. There were other symptoms of ruin, too. I started treatment . . . and by the grace of the Almighty he regained his youth.'

As a cure for impotence the clinics recommend a period during which men should avoid thinking of sex, and have a course of alternative hot and cold baths, followed by herbal medicines to enrich and thicken semen, enhanced by doses of calcium, tin and crushed pearls. To improve tumescence arsenic, saffron and musk are recommended, as well as applications of lion and bear fat, castor oil and carbolic acid. Cantharides, mustard and oil of cloves are also prescribed; and a diet including eggs and the testicles of a goat is favoured; while tea and tobacco are frowned on.

Once normal service is resumed, men are enjoined to preserve the gem of life (an Indian researcher reported recently that semen contained gold) and to enjoy intercourse only once or twice a month, avoiding the act when they are constipated.

Sexual display in India is very restricted. The advertising of women's underclothing, so familiar to westerners, is hardly ever seen. Even in women's magazines there is very little advertising of brassieres and what there is is discreet. A picture of a shapely leg advertising stockings would be pointless because most Indian women do not wear them and do not display their legs, covering them in a sari or with narrow trousers or pantaloons. For winter warmth they wear socks. An Indian girl rarely wears a western-style skirt and if she wants a western accent in her appearance she will usually choose jeans or corduroy trousers. Bombay girls, however, may be more ready to adopt western fashions.

The great majority of Indian women wear traditional costume, the artfully concealing and revealing sari with a tight blouse beneath. In the north they also wear the attractive trousers and long knee length dress known as shalwar-kameez. In the south, women, like men, wear long skirts, or lungis.

The sari is eternally in fashion, comfortable and right, and while the changes are rung mainly in colours and patterns, there are varying ways of wearing it. For example, the skirt may be worn high, or sometimes low on the hips, accentuating the belly-swell considered so attractive. Smart women in Bombay sometimes like to show some buttock-cleavage, and the blouse, or choli, may also be low-cut. The sari is a garment of languorous grace, not suited to rapid activity.

The wet sari, as seen clinging to film actresses, has in recent years come to represent an erotic ideal. In hundreds of films the director contrives ways of leading both the heroine and the bad girl to water. They fall in rivers and the sea. They get caught in the rain and sprayed by gardeners' hoses. They have large liquid eyes, bruised roses for mouths, slightly sulky, and there they stand with their garments clinging. The cinema in India is a sexual frontier, gradually encroaching on conservatism, and is partly devoted to stimulating and gratifying fantasies in a sexually unpermissive society. The giant film hoardings are remarkable, an industry and art form of their own, a colourful part of the city street scene, promising hours of thrusting bosoms, wet saris and gunfire for a few rupees. In blasé Bombay, and Delhi, Calcutta and Madras, the strictly limited eroticism of the cinema has become accepted, although there are always newspaper controversies over films that have supposedly gone too far. But in the villages many find them too strong, and men forbid women to go to the travelling cinemas.

A kiss is rarely seen in an Indian film, being too daring, and too offensive, in a society where such physical pleasures are enjoyed in private. Few Indian couples show affection in public. You hardly ever see boys and girls holding hands, and you never see canoodling in the parks. Indeed, in parks you are more likely to see groups of boys and girls sitting in sexually segregated circles, some yards apart. Thus the question of 'to kiss or not to kiss' in films is a favourite and titillating subject in magazines and newspapers.

When the Prince of Wales visited a film studio in Bombay in 1980 a young actress was persuaded by Fleet Street photographers to kiss him on the cheek, which she did. An outraged citizen took out a summons against her for dishonouring Hindu womanhood, but as with so much else in this litigious country, nothing came of it. The photographers, incidentally, asked the girl if she would care to remove the pantaloons of her shalwar-kameez outfit, for a glamour photograph, an invitation she declined. Indian girls are modest and many actresses would not only refuse to kiss in a film but would be outraged if asked to do a nude scene. Even partial nudity is rare. The camera usually stops short at a bare back or a generous thigh. Western films are heavily cut. Bosoms heave, but are not bared.

Nor, in the main, are they bared for artists and photographers. The life class in India has usually been a drab affair, lacking a suitable model, male or female. Artists have had to make do with beggars for male models and statues for female. Girls can sometimes be persuaded to pose, usually draped, but one Calcutta artist recalls that the models in his life class were ageing prostitutes. Recently a few Indian girls have posed nude for photographers and the results have been published in what is considered a daring magazine, a sort of Indian *Playboy*, but the girls looked nervous. Many photographic models are dutiful daughters of middle class parents and would not dream of embarrassing them by doing something risqué. With the one exception mentioned there are no magazines in India featuring the naked female form, although there are plenty with pictures of film stars with clothes on. Customs officers seize western magazines with nude pictures and are meant to destroy them; but a copy of *Playboy* fetches up to £10 at a backstreet stall.

Indian girls who go to the beach or to a pool dress very modestly, hardly ever in a bikini. Women swim in saris on Goan beaches, or wear pantaloons or long skirts, like Victorian belles. They perform their daily ablutions in saris and, in the twinkling of an eye, change into a dry one. They usually remain partly covered when taking ritual baths, as they do in the sea at Puri, in the lake at Pushkar, and in the numerous bathing places along the Ganges. 'We object to western television cameras lingering on our womenfolk while they are taking their ritual baths,' an Indian said. 'It is an intrusion into privacy, as if they were catching your own sister in the bath. Of course, we have a peek ourselves, but you see, we only peek. The camera stares!'

Newspapers reported in 1981 that 'a group of four well-educated girls were arrested recently while dancing in the nude on the beach at Vishakhapatnam (on the Bay of Bengal).' The titillation lay in the fact that the girls were educated as well as naked.

Given Indian reticence over sex, I was surprised to read the following verse in the *Times of India*, under the title 'Holiday Notes':

> afternoons i hug my wife
> full passion rules our life
> bearer brings the tea at three
> embarrassing her in lingerie
> evening by the lakeside
> we agree on a boatride
> fingers pluck the guitar strings
> somewhere near the church-bell rings
> meal over, velvet curtains we drew
> for the long-desired good night screw

*   *   *

I met a woman called Manbhar, a farm worker's wife. She had plucked up courage and had walked six miles across the brown Rajasthan desert to a clinic in a village school to be sterilized. She was 30 years old, slim, still fairly handsome, although wearied and dried. She wore a bright red and blue skirt and bodice, and had silver bangles on her wrists and ankles. She had had a medical examination and her blood and urine had been tested. She was nervous and wide-eyed, like the other women waiting with her. Her husband was outside looking after their three children. It was very hot and still.

Two nurses in green surgery gowns brought her into the operating theatre in a classroom next door. She was put on a bed which was canted to about thirty degrees with her head at the bottom of the incline. Her midriff, of course, was already bare: the fact that women do not have to undress and can wear their everyday clothing is part of the acceptability of this operation. Dr

Pravin Mehta, a Bombay obstetrician, gave a local anaesthetic near Manbhar's navel, and an assistant pumped in nitrous oxide gas through a small cut to clear the abdominal area. An incision was made in the abdominal wall and the doctor inserted a laparoscope. The laparoscope is an eighteen inch stainless steel probe with a pistol grip and a light source enabling the surgeon to see into the abdomen. The doctor peered through it and moved it around as he searched for the Fallopian tubes. With the first tube located he held it in the instrument's crab-like claw and, squeezing a trigger, snapped a plastic ring over the captured tube, making a tight ligature, rather in the manner of a stapler. The tube on the other side of the womb was similarly sealed; and the doctor invited me to look through the laparoscope at his handiwork, at the tube tied neater than a sailor's reef knot. The laparoscope was withdrawn and a single stitch inserted into the cut.

Manbhar was given a chit for £5.50. A balance of £2 was withheld for one week as an incentive for her to return to have the stitch removed and for an examination. In some parts of India a few women have died of infection because they have neglected to report for an inspection.

Manbhar was led to another room where about forty newly sterilized women lay on mattresses, she stretched out and some friends fanned her. Her baby was brought in to be fed. 'What I did was necessary,' she said. 'We have three children and are too poor to have any more.' She had heard about this operation, performed with what women call the magic telescope, and was persuaded that it was so quick and efficient that she would be home in time to cook the evening meal, and fit enough to work in the fields next day. The government reward of 120 rupees was the equivalent of more than two weeks' wages.

To some medical authorities laparoscopy seems the ideal method for limiting India's population. Dr Mehta had already performed 35,000 by the time he dealt so swiftly with Manbhar.

The possibilities were demonstrated by another doctor, Usha Sharma, who, at 7.30 one evening began an astonishing surgical performance, sterilizing women at the rate of one a minute. At a clinic in Aligarh, in Uttar Pradesh, she clamped the tubes of 605 women in 11 hours. The clinic was carefully arranged. From the city and surrounding villages 778 women arrived with their husbands and families, creating a crowd of 4,000. Three hundred extra beds were hired. Tents were erected in the hospital grounds, extra water laid on and lavatories dug.

There was a female medical team of eight. Every prospective patient had a medical and gynaecological examination and a blood, urine and penicillin-allergy test, and this screening ruled out 173 of the women. The 605 selected were aged between 20 and 44 and most had three or more children. The operations were carried out with relentless precision. Outside the operating theatre the patients were injected with a fast-acting anaesthetic, a sedative and anti-tetanus serum. Inside, four operating tables were continuously supplied, Dr Sharma moving from one to the other. She had four laparoscopes in use and sterilized the women in three batches, 263 in the first session, 281 next morning and 61 in the afternoon.

Dr Sharma, head of the obstetrics department at Meerut medical college, believes laparoscopic ligation is the best method of population control for rural India. 'Vasectomy is inadequate because few men volunteer for it. In my experience, once a woman hears about laparoscopy she does not need much persuading because she understands only too well the burden of endless childbearing. Once the word gets around motivation is very strong.'

Sterilization drives in the Indian countryside often employ 'motivators', welfare workers and others, who persuade women of the benefits of the operation. They are paid a fee, about thirty pence, for each women they persuade. Such a system is open to abuse, but Dr Sharma says that she checks that candidates are not dragooned. 'If you take risks, if you have a death, the word will go around like a fire and undo all the good work. I insist on strict screening and doing the operations myself. I take full responsibility and see that every case is followed up. I believe that population control is the most serious and urgent of our priorities. But I am not a machine. I am a mother myself and I feel compassion for all the women I operate on. They want me to lift the greatest burden of their lives and sometimes they come to me and beg me to help them.'

Students of India's population say that more than 4 million people should be sterilized every year if population growth is to be contained to an 'acceptable' level. Given that as a target, surgeons like Dr Sharma just cannot work fast enough. India is accepting that nothing can stop the population rising to a billion by the end of this century. The 1981 census counted 684 million people, a figure that shocked government planners who thought the total was 12 million fewer than that.

For some years after the emergency, population control was a touchy subject. The forced sterilisations left a legacy of fear; and because these brutalities were a factor in Mrs Gandhi's election defeat in 1977 the population question receded into the political shadows. But by the mid-1980s, with the fading of memories of the emergency and the arrival of a new prime minister, it was restored to the agenda. Rajiv Gandhi saw it as India's most critical problem. Hitherto, India's chief response had been to grow more wheat and rice. Indeed, it became a matter of national pride to make the country self-sufficient in food. But poverty grew with population and competition for land and water became increasingly acute. In 1986 Rajiv Gandhi launched his country's most ambitious population control drive, aiming to stabilise the population at 1,300 million by 2050. The emphasis is on sterilisation, but an important part of the campaign is the education of young women because there is a direct relationship between female literacy and family limitation. Another vital part of the programme seeks to improve children's survival chances through immunisation, so that couples do not feel the need to have more children as reserves. The government urges parents to have only two children. But couples have a strong desire and preference for sons, not only to work but also to keep them as they age. I was told of a couple who had nine girls before they finally produced a boy.

In many villages, as the old taboos and ignorance are worn away, family planning is more openly discussed. Women go for sterilization after talking it over with parents or village elders, and the first woman in a community to be sterilized is often an example enthusiastically followed. The family planning message is spread through television and the cinema, and condoms are boldly advertised. As the new population drive got under way I visited a birth control clinic and saw a large portrait of the prime minister, tastefully framed with packets of contraceptives.

3

The envoys of Kali

India's wild west: the dacoit outlaws of the valleys of death

The best thing for a bandit is a bullet.

POLICE OFFICER IN THE CHAMBAL VALLEY

THE DAY AFTER Pan Singh Tomar died the newspapers carried pictures of him as he was in his heyday, a tall handsome athlete, breasting the tape, head flung in the agony of victory. In his time he was a sporting hero, held records for long distance running and represented his country. He was a soldier for much of his life, and, on hearing of his death, one of his former officers sent a newspaper a picture of him wearing a neat team blazer, with a comment about his smartness. Pan Singh was a runner all his life, and he died running, too.

After he left the army he returned to his village and became enmeshed in the caste and land disputes that disfigure and provide an important part of the culture of the rural society from which he sprang. He killed a man in a quarrel, fled and became a bandit, a dacoit. In this, as in athletics, he became a champion, a ruthless murderer and kidnapper who was soon high on the police list of most-wanted men. His military experience helped to make him more than usually competent in his new trade. He lived by the application of terror, the brutal assertion of his will over others and his skill at evading his hunters in a long and remorseless race.

Pan Singh was a denizen of the Chambal valley region of north central India, the heartland of banditry for 800 years. Its tradition of vendetta, caste warfare and deadly squabbles over land are seemingly ineradicable, and brigandage is part of its fabric. Even the brown soil which has absorbed so much blood has its part to play in a pattern of killing and revenge.

The Chambal region is not a remote corner of India. The Chambal river flows about 160 miles south of Delhi, only 40 miles south of the Taj Mahal at Agra. The territory inhabited by bandits covers about 8,000 square miles, the size of Wales, and has a population of about four million. It sprawls across parts of Madhya Pradesh, Uttar Pradesh and Rajasthan. The chief town of the region is Gwalior, whose fortified cliffs rise 300 feet out of the plain. Over the years the Chambal and its companion rivers, with their tributaries and monsoon cataracts, have drilled the soft rock of the region into a maze of crumbling ravines between 50 feet and 250 feet deep, reminiscent of the Badlands of South Dakota. These unmappable twisting fissures and the neighbouring jungle, where deer and wild pig roam, make a natural and perfect robbers' roost. It still takes a large force of police to comb even a small area of it, and while tough Mahindra jeeps make the going easier, the advantage always lies with the pursued. It is a hot, dry and inhospitable place for much of the year and wheels and marching feet soon kick up a choking dust. In the monsoon it is wet and uncomfortable, and the rivers run brown and swollen.

Emerging from the jungle and crossing the dry scrub, Pan Singh and a dozen of his men arrived late one afternoon at a mud-walled village in a poor cobblers' community of low thatched houses and rutted streets. The people bent respectfully to touch the bandits' feet, and Pan Singh gave his orders. For his own use he commandeered a whitewashed room. Villagers showed it to me later, pointing out a simple daubed painting of a tiger on the whitewash and two charpoys, string beds, on the beaten earth floor. Pan Singh was evidently satisfied. He ordered a bottle of country-made whiskey, for 30 rupees, and a goat for his men to feast on for 150 rupees. Bandits can afford, and usually pay, high prices for the food, clothing and ammunition they buy from villagers, both sides accepting the part that brigandage plays in the marginal local economy.

Pan Singh entered the amounts he spent in a small blue diary. He was a careful book-keeper and recorded the shares he paid to his men after a robbery, or the paying of a kidnap ransom. As is the usual practice among dacoits, the chief takes half the spoils and distributes the rest according to the firepower of each man's gun. For example, a new automatic weapon rates more than a .303 Enfield rifle stolen years before from a police station. Junior members of a gang do not usually own a weapon and rent one from the chief.

Pan Singh felt safe as he ate and drank because this village of Rathiankapura, which lies up a rough dirt track off the road from

Gwalior to Bhind, was the home of one of his gang. Caste and clan loyalties are an important hedge of security for dacoits who prefer to seek shelter among their own kinsmen and caste fellows. Other castes are often their enemies and prey, and therefore a source of betrayal.

The police have developed a network of informers to penetrate the barriers of caste secrecy, loyalty and fear. Informers are sometimes paid, or are offered gun permits which are a great status symbol. Others turn informer out of feelings of resentment or a wish for vengeance. Many informers are ex-dacoits with varied motives. Some have scores to settle, or provide information in exchange for a promise by the police that they will escape being charged with a former crime. It is an ugly little world of subtle pressures and private terrors and grudges.

Dacoits, for their part, have their own spies and are ruthless and vicious with police informers, genuine or suspected. A few years ago dacoits entered a village suspected of housing an informer, dragged out ten boys and shot them in front of the assembled people. Pan Singh himself had recently dealt severely with the people of a village called Pawa, near Gwalior. There had been a skirmish with the police near this place a few months before, and Pan Singh's brother had been killed. Pan Singh retreated, swearing vengeance, certain that someone in the village had betrayed him. He returned, took five men from their homes, roped them together and shot them. The villagers of Pawa took me to the place where he had done this.

As Pan Singh ate goat and drank whiskey in his whitewashed room in Rathiankapura, a force of about 100 policemen quietly surrounded the walls in the darkness. The gang had been betrayed. A cool young police superintendent, Vijay Raman, entered the main gate with a group of his men and shooting started. It went on for hours. By four in the morning the police were 300 strong and shooting by the light of parachute flares.

All that was left for Pan Singh was a desperate sprint for safety. He ran through an alley, out of the gate and into the open where some scrub and stooks of hay provided shadow. He was running when the bullets cut him down. He was 49 and had a price of 10,000 rupees (£600) on his head, a score of murders and fifty kidnappings to his name. His body, and the bodies of nine of his men, were laid out at the feet of the police for the ritual of the team photograph, just as dead bandits were laid out and photographed on the American frontier, and were subsequently taken for display in Bhind, the nearest town. People turned out in force to stare, for a dead dacoit is a great attraction. Hawkers lit their fires and sold hot nuts, fried snacks, sweets and soft drinks, and the stinking spectacle became a carnival.

That year, 1981, the police mustered more force and determination than ever before in their war with dacoits. They took on more men and vehicles and armed themselves with the automatic weapons which would match the dacoits' firepower. They spread their network of informers. But it could never be easy. It was not simply a case of cops and robbers where the forces of evil could be seen clearly delineated. Here in the Chambal an array of social forces were at work. Police, bandits, villagers and politicians were tangled in a mesh of conflicts and interests, compounded by the forces of tribalism, history and economics.

In many societies, and the Chambal is one of them, the bandit has for a long time represented an embodiment of the rebel, the romantic freedom seeker, the righter of wrongs, the free spirit, the champion of the poor. Jesse James, Billy the Kid, the Daltons, the Youngers and later Bonnie and Clyde, were romanticized in the United States and their crimes were whitewashed. Ned Kelly filled a romantic role in Australia. And in more modern times the criminals who staged the 1963 train robbery in Britain became folk heroes. In the Chambal region dacoits (the Hindi word *dakait* means robber) are not known as dacoits at all. They are called *baghis*, meaning rebels, and for all the wretchedness they have spread down the years they have had in the minds of many the aura of Robin Hood. Some dacoits are careful to foster this chivalrous image and forbid their men to molest girls, to drink, to rob anyone but a rich man.

For centuries the broad ranges of central India were plagued by robbers and highwaymen who preyed on caravans and travellers. There were, too, the Thugs, the hereditary secret society of dealers of death who worshipped the goddess Kali, always portrayed as naked, black and bloody-mouthed, and who killed on her behalf. They joined groups of travellers, earned their confidence, and then choked their victims with a whispering silk scarf, ritually gashed the bodies, and disposed of them in wells or pits. Leading Thugs killed 300 or more people each. One man killed 931. The supposed sacredness of their work as Kali's servants earned them the support, or at least the blind eye, of the leaders of society. Other people, of course, lived in dread of them, terrified into silence.

In 1830 the British set the steely crusader William Sleeman to eradicate the Thugs and he did so in twenty years of patient and determined police work, dealing mercilessly with the thousands he rounded up. He combined zeal with the dogged amassing of intelligence and rigorous interrogation. Sleeman's accounts of his relentless eradication of Thuggee are in the bookshelves of today's dacoit-hunters. His methods are admired and remain relevant. In an area twice the size of Britain he created a network of informers, Thugs who chose to help him rather than hang, as so many hundreds did. Many Thugs were found in high places in society and Sleeman also exposed the rich men who financed the deadly rituals. Retribution came through special courts, and those who were not executed were jailed or transported to the Andaman Islands, although a number of lesser throttlers were trained under Sleeman's aegis to knot carpets rather than necks, an early experiment in criminal rehabilitation.

Sleeman's clean-up of Thuggee in central India ended a particular and ritualized aspect of crime. Modern dacoits are not the descendants of that grisly brotherhood, although many of them worship Kali and, believing that their guns are a reincarnation of the goddess, worship and decorate them. The eradication of Thuggee was the drying of a tributary of crime rather than the mainstream. The physical, historical and social factors which encouraged banditry in north central India remained and have become more acute in modern times.

The ownership of land is at the heart of it and quarrels are deeply rooted with an endless spiral of vendettas. A landlord can frighten troublesome and complaining tenants by threatening to call in dacoits, an effective threat because accounts of dacoits cutting off noses, fingers, hands and breasts are legion. People do not trust the legal process to resolve disputes because it is too unreliable, long-winded and expensive and people believe that lawyers, witnesses and judges can be bought and intimidated. Minor disputes among reasonably well disposed people can be settled by the sirpanch, or head man, of a village. But if there is bad blood the matter is more likely to be settled through intimidation or through the barrel of a gun; and once the fatal shot is fired the murderer heads for the ravines to join other outlaws. Because the police might look upon his brothers or friends as likely dacoits, or supporters of dacoits, there is a temptation for them, too, to throw in their lot with the dacoits.

In recent years social warfare caused by pressure on land has been aggravated by the demands of harijans who, as elsewhere in India, have been daring to defy landlords and farmers for whom they labour, calling for land and better wages. For their defiance they have been beaten and killed in large numbers, sometimes by the landlords' bullies, sometimes by dacoits.

As well as land as a cause of bloodshed there is caste. Dacoit gangs are often caste-based, and to their own people they are often heroes and avenging protectors. It is in this respect that the dacoits' Robin Hood image is strongest. Dacoit bands enter villages of their own caste with a swagger, to be feted and cheered, to have people fall at their feet. They buy food and bring welcome income. They may worship at, and contribute to, the local temple. It is to their advantage to impress religious people. They represent a rough and ready force for law and on arrival in a village will sort out minor disputes. They receive supplicants, hear the hard luck stories and dole out cash. Poor men with nubile daughters, but little money, are given wads of rupees and a slap on the back from the bandit kings, a sudden ending to their dowry worries. Accounts of this kind of random generosity are common. They fly round the countryside enhancing the dacoits' reputations.

Dacoits are not only helped by caste fellows on the land. Just as Thugs had support in high places, so have dacoits. Bandits have glamour and power, which appeal to those politicians whose views on the rule of law are, to say the least, ambivalent. Some use dacoits as an arm of their own power, relying on them to deliver blocks of votes. In return the bandits receive some protection because politicians can lean on malleable policemen.

Dacoits, policemen and politicians play complementary roles in the power structure in some areas. The bandit and the law enforcer are often of the same caste. The power of the gun is a significant consideration in some parts, and both the policeman and the dacoit are the means to maintain political ascendancy and the existing social order.

William Sleeman wrote, in 1844, words which hold true a century and a half later: 'These thieves and robbers of the professional classes, who have the sagacity to avoid plundering near home are always secure from the only three things which such depredators care about – the penal laws, the odium of the society around them, as long as they can avoid having their neighbours annoyed by summonses to give evidence for or against them in our courts. They feel quite sure of the good will of the god they worship, provided they give a fair share of their booty to priests; and no less secure of impunity from penal laws, except on the very rare occasions when they happen to be (caught in a place) where such laws happen to be in force!'

To complete the circle we come back to the land. The relentless erosion of soil by water increases the pressures. Every year many thousands of acres are washed away down the brown streams, so that the core of the region's rivalries is a shrinking resource demanded by an ever growing population. In the Chambal region you can see numerous ghost villages, abandoned when the surrounding land crumbled. There has never been enough land and there never will be now. There is a saying in the Chambal that if a man has three sons one will become a farmer, one will go into the army and the third into banditry.

Dacoity has been tidal and from time to time has thrown up big names, the equivalent of the desperadoes of the American frontier. In the 1940s and early 1950s Man Singh was the Chambal's undisputed king: he murdered 185 people, carried out 112 armed robberies, earned half a million rupees by ransom and had numerous gun battles with the police before his end in a shoot-out in 1954. It was estimated that ten million rupees had been spent in the fight against him. The police file on him noted: 'Man Singh is representative of the peculiar problems of this area. He is regarded as a man with no private vices. Stories are told of him in hushed voices of admiration of how he helps a good cause, kills informers and policemen only when pursued, just lifts (kidnaps) few men who have money to spare, respects Brahmins who give him blessings and occasionally coerces zamindars (landowners) to contribute to desirable objects like school buildings. His admirers often remark that he presents the high water mark of dacoity nobly practised. Officers of revenue, customs and education could run into him without fear. He could go to marriage celebrations attended by hundreds of people. His case illustrates how the natural revulsion against heinous offences can be mellowed by adopting ingenious methods.'

A resurgence of dacoity led to the curious spectacle of the great dacoit surrender of 1972. Surrender had been tried several times before as a way of dealing with the problem, the idea being that

India Gate, Delhi: a pink Arc de Triomphe

School run: Rickshaws, drawn by bicycles, are crowded with little school
children on their way to lessons

Barber shop: ear cleaners ply their trade . . . pavement barbers lather and
scrape

dacoits would admit their crimes, go to jail for a short term for a nominal offence and thereafter lead a law abiding life. It was to some extent a recognition of the social and economic causes of banditry, an attempt to apply social science to social ill. In 1957, for example, two dacoit leaders gave themselves up to the Madhya Pradesh governor and another chief surrendered to the chief minister.

The 1972 surrender was organized by Jayaprakash Narayan, a gentle soul, an idealist and disciple of Mahatma Gandhi, who persuaded the dacoits and reluctant authorities to give surrender and rehabilitation a try. In a bizarre ceremony at Morena several hundred dacoits, fresh from the ravines, climbed onto a stage and gave themselves up to the welcoming embrace of Jayaprakash Narayan, handing over weapons in the process. The ceremony was watched by a large crowd and the bandits were greeted as heroes. By and by they went to prison where they lived in scandalous comfort, enjoying the pleasures provided by the liquor and young women ferried to their cells. On their release they were given land and money.

The police were dismayed. In general they believed, and still do on the whole, that a bullet is more effective than rehabilitation. They suspected that the dacoits had negotiated a respite and had stored most of their arms against the day they would return to the ravines. The realities of the surrender were not lost on the public, either. Those who had been widowed, mutilated, robbed, orphaned and terrorized by dacoits were appalled to see bandits receiving such a welcome and rewards. 'If you kill one man you are a murderer', people said bitterly. 'If you kill ten you are a dacoit and a hero and the whole town turns out to cheer you.'

I met one of these men who had given up his gun. He introduced himself in Morena with a sardonic smile as 'Madho Singh, surrendered dacoit'. He had a chilling, almost unblinking, gaze. As we talked a group of people gathered, regarding him with evident respect. He said he had killed ten men with his own hands, and since giving up crime had worked as a farmer, and, for some curious reason, as a conjurer. His sideline was working as a ransom-broker between kidnappers and their victims' families. When I asked about other surrendered dacoits I was told of two gang leaders who were making a film about their exploits, starring themselves. Shooting of the film had, however, been interrupted because the two were quarrelling, unable to agree who should have top billing.

The ravines were quiet for a while after the great surrender, but the vacuum soon filled when bandit chiefs like Pan Singh Tomar, Malkhan Singh and Chabiram began the killings and extortion that brought notoriety and headlines. Their activities exposed weaknesses in the way the police worked and led the police to put their own house in order. The lack of cross border co-operation among independent and jealous state police forces had always been exploited by bandits who could find safety by slipping over state boundaries. But by the beginning of 1981, police communication and co-operation were improved. There was better weaponry, and the number of men and vehicles put on anti-dacoit operations was increased.

Just as importantly, the police in Madhya Pradesh and in Uttar Pradesh, a state where banditry was spreading rapidly, were strengthened by laws enabling them to detain for several months without bail people believed to have harboured or helped dacoits. It was a tough measure, capable of being employed unfairly, but it at last enabled the police to attack the base of dacoit support. The police were embarking on a form of warfare because the usual framework of justice, bail and trials was useless. Bail was easily skipped, witnesses were intimidated or bought, and without them it was not possible to secure convictions. In these circumstances, the police argued, there had to be firm measures. Only when bandits were eradicated could there be a start in changing the economic and social conditions which allowed them to thrive, a start in breaking the habit of feuding.

The police concede that it will be difficult to bring about changes of attitude in communities where caste bitterness and blood feuds are a solid tradition. But they say that the breaking of the gangs and the ending of rule by menace are necessary pre-conditions. 'Shooting dacoits, however, can only be a start,' a police superintendent said. 'Without reforms the ravines of the Chambal valley will always be a breeding ground for bandits.'

Obvious reforms would include better irrigation, land reclamation and industrial development. Roads need to be driven through ravine country to help both police and people.

But it will not be easy to end the ambivalent attitude that many Chambal people have towards dacoits, the sneaking pride in notorious bandits of their own clan.

*   *   *

On February 14 1981 a dacoit gang led by a young woman, Phoolan Devi, entered the village of Behmai, beside the Jumna river, in Uttar Pradesh. She had a sub-machine gun and carried a megaphone through which she bawled orders at the startled villagers. The village was inhabited by people of the Thakur caste. The girl bandit – bandit queen to the newspapers – was a Mallah, a lower caste, and while her gang were in the village for loot, her objective was revenge, the heads of two Thakur men who had murdered her lover. They were not there and the villagers said they had never seen them. The furious girl ordered thirty men into a line beside the river and opened fire. Twenty fell dead. It made headlines, of course, for the crime was trebly shocking: the massacre was on a large scale, it was performed by a woman and by a person of lower caste on people of a higher one. Moreover, it was said, the girl had first shot all the men in the genitals.

Phoolan Devi's place in the history of the region was secure. She was described as beautiful, although there was no photograph to judge her by, and the brutish life of the ravines is hardly an aid to beauty. Stories woven round her exploits are colourful and juicy: she is said in the magazines and newspapers to like bathing and soaping herself naked in front of men, to have been forced to submit to public intercourse with a bandit leader, to have left her first husband because he could not satisfy her.

She has joined a pantheon of lady outlaws led by the romanticized Putli, of whom the *Indian Police Journal* wrote: 'In the villages of central India people will sing folk songs for years about the exploits of a willowy dancing girl who became a dacoit and terrorized the countryside with murder and robbery. Death has wiped out our scores against her. Her cruelty and ruthlessness will be forgotten, but what will be remembered is the fearless courage of this leader of a desperate band of outlaws. Dancing girl, dacoit and nurse, she had drunk life to the dregs within the short period of 29 years.'

The dacoit war in central India intensified and during 1981–82 scores of gangs in Madhya Pradesh were wiped out. In Uttar Pradesh police guns killed 1,300 men. There were complaints here that innocent people had died in encounters with the police, that certain police officers were using the dacoit drive to eliminate a variety of troublemakers and petty criminals. The complaints

were justified. The Uttar Pradesh authorities agreed that innocent people had been killed. It was hardly surprising: given the
criminal environment, political pressures and distorted values of
this region it was inevitable that some innocents should suffer. In
other parts of India, Bihar and Tamil Nadu, for example, social
agitators and others deemed politically inconvenient have been
eliminated in 'battles' with the police and branded as criminals or
naxalites, communist activists.

During the campaign against dacoits in the Chambal valley, in
Madhya Pradesh, Mahesh Sharma, a deputy inspector general of
police, and a much decorated bandit fighter, took me with him on
a long tour of his territory. We went through fields of ripening
wheat and the first yellow sproutings of mustard, along dusty
tracks and winding ravines, over rivers and jungle-covered hills.
He was accompanied everywhere by a Gurkha policeman with an
automatic rifle, and made inspections of remote police posts
where his men turned out to mount guards of honour, and the
villagers bent to touch his feet. Much of our conversation concerned two bandits, Chabiram and Malkhan Singh, and we went
to the places where Malkhan had been operating and where, on
the edge of the Chambal river, his trail had dried up.

Malkhan was a bandit king. It said so on the headed notepaper
he used to send threats to the police officers hunting him, and on
the ransom notes he dispatched to wealthy men whose sons he
had kidnapped. 'Bandit king' was also the device on his rubber
stamp (curious that bandits, too, should employ that quintessen-
tial instrument of Indian bureaucracy, the magical authenticator).

At that time Malkhan and his gang headed the list of most-
wanted bandits, with more than 100 serious crimes listed against
them. Malkhan was an adept kidnapper, bandits having found
that kidnapping was less risky and far more profitable than
robbery. Murder, however, had not gone out of fashion and was
retained as the weapon of terror and revenge.

The police knew much about Malkhan and his movements,
and the way he lived, and much of the information came from the
people he kidnapped. They knew he was tall and thin and wore a
khaki police uniform with a superintendent's pips on the shoulders, and his name in Hindi on a black badge on his chest. This
was not mere insolence or black humour. Malkhan saw himself as
a principal and justified chief among men, deserving respect.
Uniform in any case is worn by many dacoits as an effective

disguise. Malkhan was fond of writing letters, and being illiterate dictated them to his clerk, who also read to him from Hindi newspapers. He was one of those few bandits who set high moral standards, which did not, of course, apply where murder and other crimes were concerned. He forbade womanizing and drinking, a ban which many bandits would consider would make life unnecessarily tedious, but this was perhaps as much a practical as well as a moral stance for drink and wronged women have led to the betrayal and death of many a bandit.

He took other precautions. He never slept two nights in the same place, and when he did rest he did so at some distance from the main body of the gang, with a bodyguard watching over him. He took care to maintain his relationship with the goddess Kali, using some of his loot for the upkeep of a temple in a village. He understood the importance of religion in a religious area, and made sure he and his men were seen to be devout. A dacoit who ignores this aspect of his trade will earn the disapproval of people he depends on.

He tried to keep to the habit of offering puja, obeisance, to Kali every Monday, and he and his men prayed before a raid just as the Thugs used to pray. Malkhan's men put their guns in a circle and decorated the stocks with their names in their own blood, or their victims' blood. They were also superstitious and the sight of a snake would lead to the cancellation of a raid.

One evening in 1981 Malkhan and his men slipped across the Chambal and made for a village near Bhind. There were two scores to settle, an eighteen-year feud with a farmer, and the matter of a man who, Malkhan had been told, had tried to poison one of his gang. In the village Malkhan had this terrified man dragged out from his house.

'Poisoner,' Malkhan said to him by way of explanation and condemnation, and promptly shot him dead.

He then sought out and captured the farmer's son, aged 24, and hurried off with him to his hideout across the river. Some days later, the farmer received a ransom note for 50,000 rupees (£3,000), written on the bandit king's famous headed notepaper. The victim was with the gang for nearly three months, was reasonably treated and fed, until his father sold some land to raise the ransom. Kidnap victims are not usually killed except, occasionally, to encourage rich fathers. It is the Chambal dacoits' growth industry.

Life was made harder for men like Malkhan by the extension of the police network, the growth of its manpower and number of informants, and the application of the law permitting the rounding up of a dacoit's helpers. Police have also become much better at tracking gangs through food purchases: a large gang like Malkhan Singh's had to have considerable supplies, and police try to get their informers to tell them whenever a group of men is seen making large purchases.

In spite of the pressures a chieftain like Malkhan could still enjoy the old style of an outlaw's life, holding court in villages and dispensing rough justice and cash. Villagers often say that 'the baghis have done more for us than any government' – and it remains a problem for the authorities that as they drive out the bandits they have somehow to fill the economic gap and replace the crude justice. The police often install a police post in villages patronized by bandits, not only to keep bandits out but to support the village economy by providing purchasers for food and milk.

'Watching the source of food is only one way of catching dacoits', a superintendent said. 'There are others. When a gang is in the vicinity there will be an air of excitement among the people. You will see the men of the dacoits' caste twirling their moustaches and walking with a spring in their step. A lot of people are proud of their baghis, and they feel good when they come into town. You can sense the change in the atmosphere. The people will tell you nothing, but their smiles and their moustaches will tell you everything.'

In their pursuit of Malkhan the police felt it was only a matter of time before they got him. But in the meantime the police in Uttar Pradesh cornered another notorious bandit chief, Chabiram, near the town of Mainpuri, and killed him, an event which contributed to the ending of Malkhan's reign of terror.

A short while before his death Chabiram made the police look foolish by arriving in a village with his gang and holding court there for four days, during which time he was seen by many hundreds of people. No-one betrayed him. The police did not go near the place because the state government was negotiating with Chabiram for his surrender. Chabiram was dealing with politicians and the politicians kept the police at bay, an extraordinary blow to their morale, for the police take a dim view of surrenders and political interference in the dacoit war. The fact that a newspaper reporter had an interview with Chabiram in the village where he held court made bitter breakfast-time reading for the police. But the surrender negotiations broke down and the police took up the hunt again.

Chabiram was eventually betrayed after one of his gang abducted a girl from a village after killing her parents and brother, an act which damaged Chabiram's reputation for not harming women. The police were told where he was, and surprised him. Chabiram and his men fled and were pursued for seven hours before they were pinned down and forced to a last stand. The last time Chabiram was seen alive he was calmly smoking a cigarette while the battle raged around him and bullets kicked up the sand. A cool nerve and bravado had been his trademark. He saw himself, as many villagers saw him, as a man who had the courage to take up his gun and fight for justice. 'I only rob people who have more than a million rupees', he used to say.

The corpses of Chabiram and eleven of his men were put on display in Mainpuri. Their arms were secured behind them, over staves, and in this fashion they were hauled upright on a line of poles driven into the ground, as if crucified. The newspapers reported that 30,000 people came to view the bodies. Children stared wide-eyed, young men climbed trees for a better look, women held cloths to their faces against the odour, dogs sniffed, and hawkers did a brisk trade in hot nuts.

The grisly end of Chabiram had an effect on Malkhan Singh. He saw the pictures in the papers. He began to realize that he was tired of running and he had, after all, had a long run. He was now 38, he had made a lot of money, a great reputation, and had at last killed a man against whom he had long held a grudge. Honour was satisfied. Why end up full of bullet holes, hanging on a post, while policemen gloated?

He put out feelers to the authorities about a surrender. Three journalists writing about dacoits provided a link between himself and the police, and in June 1982 he agreed to come in from the ravines. The authorities were adamant that the surrender was unconditional, but it seems unlikely that Malkhan would have given himself up without an assurance that he would not hang for some of the 110 offences of kidnapping, robbery and murder recorded against him. He calculated that a few years in prison would settle his account with society.

It says much about the status of bandits like Malkhan that his surrender was received at an astonishing public ceremony. It happened in the dusty town of Bhind. At the police barracks a dais of bricks, six feet high, was hurriedly erected, covered with a white cloth and shaded by an awning of red, green and yellow cloth. It was hung with photographs of Mahatma Gandhi, Mr Nehru and Mrs Gandhi, the prime minister. On the dais a low table was tastefully set with a pink rose in a vase and smoking joss sticks. Film music was playing loudly over a public address system. Reporters and All India Radio were in attendance, along with numerous senior police officers and state officials. A crowd of 25,000 people who had travelled on foot, by bus, pony cart and bullock cart, were in roped-off spectator enclosures.

As arranged, Malkhan left his hideout in the ravines with nineteen of his gang, paused to pray in his home village, and was taken to Bhind in a convoy of police jeeps. Meanwhile, the chief minister of the state had flown down from Delhi and had made the connecting journey to Bhind in a white helicopter. He was there to receive the surrender of the great bandit (a political fillip for him) and to give the event an official stamp. He was waiting on the dais when Malkhan arrived and the crowd was chanting 'Long live Indira Gandhi'. Few people had seen the bandit before. Even the police had no photograph of him. Now he paused for the photographers as he mounted the steps of the platform.

He was tall and thin, unlike the usual fat-bellied dacoits, and luxuriantly moustachioed. He wore the khaki uniform of a police superintendent, and a cap, and was as hung about with weaponry as a caricature brigand. He had a rifle, a revolver, a long curved dagger, a bandolier, a cross-belt of pouches, and a whistle.

The seething crowd pressed forward, Malkhan fell at the feet of the chief minister and touched his shoes in homage. He then turned to the crowd holding his rifle above his head. He placed it reverently on a chair on which there was a picture of the goddess Durga, and added his revolver, dagger and belts. The rest of his gang followed suit and Malkhan's long reign of terror was over.

He made a short speech to the crowd, justifying his actions as an attempt to right wrongs done to him and others. Some firm-jawed policemen looked as if they were wishing he were standing on gallows planks rather than this platform of triumph. A message from Rajiv Gandhi, the prime minister's son, was read out. It expressed a hope that there would now be peace in the region.

Malkhan was taken off to jail in Gwalior. He had left sixteen of his gang in the ravines, an insurance policy should any prospective witnesses need a little terrorizing. The ceremony was over and the crowd dispersed. Some people said they were relieved that such a terrible man was now in custody. Some deplored the effect of such a ceremony on impressionable young people. 'A big bandit gets a big minister', a man said wryly.

The chief minister, officials, police officers and reporters adjourned to the circuit house where lunch was served in a large tent. It had all gone off well, a perfect bandit surrender. Seven months later Phoolan Devi, voted 'bandit queen' of India by the press, followed Malkhan's example and laid down her arms in a similar public ceremony. She was defiant and truculent, but sometimes gave a cheeky grin. Her red bandanna gave her the appearance of an Apache. She, too, went off to jail; and in Bombay the finishing touches were put to a film based on her life. For the time being there was a lull in the gunfire in the Chambal valley.

4

A hundred versions

Gods and the guru business

We spend more time in the pursuit of religion than any other people in the world.

KHUSHWANT SINGH

THE GREAT GOD Juggernaut was roused from bed long before I was. I dozed under the mosquito net in the South Eastern Railway Hotel, while Juggernaut was made ready for his big day. He is a grotesque monster, a white-faced legless wooden idol, five feet tall, with glaring eyes and stumpy arms emerging from his head which has a large diamond set in it. He lives with his black-faced brother and yellow-faced sister who are equally hideous, like a child's crayoned depiction of nightmare goblins. But their popeyed fiendish faces are relieved by impish grins and fairground colours, making them seem almost amiable. They are the rulers of, and the reason for, the great temple at Puri, one of the four most hallowed of Hindu temples and a goal for countless pilgrims. Its telephone number is Puri 1.

At the Railway Hotel, a considerable timbered establishment on the Bay of Bengal, like a transplanted Surrey golf club, I had porridge and eggs. About two miles up the road Juggernaut was being attended by a chosen few of the 6,000 servants who devote their lives to him. They cleaned his teeth, washed him, dressed him in fine clothing and placed in front of him a light breakfast of rice, sugar and wheat. They similarly attended to his brother and sister. The traffic restrictions in the town were relaxed for vehicles carrying food for the Juggernaut family.

Although this was an important day, the annual journey of the gods to their summer house, the washing and feeding are a daily ritual which has been carried on for at least a thousand years. Those who serve the gods are divided into thirty-six orders, a mysterious complex of hierarchies, performing sixteen daily ceremonies, including teeth cleaning, feeding, making offerings, dressing and undressing, and putting the gods to bed for their siesta after lunch. None of the ceremonies may be witnessed by a non-Hindu and the entire temple is a forbidden citadel to outsiders.

Outside the temple, in the town and on the roads leading to it, there was excitement in the air. There was an increasing noise made by a surging orchestra of creaking, tinkling rickshaws and pilgrims' sandals slip-slapping on the road. Many people peeled away from the main bodies of marchers and crossed the hot sand dunes to the sea. A local guide book says: 'A dip in the sacred sea brings broadness of mind, doing away with all meanness.' There were several hundred dunking themselves under the supervision of fishermen dressed in loincloths and conical winkle-like wickerwork hats who charged two rupees to lead pilgrims into the surf. Men bathed in their pants, women in their saris, and a wave would sometimes knock them all down and, as it receded, would leave them gasping and giggling in the froth.

It would be impossible to say how many were in Puri that day. People talked of a million or more. I guessed there were at least several hundred thousand who had been gathering since long before dawn. On the roads the authorities had set up cholera inoculation stations and had sprinkled the narrow streets with disinfectant. As the crowd swelled and seethed in the broad main street men patrolled up and down with sprays, squirting into the mass like gardeners attacking aphids. People crammed every window, balcony, rooftop, ledge, tree and hoarding, and I paid a few rupees to get onto a roof packed with squirming bodies. There was a strong smell of sweat and camphor and sandalwood. It was as hot and humid as the devil's laundry. Down in the street cows and bullocks ran amok and people shouted and scattered, an Indian Pamplona. Several people fainted and were borne aloft by stretcher bearers who ran through the seething congregation preceded by men with red flags and whistles.

Excitement grew through the afternoon. More pilgrims pressed in, their foreheads daubed with paint. Men jigged incessantly to the beat of drums, becoming steadily entranced. Hundreds of women had cut off their hair and brought their shining tresses in offering. There was a constant cracking and spluttering as people smashed coconuts on the ground and anointed themselves with the milk, falling to their knees in prayer.

All eyes were on three monstrous vehicles standing abreast

outside the Lion Gate of the 12th-century temple. They are called cars, but the word does them injustice. These are great chariots as large as houses, surmounted by decorated pavilions in which the three gods ride to their summer house. The largest is Juggernaut's, with a platform 35 feet square mounted on 16 painted wooden wheels each 7 feet in diameter. It has a red dome and the whole gaudy structure is 45 feet high. The other chariots are only slightly smaller. Every year, in June or July, the chariots carry the gods on their mile-long journey to the summer house, and transport them back after eight days. The chariots are then broken up, new ones built, and the discarded timbers are sold to the people as sacred relics.

At last, to a roar from the multitude, Juggernaut and his siblings were brought in litters from the temple and installed in their transport. They are the focus of a remarkable veneration and love. A man next to me said simply: 'It is the Lord. Everyone loves the Lord.'

In Sanskrit Jagganath means lord of the universe. It is one of the names of Krishna in his incarnation as Vishnu, and one of the main reasons for his popularity is that all castes are equal before him. As the sixpenny guidebook says: 'Jagganath stands amidst them in his Olympian height. He mingles himself with the people even at the grass roots. People love him. He is their inseparable loving comrade in their weal and woe. The name of Lord Jagganath is to conjure with every sector of the people of the world irrespective of their caste, creed and religion.'

At about five o'clock long thick ropes were attached to the chariots and men rushed forward to grab them. By tradition 4,200 men pull each wagon, but there seemed to be more of them than that struggling and shoving for the honour of dragging the gods in a commemoration of a journey that Vishnu once made.

At last, the chariots began to tremble and move. The din was terrific. Wheels shrieked in torment and the contraptions groaned like primeval monsters awakened. The platforms shuddered and the ground shook. It was clear at once how Jagganath entered English as Juggernaut, meaning a dreadful, inexorable and destructive force. This was no half-hearted carnival, but a manifestation of India's religious energy, an event of great power whose participants were singleminded in their devotion and enthusiasm. The platforms of the chariots were crowded with musicians playing cymbals, drums and horns in wild abandon; there were scores of half-naked priests jumping up and down, gesticulating and shouting to the crowd, the mad banging blaring music at times drowned by the scream of tormented wheels. The people surged forward and tossed rice, marigolds and coconut shards at the wagons, and scooped up brown dust where the wheels had passed and rubbed it onto their heads. The eyes of men and women were wide and shiny with adoration, tears blobbed their dusty faces. The chariots moved a few yards at a time and then paused while the draggers drew breath. By nightfall they were halfway and the progress stopped while the weary hauliers slept. The journey resumed next morning. This time I watched from the street. I have an indelible memory of the towering monsters advancing and people running from the grinding wheels, under which, years ago, some of the devoted used to hurl themselves in sacrifice and to achieve an ultimate bliss.

The extraordinary spectacle of Puri is merely one of many epic demonstrations of the strength of belief in India and an aspect of its awesomeness. There are many other festivals, ritual dunkings and anointings, that draw people by the million. Just as importantly, there are innumerable and commonplace rites, celebrations and observances. On any city pavement you may have to skirt a religious painting, fashioned with powder, chalk and petals, and perhaps finished off with a small brass oil lamp and incense straws: a small act of devotion. There are numerous small shrines in the streets, where candles burn and homegoing workers stop to offer puja or homage, just as there are in almost every village in the land. Religion is a dominant force in the country and its influence and symbolism are embedded and pervasive. Taxi dashboards are often decorated with religious images, and cars, lorries and rickshaws are painted with swastikas, the most ancient of Hindu religious symbols. Many homes have shrines and the wealthy may have a small room set aside for worship. The calendar is peppered with religious holidays, and there are only a few secular ones. Most Indians, about 83 per cent, are Hindu and whether or not they profess atheism or agnosticism their lives are affected to a greater or lesser extent by one of the world's most powerful religious forces, the core of India, the heartbeat of the secular republic, with its roots in the Aryan books of knowledge first written about 3,000 years ago.

It is difficult for anyone with a western background to explain Hinduism satisfactorily in western terms, probably impossible,

and I am unwilling to venture beyond what little I have observed
of it; although, as I have indicated, I saw something of its influence
almost every day I spent in India. Religion is a daily business,
seamless and pervasive.

Hinduism is both a religious and a social system, the religious
part being no more important than the social, and no aspect of it
being more important than another. It is indivisible and all
embracing, so that the esoteric part is no more significant than the
material. It is a framework for dealing with natural and supernatural, providing places for all manner of beliefs and superstitions. It is a sponge, admitting far more than it prohibits, and sets
little store by dogma. The existence of an omnipotent force is
recognized, but this god-alone is by no means the central exclusive focus in a religion which admits millions of gods and allows
immense freedom of worship. The spiritual and superstitious can
be blended, permitting limited notions of heresy. You can shout at
your god if he or she displeases you, and withhold your offerings
as long as your sulk lasts. The incomprehensible ultimate force is
not worshipped and its existence is considered only by a few
sages. Hindus are too practical to want to spend much time
considering the esoteric. The lesser gods and forces are more
comprehensible and relevant, and include the sun, the sky,
planets, mountains, rivers, snakes, trees and the phallus, the
creative force. People may worship ancestors, and have regard for
ghosts.

Hinduism is based on birth and behaviour in life, the religious
and the social elements being stitched together by the idea of
dharma, the fulfilling of one's duty dictated by conscience, social
background, personality and custom. It is a powerful idea, being a
code for living, and is linked with karma, the idea that present
actions affect future existence, the soul being eternal and going
through a cycle of births, deaths and rebirths, so that marriage, as
the preliminary to birth, is pivotal. Hinduism offers solace and
hope, a belief that present troubles are the wages of a former life's
sins, that the future may be mitigated by unselfish and dedicated
actions. And, if these actions are truly altruistic and not performed for the satisfaction of ego or conscience, they may lead to
a form of liberation. This serene state may also be achieved
through various pilgrimages, worship and meditation.

Nevertheless, the esoteric aspect of Hinduism has for many
years been an attraction to certain westerners. But it seems

unlikely that Hinduism is a source of a wisdom of an extraordinary kind or of wisdom superior to others: if this were so,
India would presumably be a different sort of society. Indians tell
me that the mysterious aspect, the esoteric, the supposed harness-
ing of forces through meditation and other forms of yoga, are not
the most important part of Hinduism. It is a religion with its feet
on the ground, a way of living in the world of flesh, money, food,
fellows, sickness and difficulty. It enjoins its adherents to be
materialistic, to create wealth.

Still, India's reputation as a spring of mystic wisdom makes it
the goal for a variety of metaphysical tramps, lost souls in various
stages of confusion, and those who suppose themselves refugees
from the decayed and materialistic values of western civilisation.
In India they seek solutions to the mysteries of human existence,
an unravelling of spiritual knots, an ordering of their own per-
sonalities. A flourishing enlightenment industry has grown up to
accommodate them and to minister to their needs. Like Hinduism itself, it has its feet firmly on the ground. A number of gurus
and godmen have grown wealthy on the proceeds of the institutions that have sprung up around them, finding in the suggesti-
bility of westerners a thick lode.

One bright summer morning I visited the ashram, or commune, of one of the more celebrated of these masters. This was in
Poona. Its ornate wooden gate was easy to find, just past Dr
Bumb's acupuncture clinic, as I had been directed at the hotel.
There was a surly looking young man in a red robe guarding the
gate and he allowed me in with some reluctance, ordering me to
maintain silence. Inside there were numerous buildings set
attractively among trees and shrubs as well as several hundred
people sitting around in the dappled shade, gazing vacantly as if
struck into stone. The women were dressed in robes or shifts of
saffron or maroon. Some of the men wore long shifts, too, or long
shirts and trousers, all of the same reddish or orange hue. Both
sexes wore brown beads around their necks.

This was the morning meditation hour and there was only the
sound of birds. In a pavilion, a sort of dance floor under a large
canopy, a crowd was squatting and kneeling, either staring ahead
or with eyes closed. Under trees, or on steps and in alcoves,
people sat, lay or leant, with blank or reflective expressions, their
still and statuesque poses making them seem excavated from
volcanic ash. After a while there was some stirring. The hour was

almost over. People rose, clutched hands and embraced. A man and a woman met on a pathway and kissed passionately. Two women, holding hands, met a man and hugged him warmly, planting kisses on either cheek while he encircled them with his arms and affectionately rubbed their bosoms. A girl emerged onto a balcony, sleepy-eyed and naked, and, with arms outstretched, like the statue of the spirit of ecstasy on a Rolls Royce, strained towards the sun.

This was the ashram of Rajneesh, a notable Indian godman of the time, whose white-bearded, sepia-eyed and photogenic face made him look like the traditional picture of a saint. His followers called him master and some, I learnt, imagined he was god.

For seven years or so his ashram in Poona had been a goal for thousands of middle class westerners, mostly Americans and Germans, who had streamed there in search of bliss, inner peace and repair to damaged psyches. Many seemed to be refugees from the late twentieth century and what they regarded as repressive, tumultuous and distorted western society. Some fled collapsed marriages and stifling jobs. They jumped from their unsatisfactory ships and swam to the island of the ashram.

They removed their trousers and skirts, blouses and shirts, brassieres and jeans, sold them on the streets of Poona for as much as they could get, changed into the orangey garb prescribed by the master and became sannyasins, followers. 'Orange clothes are indications that the sannyasin is ready to plunge into the unknown', said the master. 'Orange has no other meaning. It is a love affair.'

Having a range of allergies he would permit no-one near him who was wearing perfume or smelt of strong soap. His acolytes therefore sniffed all those entering the presence in an intimidating olfactory frisk.

The six-acre ashram was truly an island, fenced and hedged, with India kept out. All the work except the washing was done by commune dwellers. They delved and span, cleaned, cooked vegetarian food, baked, wove, sculpted, made slippers and lovingly boiled up soap for sale at high prices, seeking nirvana through saponification. The administrators worked, with evident dedication, in some of the best-equipped offices and studios in India, manning the godman's telex and his publicity machine.

It was said that Rajneesh had about 200,000 followers throughout the world and, at the height of its popularity, the Poona

Mass marriage at Dharmastala near Mangalore: a way of ending the financial burden of marriage ritual while providing the dignity and sanction of a 'proper' wedding

Monsoon, Bombay: the warm rain seems ceaseless . . . the slum dwellers are
as wet and uncomfortable as soldiers in trenches

Street scene, Delhi: the true Indian motif is not the Taj Mahal or the
elephant, it is the crowd

ashram was the base for about 6,000 people. An elite among them lived inside the compound, even heaven having its castes. The rest contributed to the town's economy by renting rooms and staying in hotels, eating in the little restaurants and tea stalls. Every morning they entered Rajneesh's leafy paradise of love and beauty, music and discarded inhibitions; and learnt to endure the bane of the place, jaundice and diarrhoea.

Dressed in an ankle length white gown Rajneesh used to arrive every morning in a Rolls Royce and sit in a chair to face his adoring followers, hunkered down in their hundreds, the men mostly bearded and long-haired, the women long-haired with adoring misty eyes. This was the master's morning discourse, an outpouring over the years of 33 million words, a mixture of pop psychology, recycled hippy philosophy, scraps of Hindu teaching, and nonsense and contradictions to provide provocation and a sense of rebelliousness, the equivalent of a naughty child saying 'bugger' to its mother. For example: 'I teach you to be free of the clutches of knowledge. I teach you to be selfish because only out of true selfishness is altruism born. I want to give you emptiness. Duty is a dirty four-letter word, husband and wife will become dirty and ugly words. I am God because I am not. Even if I make illogical statements I make them logically.'

Little in the ashram was free of charge; certainly not the morning discourses, the entrance fees for which helped to put the Rajneesh business on a sound financial basis. The 33 million words were rendered into 336 books and 4,000 hours of tape, all for sale along with the soap, clothing, jewelry, stationery and slippers. The ashram's turnover was estimated at £2 million. Rajneesh never uttered a word without profiting, and smart and jokey titles like *Ninety Nine Names of Nothingness* and the *Madman's Guide to Enlightenment*, the sort of thing found in baffling California bookshops, were on sale for £10. A hand-bound coffee-table volume of photographs of the sage could be had for £200.

Rajneesh's people were, typically, westerners over 30, of reasonable financial means: teachers, doctors, lecturers, lawyers and the like, usually single. In the ashram they changed their way of living completely. I met a veterinary surgeon who was happily spending his day making pizzas, and a young woman who was my guide had been a computer specialist whose marriage had soured, now content to spend her life at Rajneesh's feet. She said she had now rejected her parents, and would never see them again, because they were no longer relevant, and she had told them so. But she had a face perpetually sad. A Californian doctor, treating the jaundice and diarrhoea patients in the ashram's clinic, said he felt fulfilled and had no desire to do more varied medical work. 'I can't treat the whole damned world, man, can I?'

The ashram had a reputation for being an island of sexual licence. The landlords, rickshaw drivers and stallholders of Poona benefited from the ashramites' spending, but many people were scandalized by the reputation for free love and the sight of westerners upsetting local sensibilities by cuddling openly in the streets. The manager of a hotel said he had had to rebuke a girl who appeared on his premises bare-breasted. 'I told her it may be all right in America, but in India we don't do that sort of thing.'

The ashram provided group therapy sessions where you could stand and scream, and massage and encounter groups, as well as various other facilities thought to aid catharsis and the search for inner peace. Some of these techniques owed much to California mind-doctors.

I never saw a violent session in the flesh, but I did see a film which was decidedly unpleasant and disturbing, showing naked men and women shouting and screaming at each other, men hitting and kicking women, and women rolling on the ground shrieking. I was not surprised to hear that local doctors complained of having to treat mentally disturbed ashramites.

The only event I witnessed was an evening meditation session in which several hundred people obeyed the instructions of a master of ceremonies. They began with a twitching session, shaking their hands and heads like aspens for fifteen minutes. For the next fifteen minutes they engaged in abandoned dancing. Then they sat fixed like Easter Island statues, contemplating while an electronic fugue was played. For the last quarter of an hour they were supine, eyes closed, and during this time the master of ceremonies sat in a chair with a girl on his lap and kissed and fondled her passionately. The ashram was a temple of tactility, where people broke off frequently from what they were doing to embrace and nuzzle. Its inhabitants assured me it was a secure, warm, loving place where they would stay forever; a sort of permanent Club Mediterranée. But it was a bolt-hole, stiflingly introverted and parochial, with its own jealousies and elites, its suggestible inhabitants breathing an artificial atmosphere.

Questions made them uncomfortable: they fenced, became with-drawn and lied, as if afraid the whole enterprise would not bear the weight of examination and frankness. There was withal an atmosphere of selfishness and deceit.

I never saw Rajneesh. In full page advertisements in the news-papers he had made what he called an historic declaration, that he had 'entered the ultimate phase of his work and would speak only through silence, the language of existence.' The newspapers speculated that he had a bad throat. He Rollsed to his morning discourses for 'wordless, heart to heart' communion with his devotees, lasting an hour, and tapes of this silence were made available for sale; but, curiously, no books.

Then, in a puff of Rolls Royce exhaust, Rajneesh made his celebrated disappearance. Without a word to the ashramites he and a few of his acolytes flew to America, to set up shop in Oregon, with four Rolls Royces for comfort. The ashram publicity machine would tell no-one where he had gone and hotly denied that he had fled to evade tax demands. In Rajneesh's discourse chair in Poona there was now a photograph of the master, and I saw hundreds kneeling in worship before it. But the show had moved on, leaving the ashramites stranded on their island of love and truth with their heads in the sand.

Swami Muktananda, on the other hand, did not have a Rolls. When I saw him in Bombay he was making do with a more modest midnight blue Lincoln Continental with smoked glass windows. He was a considerable celebrity, the head of a large yoga and meditation empire, with branches in India, Australia and the United States, worth many millions of dollars, and with a world-wide following of a quarter of a million people, according to his publicists. Unlike Rajneesh he did not indulge in the vulgarity of charging people to hear his discourses. His wisdom was free, and living in his ashram in the hills fifty miles from Bombay was cheap. His empire prospered through the sales of his books and through the donations of his grateful flock. The brochures say the ashram has room for 2,000 people and is dedicated to the attain-ment of supreme bliss . . . although reveille is at 3.30 am. There was a warning that Baba Muktananda was 'stern with idlers, escapists, pretenders and statue-mongers.'

Like others in the godman business, Mr Muktananda was considered by his devotees to be a saint. Moreover, he was a realized being, as opposed to an ordinary being, and so there was a sense of excitement in the ballroom of the Bombay hotel where more than 1,000 people waited under the chandeliers to hear him speak. He drove down from his ashram and was half an hour late, heightening anticipation. Outside the hotel a scruffy man paused to stare at the welcoming party, but the security-wallah shooed him off with the Bombay vernacular equivalent of 'Buzz Off'. The last thing you want when a living saint is about to arrive is some tattered citizen cluttering up the pavement.

At last a car drew up, spilling the saint's aides like shelled peas, and almost at once the Lincoln berthed alongside and willing hands reached into the dark recess to pull out the saint, as if rescuing him from a whale's belly. Nikons opened fire as the Realized One emerged into the sunlight. He wore a simple short frock of pink silk from which protruded surprisingly dainty legs and which offered a glimpse of the saintly patella. He had an incipient beard, glasses, a red tikka mark on his forehead and a rather jolly smile full of excellent teeth. He was 73 and could easily have passed for 65.

'Baba is coming, Baba is coming,' went the urgent whisper into the hall. Through a rippling blitzen of camera flash and the thunder of a standing ovation he ascended the podium and tucked his heels into his groin. His adoring followers, shaven-headed westerners in tangerine togas, sat at his feet with the shiny and eager faces of children about to be dosed with their bedtime Virol. Electric fans breezed up his pink dress, making him seem a gnome in a wind tunnel. His interpreter, a beautiful statue of a girl in a sari, stood beside him as he launched into his patter.

It was about knowing one's mind, one's inner self, in order to know real truth. It was banality piled on triteness, and quite soon three people were asleep. By and by a young woman ran from the hall, uttering loud sobs, and sat outside bawling while Californians in saris stroked her head, and tears wetted her tee-shirt. I enquired what had happened and someone said she had been caught up in the swami's energy field and her equilibrium had been disturbed.

'It happens. Some people just get over-energized by Baba. We'll give her a lump of sugar and see if that helps.'

I attended the swami's press conference, organized by his indefatigable publicist, a large Australian with a smile that never wore off. The first question was: 'What is the significance of the alignment of the planets on March 10?' Through the clatter of camera shutters Swami said that planets were not important. What counted was the maker of the planets. His acolytes nodded gravely. The next question was: 'Why are you here?' And the Swami said it was because he had been invited. The acolytes laughed to see such fun. After half an hour of this the publicity man called through his smile for the last question, and someone asked: 'What is it like to be a realized being?'

The saint rose to go. 'You should have asked that at the beginning,' he said, departing with his tonsured admirers for the prosperous ashram in the hills. Some months after this he died and was buried, sitting upright, in mud and salt.

Under the shade of an awning set up by the Red Fort in Delhi a large crowd gathered to bid farewell to an urn. No ordinary urn, this. It was six feet high and about eight in diameter, a gleaming copper vessel, heaped with flowers. It stood on the back of a lorry, protected by a silver umbrella, and was seen off by priests, prayers and the prime minister. I last saw it heading down Chandni Chowk with crowds of people cavorting around it and bands thumping and blaring on that hot afternoon.

The urn trundled through India for more than 1,500 miles, taking six months to reach the town of Sravanabelgola, about ninety miles from Bangalore. It was feted in every town and hamlet along the way, for it was the largest and most important of all the urns employed at the ritual bath of the statue of Lord Gomateswara.

The statue is fifty-eight feet tall, cut from a single granite rock 1,000 years ago, and stands, nude and at attention, on a hill. On a day chosen by astrologers and holy men it was ceremonially washed in milk, water, clarified butter and curds. It was showered with flowers and gold and silver coins and anointed with saffron and vermilion. This washing ritual, which normally takes place every twelve years, was watched by a million people.

It was another remarkable example of India's faith. In this case it was a festival of the Jains, a religion of severe asceticism, followed by about 3.5 million people, pledged to abstain from taking life in any form. This leads some of them to wear masks over their mouths to prevent them breathing in insects. Occasionally, you see them walking like small groups of ready-masked surgeons. These devotees do not eat after dark in case insects should get into their food and die. They run bird hospitals, drop grain near anthills for the ants to eat, and do not engage in agriculture for fear of killing worms. Some Jain monks, known picturesquely as the sky-clad, go naked in the belief that the achievement of nirvana, ultimate bliss, is inhibited by attachment to earthly things like clothes. All this, however, is rather like writing of Scotland and focusing on the kilt: Jains are significant and influential in the business world, as traders and bankers; and their commercial skills make them an important minority.

Sikhs, in contrast, have a distinctly martial mien and tradition. They are the most distinctive of India's minorities. They are proud, enterprising, assertive, pragmatic. Not too privately, they consider themselves a cut above the rest; and there is some justification in their swagger.

Although Sikhs make up only about two per cent of the people of India their contribution in many fields of national life is in much larger proportion. The turban is rarely in the background. As a soldiering people they retain a strong presence in the forces, about a tenth, and are also strongly established in the civil service, medicine, engineering and sport. They are in the forefront in commerce and in farming and are the champion cereal growers of India. They are the major road hauliers of the north and they provide many of the lorry crews, too. Most of the taxis in Delhi are driven by Sikhs with the light of battle in their eyes.

The Sikh religion was founded in the 16th century, originally as a pacifist, caste-rejecting offshoot of Hinduism, a rebellion against Brahmin dominance and dogma. It is based on the teachings of ten gurus and its heart is the book of scriptures known as the Granth Sahib. Sikhs became a military community at the end of the 17th century in response to Muslim persecution. To distinguish him from other men every Sikh was at that time enjoined to observe and wear the five kakkari: kesh, uncut hair and beard; kachh, short boxer pants; kara, an iron bangle; kanga, a wooden comb; and kirpan, a dagger. The turban is not compulsory but it became an essential part of Sikh distinctiveness. Sikh men were told to adopt the name of Singh, meaning lion, and women the name Kaur, meaning princess or lioness. Conflict is part of the Sikh tradition. In the Golden Temple in Amritsar, the faith's holiest place, there is a museum with numerous paintings of Sikh martyrs dying painful deaths at the hands of their oppressors. Children gape at the pictures of severed heads and butchered babies, and at the photographs, with enhanced blood, of more recent victims, the enshrinement of the tradition of defiance and blood sacrifice.

Sikhism exists alongside the massive bulk of Hinduism and for years some Sikhs have felt that there is a danger of their faith being absorbed by it. The story of modern Sikhism, particularly the tragic, bitter and violent developments of the 1980s, is rooted in this crisis of identity. When India was partitioned, Punjab was halved by the partition line and more than two million Sikhs poured across it to settle in Indian Punjab. Inventive and energetic, they made Punjab the most prosperous state in India, the wealthiest, healthiest, best-fed and best-educated. Drive along the Grand Trunk Road out of Delhi and on the Punjab border you see a sign saying: Punjab, Land of Milk. Punjabis drink five times more milk than the national average and buttered toast here means no boarding-house smear but a generous load. The view from the road is of a fertile land, of plump buffaloes and numerous busy tractors. It is a prospect that many Indians envy and they do not think Sikhs have much to complain about. But in the late 1970s a minority of Sikhs began to express grievances with an ever-insistent voice.

Sikh fundamentalists had noted that the dividing line between Sikhs and Hindus had grown less well defined. Sikhs and Hindus readily intermarried and it was a custom for years for one of the sons of a Punjabi Hindu family to be brought up a Sikh, a way of protecting the family. Sikhs worshipped in Hindu temples and vice versa. For certain orthodox Sikhs these customs, the close and amicable relationship with Hindus, were disturbing. And perversely, prosperity and modernization blew on the small coals of discontent. Many young Sikhs decided that Sikhism and its trappings had little relevance for them in the modern world. They opted out of the faith by shaving, cutting their beards and discarding the turban, so that they looked just like other Indians; and these departures added to the anxieties of orthodox Sikhs.

Sikh extremism developed from and fed on those fears. Fundamentalists said that the close relationship with Hindus was smothering the faith, that survival lay in being separate and manifestly different. Thus, among other things, they created a politics of beards, jeering at Sikhs who trimmed their whiskers, saying, in a more-Sikh-than-thou way, that only men who let their beards grow freely could be true Sikhs. They found a leader in a young preacher, Jarnail Singh Bhindranwale, whose name was to become burnt into Indian history. His rapid rise from obscure, itinerant holy man was powered both by the growth of fanaticism among a minority of Sikhs, and also by the cynical political manipulations of Sanjay Gandhi, Mrs Gandhi's younger son, and of Zail Singh, who had an immense knowledge of Sikh politics and who was later to be the first Sikh president of India. These two promoted Bhindranwale in order to destabilize and discredit the all-Sikh Akali Dal party which ruled Punjab, in coalition with the Janata party, after Mrs Gandhi's electoral defeat in 1977. Sanjay's aim was to undermine the cobbled-together components of the Janata government which took over from Mrs Gandhi, and restore his mother and her Congress party to power. It was not difficult to exploit the cracks and rivalries in the Akali party. Wealth and education had not changed entrenched power patterns. Punjab has always been a land tied to codes of honour and personal vengeance. And while Sikhism's followers rejected the Hindu caste system, caste is a fact of Sikh life. The dominant group are the jats, farmers who form three-fifths of the Sikh people, and who hardly ever marry out of their caste. And the Akalis are essentially a jat party.

Bhindranwale was launched on his fanatical and terrible path. Fighting broke out between fundamentalists and Nirankaris, another Sikh group condemned as heretics. A new party of extremists was founded to confront and harass the Akalis. This group, Dal Khalsa, which was always associated with Bhindranwale, called for a separate Sikh homeland, Khalistan, an idea backed by some Sikh expatriates in Britain and north America, but never strongly supported by Sikhs in India.

After Mrs Gandhi's return to power in 1980, Bhindranwale became increasingly dangerous and his devoted followers ran a campaign of terror and murder against Nirankaris and Hindus. Opportunist leaders of the Akali party courted him for their own ends as they pressured Mrs Gandhi for autonomy for Punjab. Bhindranwale became a monster, and Mrs Gandhi's indecisiveness allowed him to flourish. His unchallenged existence and the reign of terror he conducted from the Golden Temple became an unendurable affront to her authority and credibility. He fortified the Golden Temple against the inevitable showdown. On June 5 1984 Mrs Gandhi ordered tanks and soldiers of the Indian army to clear the terrorists out of the Golden Temple: Operation Blue

Star. Bhindranwale was among the hundreds killed in the fighting. Most Indians were relieved that the government had acted at last, and while many Sikhs were privately glad that the terrorists had been smashed, the attack on the Temple, the base of their faith, caused a roar of rage and anguish among Sikh people. It was a desecration that many found unforgivable. They mistakenly saw Blue Star as an action against their community, rather than as a blow against terrorists. The extremists vowed revenge and five months later Mrs Gandhi was murdered, a killing which led to Hindu mobs slaughtering hundreds of Sikhs in a frenzy of murder in Delhi.

In the aftermath of his mother's death, and the communal violence, Rajiv Gandhi laid the foundations for a political, and Sikh, settlement of the Sikh problem in Punjab. He saw to it that an Akali government won power in an election so that Delhi could distance itself. But the Punjab question remained formidable and dangerous. Sikh terrorists roamed parts of the countryside, murdering indiscriminately to keep up the tension, to frighten Hindus away and to emphasise their secessionist demands. It was a sad aspect of Punjab's tragedy and torment, of the great convulsion in the Sikh faith, that Hindus and Sikhs, who had traditionally lived together in considerable amity, now found their relationship soured by suspicion and fear.

The largest religious minority in India are the Muslims. Their population, 77 million, is almost the same as that of Pakistan. They are the rather unhappy remnant of a once powerful people whose forts, mosques and domes dot the landscape and remain among the most distinctive of Indian images.

The Muslims are, on the whole, a shattered people who have yet to rebuild themselves, following the departure of so much of their talent and vigour to Pakistan. Today they are among the poorer sections of society, virtually leaderless and apathetic, lacking the dynamism that was once their stamp. They are divided and demoralized. They do not get their share of jobs in the civil service, nor their share of seats in the legislature. Politically and economically they are towards the bottom of the pile.

Their position in Indian society is anomalous and sometimes difficult. They have been made well aware of the increasing emphasis on the Hindu character of a country ostensibly committed to secularism. They have had to adjust to the idea of their fellow-Muslims being foreigners and suspect neighbours, and to the idea that the Hindus they once ruled are their compatriots and are in the ascendancy and will remain so. They have had to get used to the notion that when relations with Pakistan are bad they are held in some suspicion. At the same time they have generally had the worst of the communal riots that so bloodily punctuate Indian life.

Tensions often run very high where Hindu and Muslim quarters in a town adjoin. It needs only a rumour, a scuffle, some imagined insult to do with a pig or a cow, and scores of people can very soon be beaten and shot to death.

Muslims are scattered throughout northern India. Only in Kashmir are they a regional majority, and in Kashmir they had the great Sheikh Abdullah to speak for them for more than fifty years until his death in 1982. Elsewhere they have no-one who can instil the kind of self-respect that Kashmiris have and which was, perhaps, the sheikh's most important gift to his people. Muslims were loyal to the Congress after independence, because it ruled and because it was avowedly secular, certainly under Nehru. Some of that loyalty has waned and Muslims have grown disillusioned; but, in common with other poorer people, Muslims have tended to vote for Mrs Gandhi, who has always made it her business to keep in close touch with people whose lot is meagre. Certainly the Muslim vote was an important factor in her sweep back to power in 1980. Today these people are looking for the better deal they feel they deserve.

Muslims are outside the Indian mainstream in another respect: they do not have the feeling that their fellow countrymen have for astrology. Most Hindu people accept the importance of rituals like bathing in rivers and lakes and wearing sacred threads on their wrists and around their necks. They also believe strongly that the movements of stars and planets play a part in their existence, and, accordingly, astrologers, palmists, physiogno-mists, assorted seers and peddlers of superstition make a singular contribution to Indian life.

'You may notice', an MP said to me, 'that many politicians wear a pearl. They have been told to do so by their astrologers, for the pearl is considered to be connected with political advancement.

Many MPs wear a pearl and dream of getting a ministership.

'You have to understand that ours is a multi-polar society. There are many gods and there is no single scripture, no single prophet. Life has many colours. Astrology is only one of many factors operating in a man's life. Belief in the stars helps people to get through their lives. It is a form of cushioning, a comfort that helps to make life more bearable. Indians are no different from other people in that they require hope to help them survive, and their astrologers help to give them hope. A woman, yearning for a son, consults her astrologer. He says: You will have a son within three years. That gives her confidence, anxiety subsides. We all know that anxiety can play a part in conception, and perhaps she will have a son. It is, after all, 50-50. Similarly with precious stones. The astrologer tells you to wear one and you somehow feel yourself more dynamic and effective, even protected. Astrology has its place in politics, and we Indians are rather sensitive about it because we know some people think it is very foolish for a society which aspires to be considered modern to be affected in its actions by astrologers. But the fact is that we believe in an order in the universe and we cannot escape beliefs that are strongly rooted in our traditions.

'The most sensible and highly educated politician will check that elections and other important events happen on auspicious days and he will wear the appropriate stones and perform the appropriate rituals. The westernized businessman, as at home in New York or London as in Bombay, will consult his astrologer before going on a trip. A scientist who you think would know better will ensure that the stars are right before he launches some experiment or process. Everyone knows the importance of having an auspicious day for a marriage. And I would guess that a man's horoscope is the most precise document you will see in India. As I said, astrology is not the dominant force in life: it is one of the factors that people in India consider. It is more important to villagers than townspeople because they are closer to nature and need more help when deciding to plough, reap and sow and sink a well. But for most of us astrology is a kind of helping hand. You in the west, after all, have your psychiatrists and pills.'

Astrologers of all prices abound. One of them advertises in the newspapers: 'If you are fully disheartened, consult Professor P.G.A. Nath . . .' and offers consultations ranging from Special, 1,200 rupees, to High Super Delux Power, 3,400 rupees.

Mr Sarathy, an astrologer with a consulting room in one of the major hotels of Delhi, learnt his science from his father and started in business on a three-questions-for-two-rupees basis. Now he charges about £5 for a consultation. He said it was not unusual for bank managers to bring their loan-seeking customers to him. 'Such people believe it makes good business sense to get me to check the horoscopes and palms of borrowers. I recall one case in which I noted that a man brought along by his bank manager had not long to live and would not, therefore, be able to repay his loan. So he did not get one. A few months later, I am sorry to tell you, I learnt that the man had committed suicide.'

Mr Sarathy bit reflectively into his breakfast dosa, a crispy southern pancake, and flicked the crumbs from his snow-white gown. He said that many businessmen consult him before starting a new venture or taking a long business trip. Men contemplating going into a business partnership often go to his consulting room with the prospective partner's photograph and birth date. Mr Sarathy stares hard at the pictures to gain some insight into the man's character. 'Some European firms consult me, as well as Indian ones, and send me photographs of men who are under consideration for jobs. I am also consulted by people thinking of taking matters to law. We are a litigious people, and obviously clients want to know if they are going to win. Builders and civil engineers will seek help in determining the best day to lay a foundation stone or start a bridge. No-one would dream of starting anything on the eighth day after a new moon.'

Nor would most people attempt anything new or important at the time of an eclipse. Many prefer to stay indoors at such a time and insist that all their crockery and cutlery is washed, and they blindfold their ponies and donkeys.

All great events in India, and many smaller ones, are attended by astrologers. At an astrology conference in Delhi the chairman, a member of the cabinet, called for the establishment of a university chair of astrology and said that a seat in the upper house of parliament, the Rajya Sabha, should be reserved for an astrologer. Officially governments have nothing to do with soothsayers, but parliaments tend to open on auspicious days. And great political events, accidents and disasters are always followed by a crop of newspaper reports quoting astrologers, seers and sundry wizards saying: 'We told you so . . .' and claiming to have divined it all in the palms, cards and stars.

5

The power in the land

India and the house of Nehru

Mrs Gandhi asked newspaper editors not to call her an empress.

NEWSPAPER REPORT, 1982

A few critics grumbled at the way Rajiv Gandhi was hurriedly sworn in as prime minister the day his mother was murdered. To them it was a dynastic succession, an unseemly contradiction in a country so avowedly democratic. And this man had hardly any political experience, had held no government job. Indeed, Rajiv Gandhi had been, until fairly recently, the unknown member of the ruling family, content in his backwater, with his flying career, his Italian wife and son and daughter. He had shown no interest in politics and his friends knew only of his disdain for it. Now, over his mother's spilt blood, with the country in crisis, he was the new leader of India. It was not the first time that people had declared themselves affronted that India seemed to have an imperial family. But almost everyone recognized that it was the mystique of this family that in a critical moment provided India with a vital sense of continuity and stability. The swift succession was greeted with relief. There was no sensible alternative. This grated with some, but in that fact lay part of the story of the development of modern India; the astonishing house of Nehru has provided leadership for almost all of the years of independence. In India, and to the outside world in particular, the family has been the predominant presence of Indian politics and its fortunes have been to Indians an enthralling, sometimes entertaining, but always central part of their own evolving drama.

With Mrs Gandhi's death India made a certain break with its past. It was, in a particular way, a leavetaking. The Nehrus were strongly involved in the struggle to end British rule; they were intimately connected with the Mahatma Gandhi epoch. Motilal Nehru, his son Jawaharlal, his granddaughter Indira, as well as other members of the family, had gone to jail in the nationalist campaign. They were all 'freedom fighters' – the name given in India to those who worked for the independence cause and went to prison.

But Rajiv Gandhi was one of 'midnight's children'. If not exactly one of those born at the midnight hour of independence on August 14, 1947, he was certainly a man of the new India, of the generation for whom the freedom struggle was not part of personal experience, but part of history. He was an inheritor. And he was also, in a unique way, an inheritor of what his grandfather and his mother fashioned.

When I talked to him in Delhi he said that his grandfather's life is an inspiration to him, that almost everything in modern India is based on foundations that Nehru laid. I asked him, considering that India's population is twice what it was at independence and that its problems remain formidable, whether he thought the prime minister's task more difficult now than it was in his grandfather's day. In some ways, he said, yes: in those early years India rode the euphoria that accompanied independence. There had been a great struggle and the people had the satisfaction of winning it and they were united. In forty years that wonderful feeling had gone and the question now was how to replace that spirit, to fill the gap. 'It's the most difficult thing. One of our weaknesses now is that we have not been able to provide an ideology for our people. There has to be something they can work for.'

One of the problems, he said, is that India's economic and social progress had raised expectations. 'Difficulties erupt where a lot has happened. Go to those parts of India where little has happened and there is no trouble at all. What is happening in India is what you in England were able to do over more than 300 years, which gave time for society to change. We are trying to push it all into a few decades and it isn't easy.'

A few years earlier I had talked with his mother in the same room. In those days there was little of the security apparatus that now envelops the prime minister. There was no bullet-proof shirt, or lectern enclosed by armoured glass, or large teams of security men. Rajiv Gandhi and his wife were plain untroubled citizens. Today it is too risky for their own children to go to school.

Mrs Gandhi set much store by presenting herself physically to the people as often as she could. She travelled more widely in her own country than anyone else and until the army's storming of the

Golden Temple in Amritsar she was usually accessible and visible, not hemmed in by security men. No major political figure in the world had so much physical contact with those she led. Her father was prime minister for seventeen years. She held the job for sixteen. In Indian cartoons she appeared in a variety of roles, as mother, teacher, landlady, wife, big sister and empress. Empress is what writers, both western and Indian, sometimes called her and she protested that it irritated her. When she visited London in 1982 she asked newspaper editors not to use the term. That was because, in her sensitive way, she imagined that it was always employed pejoratively. But no single person in history ran India so completely as she did. No Moghul emperor, no viceroy, had so much territory, population and responsibility to manage.

She was keenly aware of the charismatic nature of her leadership. Even when she was out of office after losing the 1977 election many Indians believed she was still prime minister. She took care to remain a national figure, constantly going out to meet the people, with particular attention to those near the bottom of India's economic and social structure: Muslims, harijans, the rural poor. Where there was trouble in the form of a flood or cyclone, there was Mrs Gandhi, consoling. Throughout her career she provided lessons in the politics of popular appeal and, as did her father, derived a personal charge from her meetings with crowds. She had a genuine interest in the villagers who make up the majority of the population. 'In many parts of the country,' she said, 'I am called mother, and I regard India as my family.'

There is a photograph of her speaking at a meeting and at her feet is a woman in an attitude of prayer and adoration. People everywhere had respect and awe for the embodiment of power and its hierarchical structure. What an impression she created during the 1980 general election when she dashed from village to village, from crowd to crowd, riding her comber of revived popularity. People waited into the small hours for her. At night she sat in the front of a jeep and held a spotlight in her lap, shining it onto her face as she drove through the villages; an exciting vision, a goddess on the move, rushing through the darkness.

She was no orator. Few Indian politicians are. She spoke softly in stilted sentences to the people who turned out to see her. She usually expressed a few simple ideas, urging greater productive effort, unity and vigilance against unspecified enemies. If these routine speeches seemed trite, it should be remembered that the people had not gathered to hear stirring words reeking of midnight oil. They had come to see, and be in the presence of, the prime minister, to be satisfied that she cared for them, to take part in the enjoyable and monotony-breaking aspects of a gathering: the gossip, snacks and shoulder-rubbing as well as the pleasures of anticipation. Nor were these events the right place for the exposition of complex political and economic ideas. Mrs Gandhi's words had to be simple and illustrative, like parables. In many parts of the country she could not be understood by most of the people who flocked to see her.

These encounters with the millions were not the sum of Mrs Gandhi's showing of herself. There were also her darshans, morning audiences held in the grounds of her prime-ministerial residence. Every morning between 100 and 200 people were admitted to the garden to meet the prime minister and to bring their problems to her. The grievances were often small for a prime minister's attention: land quarrels, landlord persecution, some immovable human or paper clot in the bureaucracy. But a prime minister can crowbar obstacles at a word – Expedite! – and her actions in handling small grievances were important.

These audiences were sometimes held up as evidence of her autocratic, Moghul style, as an anomaly in a democracy. But the darshan is an Indian tradition. This is a society of hierarchies where the monarchical idea persists, and people have always had to work through the hierarchies to vent grievances, have wrongs righted and get things done. The grafting of democracy onto such a society was hardly likely to change it, and will not do so now. The growth of democratic politics has simply created new hierarchies and power centres with which people must deal, along with obstacles created by a tangled and inefficient bureaucracy. There is always a need for access and for circumvention, a channel for consultation, complaint, petition and justice, a method of pulling wires. In India people felt they could turn to Mrs Gandhi, just as people in England once felt they could turn to the monarch for justice. Tradition, and a legal, political and bureaucratic machine unable to provide redress and justice, make direct access to the prime minister important. This has its feudal aspect but it is a safety valve. It is uneven and arbitrary but it is one of the things that makes India work. But the old open-ness has been affected by the demands of security.

The hierarchical structure also makes people fawn. Sycophancy is woven into Indian politics and public life. Mrs Gandhi was the focus of gushing idolatry and some politicians abandoned any pretension to dignity as they danced attendance. They wasted much time and money travelling to the airport to see the prime minister off on trips, and being there with garlands and flowers when she returned. In 1981 the *Hindustan Times* rebuked the chief ministers of ten states who flew to Delhi at public expense to greet Mrs Gandhi on her return from an overseas journey. 'Servility', the newspaper said, 'is not loyalty. The Uriah Heeps of Indian politics are a disgrace to the nation.' Mrs Gandhi often looked testy when she spied the fawning benedictory courtiers, simpering on the tarmac, and from time to time scolded them for wasting flowers, and for being away from their desks. In government offices they told a joke to illustrate the craven nature of her followers: had she declared, on a bright morning, that night had fallen, her ministers would have rushed to the windows exclaiming: 'Yes, Madamji, we can see the stars. And look – there is the moon!' (The suffix -ji is added to names in India as a mark of respect and sometimes affection. Mahatma Gandhi is still referred to as Gandhiji. Mrs Gandhi was known variously as Mrs G, Madam, The Madam, Madamji, Mataji and Indiraji. Once it was known that her son Rajiv had installed a computer in his office he was labelled Computerji.)

Although servility is ingrained in certain Indians, Mrs Gandhi was herself responsible to some extent for these unseemly displays. Her upbringing and experience led her to prize loyalty above most other qualities, even if accompanied by an oily devotion.

　　She was quite different from her father, just as her son is markedly different from her. Her personality was marked by suspicion and insecurity, which stemmed from her experience in politics; an expectation that people would disappoint or try to use her. More deeply, her fears originated in an anxious childhood, as the only child of an emotionally buttoned and often absent father and an adored mother who died young of tuberculosis. The independence struggle filled half her life and helped to stoke tensions in the extraordinary family that shaped her. Her grandfather, Motilal Nehru, a lawyer, made a courageous commitment to the cause. Her father was frequently away at meetings or serving the prison sentences which totalled nine years. The atmosphere of the family home in Allahabad was charged with political arguments and personality clashes, by meetings, visits from political leaders, and from the police. Indira's mother was ill and, as Indira saw it, humiliated by other female members of the family for her lack of Nehruvian sophistication. Indira emerged insecure and shy and embarked upon a disrupted and unsatisfying secondary education in India, Switzerland and Britain. She grew up not well-read and a shade suspicious of those who were. By the time she reached Britain, to study at Badminton and at Somerville College, Oxford, she was already committed to the struggle – and also to the sari – her family having burnt their western clothes on a nationalist pyre years before. The knee socks, coats and frocks she was so often photographed in as a little girl were consigned to the flames. As a more personal act of dedication Indira cremated a doll, beloved but British.

In London she was courted by Feroze Gandhi, an amiable Parsi journalist, and married him in India in 1942, the year after her return. It was an act of a determined woman of independent mind. It was a love match, not an arranged marriage, and it was unusual for a Hindu girl to marry a Parsi. In conservative Hindu circles it was disapproved of and people wrote insulting letters to Indira and her family. Nehru was not happy about his daughter's action but he did not oppose it.

There were two sons of the marriage, Rajiv and Sanjay. Mrs Gandhi also gained one of the magical surnames of India, a lifelong asset. It was not only in the west that people still believed her to be the daughter or grand-daughter of Mohandas Karamchand Gandhi, the Mahatma, or 'great soul'.

Her marriage did not bloom as it might have. Her father became prime minister and needed a chatelaine and consort. To her husband's consternation and anger she became her father's hostess and moved into his house. She and her husband quarrelled often. It was not easy for him to be Nehru's son-in-law and Indira's husband. He became a member of parliament for the Rae Bareilly constituency in Uttar Pradesh, and built a circle of admirers. He died of a heart attack in 1960. His son Rajiv bears a strong physical resemblance to him.

By the late 1950s Nehru wanted his daughter to shoulder greater responsibilities. She had begun by being his hostess. She now became confidante and conduit, began to sit on committees and to deal with ministers and visitors. She travelled widely with her father and was privy to his talks with national and international leaders. She had a unique vantage point and a long political education at the seat of power, as the chief engineer gradually gave his apprentice more to do. He put the management of the Congress party into her control and in 1959 she was elected its president, the third Nehru to hold the position. She developed skills as a manager and alliance maker, and strengthened her relationship with ordinary people by touring the country and identifying herself with the aspirations of harijans and Muslims. She showed political muscle by being instrumental in the dismissal of the communist government in Kerala. She also made a good impression with the services by visiting the war zone in the 1962 conflict with China. This quarrel over frontiers was a demoralizing blow to her father's foreign policy which depended in part on a good relationship with China. It knocked the spirit out of him.

On Nehru's death in 1964 Lal Bahadur Shastri became prime minister, and Mrs Gandhi was in the cabinet as information minister. When Shastri died in January 1966 the Congress leaders, the so-called Syndicate, saw Mrs Gandhi, whom they disparaged as 'the dumb doll', as ripe for manipulation, and favoured her for the premiership. In the ballot she beat Morarji Desai.

Those who imagined she could be manipulated were mistaken. She soon dispatched the pompous kingmakers of the Syndicate and neutralized her opponents by splitting the Congress party. She also worked steadily to weaken the party's regional leadership so that her hold on the states became stronger. She knew the jungle well and revealed herself as a shrewd political operator with a good knowledge of the weaknesses and ambitions of men. She never had illusions about the sordid aspects of politics and the corruption and shallowness of many of its practitioners. 'She has few peers in the cold-blooded calculation of the elements of power,' Henry Kissinger once wrote of her.

The insecurity which she herself described as a theme of her childhood never left her. It shaped the woman and the leader. Her career was notable for her pursuit of unassailability, for her determination to be independent and always in command. She saw to it that her collaborators did not grow too powerful.

Her growth in the leadership answered a deeply felt need for a focus in the country, and reinforced in her own mind an idea of the destiny of the Nehrus. She established herself firmly in control through her landslide victory in the 1971 general election, and achieved the pinnacle of her premiership in her handling of the war later that year in which the Indian army played the decisive part in securing Bangladesh's independence. In other circumstances she had been bruised by the failure of expert opinion and decided that in this war she would trust her own judgment. She was clear and confident. The military operation was firmly directed and the Indian army's swift withdrawal after the fighting was an act of wisdom. The affair was a triumph, restoring Indian self-respect damaged in the 1962 China war. Pakistan was cut in two. At home and abroad Mrs Gandhi's stock was high.

Inevitably, the Bangladesh effect wore off. The economy stagnated and there was serious inflation, strikes and agitations, and food shortages leading to agrarian unrest. Mrs Gandhi had campaigned in 1971 under the slogan of 'abolish poverty,' an exciting message at the time, for such a social aim had not been so dramatically expressed before; but poverty was too entrenched for slogans and she raised expectations while having little ability to satisfy them. The oil crisis of 1973 added to economic torment. Prices rose, disturbances proliferated and a sense of insecurity increased. By 1974 the country seemed, to critics of the government, to be directionless. The tone of complaint in the press grew sharper. Among the bourgeoisie there was a feeling that anarchy had been unleashed. A protest movement against the government was started by the Gandhian romantic, Jayaprakash Narayan. Mrs Gandhi sensed, too, that rising discontent in her own party might threaten her leadership.

Against this background she snagged herself on a legal thorn. She had been found guilty in the Allahabad high court on two charges of malpractice in the 1971 election. By Indian standards they were trifling: she had used government staff to help her run her campaign. But the court ordered her exclusion from parliament for six years. The opposition roared for her dismissal and a national civil disobedience campaign was called. During the night of 25 June 1975 she pulled the plug, ordered a round-up of her opponents and critics and, next day, declared a state of emergency, suspending basic rights and freedoms.

This was not the outcome of a simmering plot, but the instinctive political reaction to a threat, the spring of a cornered tigress determined to survive and keep her grip on what she had.

The coup's swiftness snatched away the breath of protest. Some justices and lawyers spoke out, some journalists, too. But the imprisonment of politicians and journalists, and censorship of the press by foolish and petty men, left a frustrated silence.

Many accepted Mrs Gandhi's story that the emergency was a necessary way of saving democracy, public order and Indian unity. (There are people today who say it was right and beneficial and that, moreover, India would benefit from another dose. 'We have to get some discipline into our bloody country', they say feelingly, shouting against history and wishing their land were not the functioning anarchy that John Kenneth Galbraith called it.)

The emergency seemed to promise action to rid the country of so many trammelling irritations. A crackdown was ordered against black marketeers, criminals and hoarders. Prices were stablilized, production improved. It was announced that the trains were running on time. There was an emphasis on the most unIndian of qualities, discipline; and with it a feeling of a new start, as if India were a man on new year's morn setting out to cut smoking, drinking and paunch.

The personification of this mood of excitement was Sanjay, the prime minister's second son, leader of the youth wing of the Congress. His bespectacled sideburned face soon became almost as well-known as his mother's. He had risen, with little trace, from patchy beginnings. He was contemptuous of routine politics, impatient of criticism and ruthless. His steamrolling and unsuccessful attempt to set up the Maruti car factory showed the lengths to which he would go to get his way. He had a strong instinct for power and knew how people could be managed. He was despised for his arrogance, his scorn for convention, for his lack of philosophy. But it was just these qualities that many liked. He set out to reduce the population, clear hovels, plant trees, fight dowry; and rode roughshod over restraints. His pursuit of population control was hamfisted: through him the authorities brandished a knife. Forced sterilizations spread terror among the poor and illiterate. Village men fled at the sound of a jeep. In population control, as in slum clearance, officials felt licensed to act as brutally as they wished, as if the end justified even the cruellest means.

Sanjay had no formal office, but that did not matter. He was in the cockpit of power, at his mother's side as manager, confidant and fixer, answerable only to her. To his critics his rise during the emergency cast a shadow more forbidding than the emergency itself. His supporters, though, hailed him 'India's man of tomorrow', the embodiment of an abrasive order, of a brave new India, harnessed to science, technology and vigorous free enterprise, impatient for change. Close by him stood his myrmidons, a new breed of men, some of them MPs owing everything to the Gandhis, committed to no ideology, as politically unfettered as their master and, one or two of them, not averse to a little gangsterism.

Western governments (though not all western politicians) disliked the emergency and newspapers were hostile to it. In some parts of the world the emergency was considered an internal political crisis; but in the west it was viewed more as a moral one and Mrs Gandhi was reviled as a traitor to democracy and branded a tyrant. India's faults and weaknesses came under unsympathetic scrutiny. In part the anger was a mark of the high regard in which India was held by many in the west. Much hope had been reposed in it by those who saw it as a flag carrier in a world where democratic values were so often trampled by ambitious soldiers, autocrats and thugs. Hence the disappointment at Mrs Gandhi's abrupt action, and the concern at the surfacing and rising power of her son: the cruelties of the emergency seemed a particularly painful betrayal.

Mrs Gandhi did not wish to be a permanent dictator. Democracy is important to India and especially to Indians of the westernized and educated middle class. It is a bridge to societies and cultures Indians admire, and they rather like being in a club with challenging rules. It enables them to look the west in the eyes, as equals. Through the emergency they lost face. Mrs Gandhi also knew that although democracy might be hard to manage the alternative might be harder.

So, after nineteen months, she brought the unhappy episode to a close and called a general election, believing she would win. She lost. The people reacted to the emergency's oppressions: the ruthless clearances, the high-handedness of officials and their authoritarianism. They were angry about jailings and detentions, the loss of rights, the growth of a police state apparatus. Censorship of the press, which led to the prime minister being ill-informed, closed a popular means of airing grievances. The emergency also caused frustration by upsetting, through the creation of uncertainty, the traditional hierarchical system of consultation and ways of applying pressure. Above all there were the sterilizations (the reality and the rumours of them), which created such fear and seemed such an invasion to the humble people of northern India. Mrs Gandhi always prided herself on knowing the people of the countryside who called her mother; but in their millions they turned their backs on her.

The emergency showed how fragile democracy was, in that it could be suspended at a stroke by a cornered leader. it also showed how strong it was, for the emergency jerked people awake, brought them face to face with the issue of what the country should be. The excitement of the emergency faded and improvements were illusory: it demonstrated the importance of democracy as a way of running India; that democracy had, indeed, taken root.

India elected the Janata coalition of opposition parties. It might have been a turning point in Indian history but the Janata ensured it was not. After heady early days the stored-up hopes vanished like gas from a leaking balloon. The people lost patience with rulers whose attention was diverted by internecine quarrels and an unseemly hounding of Mrs Gandhi.

If there was one bizarre incident which typified the condition of politics at that time it was the case of the exhumed time capsule. The vessel contained, among other things, a history of independent India, and had been interred at Delhi's Red Fort in 1973, during Congress rule, for the enlightenment of historians 5,000 years hence. But the Janata believed the history was biased in favour of the Nehru family and ordered it to be dug up.

Mrs Gandhi did not brood for long on her humiliating defeat in 1977. Urged on by Sanjay, she assiduously fought her way back, tended the roots of her support, comported herself as a leader-in-waiting and split the Congress again to create a completely loyal machine. A cartoon by R.K. Laxman in the *Times of India* showed her as a stage hypnotist telling an audience: '. . . You can't remember a thing! There was no emergency! Nobody suffered! Nobody was hurt! Everybody was free and happy . . .'

In the 1980 election, at the head of her eponymous Indira Congress, she took power thirty-three months after losing it. 'India is Indira, Indira is India,' the slogan said. She won because Janata made a hash of ruling, because she offered leadership, because she seemed to be 'the only one'. It was a remarkable comeback, a complete rehabilitation, a journey from the ashes of defeat to the roars of popular victory. She was mistress of India again, unchallenged leader of 700 million, a world figure once more; and Sanjay was entrenched at her side.

Six months later the wheel turned cruelly. Soon after he took off from Delhi flying club at the controls of an American aerobatic biplane on June 23 he attempted a difficult manoeuvre, without having enough height, and he and his passengers were killed. The next day a multitude witnessed a prince's funeral. He was cremated on a sandalwood pyre while his mother sat on the ground staring at the fire until the sun sank and only the flames lit her sad and stricken face. The ashes were divided and taken to rivers and lakes for immersion. India was never to discover how Sanjay's power seemed ominous. At a stroke his ambitious young followers were headless and finished.

Maneka Gandhi lost not only a husband but also her place in the limelight at court. Resentment soon took root and she eventually left the prime minister's home, in a melodramatic departure well-covered in the newspapers, to become a political maverick, a focus for some malcontents, a girl armed with ambition, bitterness and the potent name of Gandhi.

For Mrs Gandhi so much seemed to vanish with the smoke of the pyre. She withdrew, almost into catalepsy. Her elder son moved to her side. Inevitably his own flying career was ended by his brother's fatal misjudgment. Rajiv was then 36 and had stayed in the background, eschewing politics and pursuing a satisfying career as a pilot with Indian Airlines. He devoted his spare time to his son and daughter and his wife Sonia, whom he had met at Trinity College, Cambridge, the college where his grandfather, Nehru, had studied. Many were hardly aware of his existence while Sanjay lived. He was plucked from pleasant obscurity to light his brother's pyre; and thereafter emerged as the person his fiercely independent mother needed, a loyal aide and go-between who could protect and inform her. He moved to the house next door. His key qualification was that he was his mother's son and therefore trustworthy. It underlined the importance of the family in India. 'The way I look at it,' he said, 'is that Mummy has to be helped somehow.'

A year after his shy debut I travelled with him in a jeep bouncing around the Amethi constituency, Sanjay's seat, eighty miles from Lucknow. He was fighting the parliamentary by-election there, and taking it very seriously, although there was no doubt he would win. This is the most backward part of a poor region of the northern plain, its one million people living in thatched mud houses in a region more than one third barren, punctuated with scrub and green copses. Roads are few and villages are linked by dusty tracks. In the jeep the dust was thick and stinging and Mr Gandhi sucked a clove to moisten his throat, the better to address the large crowds which waited for him in the villages under large posters carrying his mother's picture. He made his speeches, received petitioners, heard about local problems and then was off again, cries of 'Zindabad!' ringing in his ears, in a swirling plume of dust across the scorching plain.

In Delhi people asked what a nice fellow like Rajiv Gandhi was doing in politics, for Indian politics can be a rough and cynical trade, not at all for the mild. Sanjay had loved the political melee and the odour of power. But Rajiv's disgust at the murkier side of politics was evident. He was mannerly, unassertive, his integrity a marvel in a political world where so many danced to the music of graft. How, people wondered, would he survive?

With Rajiv an integral part of her court, holding his own morning durbars, learning political management at her side, accompanying her on trips abroad, Mrs Gandhi was once again complete. Two years into her new premiership her personal popularity, according to the polls, had hardly declined. But her ability to govern well was hobbled by her failure to build a team of talented, trusted advisers and to improve the morale of the bureaucracy. There were plenty of sycophants around, but too few people with the courage to tell her things she might not like to hear.

She found it hard to trust anybody and her suspicious nature was an obstacle in the way of recruiting suitable close collaborators. She was wary of people with their own power bases and nervous of having a coterie of advisers who might grow to like power. Like other people in power for a long time she became isolated and met few who would speak bluntly to her. She was the ultimate decision maker because so many of her subordinates were afraid to take decisions. But there were times when Mrs Gandhi was not at all decisive, so that her administration lacked direction. One sometimes saw in her pictures and on her face the expression 'Do I have to do everything around here?' She boasted of India's seam of ability, its ingenuity and flair, but did not quarry it herself.

One of India's pressing needs was to galvanize its management and planning. But Mrs Gandhi seemed unwilling and unable to move incompetents in the bureaucracy, the states and in industry; for one called a tyrant by her opponents, she did not seem to be half ruthless enough in vital areas. Many of her Congress chief ministers in the states were running rotten regimes; but she defiantly resisted criticism of them, even when their crimes were blatant. They were loyal, and loyalty was what she prized.

Her task was immense and the pressure huge, the conflicts

numerous and contradictions painful. No ruler had had her range of problems. India is a gathering of disparities whose nearest equivalent would be a united states of Europe. The centrifugal tugs are powerful. A prime minister has to be like a juggler who keeps a dozen plates spinning on a stage. There is the gulf between rich and poor, the gap between impatient, scientific and business India and ground-down medieval India. There is the oppression of harijans, linguistic and regional rivalry, enduring religious and caste tensions.

Although Indians had hoped for progress towards a casteless society, and there is a constitutional commitment to one, caste plays an increasingly important role in politics and the power structure. Caste is the enduring and resilient basis of social organization and provides politicians with ready-made groups, interests and loyalties, easily mobilized. It is through group power that people feel they can get things done. Even voting is a contradiction, an individual action in a society where most actions are collective. The country is committed to helping harijans, lower castes and tribal people by reserving places for them in colleges, government offices and legislatures. But this positive discrimination, a means of economic advancement, creates incongruities and resentments. Jobs go on quota grounds rather than merit and 'backwardness' has become a vested interest. The economics of caste, the caste block vote, and the fight for advantage among the quotas, is central. It would be unrealistic to expect representative politics to develop in India except on the basis of caste.

All this adds to the rumbustious nature of Indian politics. Uproar is a frequent condition of the lower house of parliament, the Lok Sabha. 'Opposition storms out in fury' is a headline no doubt kept permanently in type. On many occasions final results in elections have been dependent on the numbers of candidates who agreed to defect, for the right fee or favour, to a particular party. Many electors have found little wrong in their politicians being Vicars of Bray, for party switching is part of the game. After the states elections in 1982 Indian watched fascinated as rival politicians engaged in fierce horse-trading and fisticuffs.

At the same time the natural suspicions built into the Indian character, a reluctance to combine except with members of one's own close group, have formed the background of the endlessly fragmenting opposition parties. From time to time they talk of forming a united front to challenge the government and end up being more splintered and confused than ever. most of the non-communist parties have no economic or social programme and no philosophy and are led by old men with small followings. The best organized opposition is the communist party of West Bengal. Communism, Bengal-style, is one way in which Bengalis assert their identity. Few communists can ever envisage their philosophy penetrating the Hindu bulk; in any case such ideologies as communism and socialism, as they are understood in the west, have never really taken root in India and exist mostly as labels. In India caste and religion and language are the more important stuff of politics for ordinary people.

The congress party, the principal engine of political movement and change in India, ceased, under Mrs Gandhi's manipulations, to be a great democratic movement. It withered as she dug a moat around herself.

From the mid-1930s the Congress involved peasant communities in electoral politics and people from this stratum grew powerful in the party in the 1950s and 1960s. It was this power, the ascendancy of regional barons, that Mrs Gandhi shattered as she remoulded the party to her own design from 1969 onwards. She drove off a generation of older politicians and destroyed the Congress parties in the states which were democratic forcing houses, resources of political skill and organs of political expression reaching down through society. In breaking up regional power bases, and appointing her own men as state leaders, she emasculated Congress so that it was no longer a great vote-mobilizing and fund-raising machine. Thus Congress's central core became identified with getting cash, and that can be a murky activity. The proximity of chief ministers to the centre made them harder to punish.

The argument about her achievements and failings is endless. Her route to power was extraordinary, and she arrived at the top with no philosophy, the prisoner of no ism, without policies, with no urge to reform, a tactician but no strategist, a merely political creature, steely and determined and clever, but untouched by any genius. 'My father was a statesman, I am a political woman. My father was a saint. I am not,' she said once.

Haunted by insecurity, she spent much time consolidating her leadership. But once she was secure, the critics asked, where was the broader vision, the social reform, war on corruption, strengthening of institutions, popular control? Her mastery gave her opportunities. Yet she hesitated, failed to make more of India's resources, allowed bad men to flourish and fester under her aegis, and left a feeling that more might have been achieved. Mrs Gandhi responded by talking of agricultural advances, a great nation feeding itself, industrial and scientific progress ... nuclear, space-age India, a force for peace, non-aligned and independent, taking its strong and rightful place in the world community.

She might also have argued that her long tenure of the leadership was a critical factor in the forging of the national unity and a sense of nationhood so important in a newly independent country. She was a force for stability at the centre. Look at other countries, she might have said, torn by internecine feuding, unable to form stable governments. At least India remained a democracy.

This stability, however, was achieved at the cost of much damage to the Congress, which should have been developed as a central part of India's political vitality and long-term stability. Her dedicated accretion of power and weakening of Congress was a disservice to democracy, for it would be difficult for anyone to restore the machinery. Mrs Gandhi became increasingly isolated, could not easily control events and was vulnerable to unpredictable political storms. She talked vaguely of enemies: the ubiquitous foreign hand, the press, the judiciary.

Perhaps Mrs Gandhi's importance and main contribution lay in the idea of India she expressed at home and abroad, something her father did well. Abroad, she was an attractive and successful representative of her country. At home, she embodied India, an India united, with a sense of continuity from ancient past to present strength, a varied but single nation, justifiably proud. She had a feeling of mission about her role, a sense of the place of the Nehrus in India's long march. Part of her strength was in simply Being There. For many millions what Indira Nehru Gandhi did and said was enough. She had a remarkable relationship with the people, and it was this, rather than performance, that was always the core of her continuing popularity and power. Nevertheless, her policy of central rule, imposition of satraps of dubious worth on the states, and wasting of talent, proved to be weaknesses of her raj.

In the end she was overtaken by the storm that rumbled and then raged in Punjab. The fanatical Jarnail Singh Bhindranwale, who had been promoted by her own son Sanjay, and her own party, as a means of making political mischief among the Sikhs, grew steadily more monstrous and uncontrollable as he stepped up his terror campaign against Hindus and his moderate Sikh enemies. He was openly contemptous of Mrs Gandhi, 'that Brahmin woman' as he called her.

Sikh leaders failed to stand up to him and some of them sought to channel his poison for their own political advantage. The Congress government could not tame him. And at a critical time, when Bhindranwale could have been crushed, Mrs Gandhi held back, indecisive. She was losing her grip and she had few strong men around her at a time when she needed help: now she paid the price for keeping outstanding people out of her cabinet, for allowing herself to become isolated. The tigress had become tired and vulnerable. Late in the day, and by now desperate, she had little choice but to launch the attack on the Golden Temple to rid it of Bhindranwale and his men.

On October 31 1984 her Sikh bodyguards avenged the violation of the Sikh faith's core. She was shot down in her garden and Sonia, her daughter-in-law, cradled her in the back of a car in the hopeless drive to hospital. She was 66 when she died. Part of her legacy to her son was the mess of Punjab and many alienated and embittered Sikh people. Like his mother, Rajiv was a target for Sikh extremists.

His arrival in the leadership was acclaimed and cemented in an election victory at the end of 1984 in which he won a majority larger than his grandfather or mother had ever obtained. He was in a strong and unique position – a prime minister without a political past, free of the debts and stains of a political career, a modern man, modest and practical, the new India personified, nicknamed Mr Clean for his noted dislike of the corruption and manoeuvring of politics. One of his first acts was to rebuke the Congress party for allowing itself to be corroded by corruption, a speech that did not find favour with some old hands.

Somewhat to his relief the euphoria which surrounded his debut faded as people made a more realistic assessment of him, and he made his first mistakes. He set out to be a moderniser, to put vigour and relevance into the Congress party his mother hobbled, to battle the vested interests and the bureaucracy he described as 'one of our biggest strengths and biggest hurdles in getting things done'. He had drawn his own conclusions from his close observation of his mother's administration, her political attitudes and her end. The third generation of Nehrus to lead India promised a quite different approach.

6

The Indian rhinoceros

Losers and winners from corruption

He will not kill cows, but he can watch thousands of imprisoned
human beings wither before his eyes.

K. F. RUSTAMJI

THERE IS another India. The manifestations of it, eruptions
of cruelty and savagery, enduring injustices and callousness,
always lead to public displays of bewilderment, shame and
sorrow. When social sores are uncovered there are appalled cries
for reform. In smaller, more homogeneous societies than India,
with different traditions and structures, reforms may be successful, and the effect of law, education and practice can whittle
prejudice and bring about change. But the unique nature of India,
its conservatism, massiveness, passivity, opaqueness, apathy and
nearly sanctified prejudices and rivalries, make it resistant to
change. The injustices which shriek mockery at the ideals of the
modern state's founders seem too widespread and embedded to
be changed, almost too ugly to confront. It is true that there is care
and compassion in India, and honest rage at offensiveness and
hearts yearning for reform. But not enough. Minds cannot
grapple. Anger evaporates. The people shrug. The rhinoceros
skin of indifference thickens.

In the jails are many thousands of people condemned to hopeless years awaiting trial. The democratic and legal processes have
failed them and only a few people care very much. These untried
prisoners are buried in a system breaking down under the pressures of numbers, the failures of a harassed bureaucracy and the
incompetence and cynicism of its administrators, including the
judiciary, the magistracy and the lawyers. 'Our legal system is on
the verge of collapse, living on borrowed time', said Mr Justice
Bhagwati, of the supreme court, in 1981.

One victim of the grotesque failure of legal and penal management was a man called Ram Chandra. He was arrested in 1952

for riding on a train without a ticket and spent thirty years in a Bihar jail awaiting trial. The police had forgotten about him. His case papers were lost. The authorities confined him, fed him, exercised him and watched his mind deteriorate for all those years without apparently wondering why he was there so long. Had his case not been unearthed by a civil liberties group, and his release ordered by a high court judge, he would be locked up to this day. He is now free and a wreck.

A report in 1979 showed that more than half the people in the country's 1,200 jails were awaiting trial and many had languished in cells for years with little immediate prospect of being tried. In some jails up to nine-tenths of the inmates were awaiting trial. Thousands had been waiting in prison for much longer than the maximum sentence for the offence of which they were accused. Action by a concerned barrister in Delhi led to the supreme court ordering a clearing of the jails, the release of just such prisoners. People on bailable offences were also set free and, in all, more than 30,000 emerged blinking from the prisons.

That progress, however, was not maintained. It was a gesture and not a policy or a reform, India being a society where gestures rather than policies are practised. There are now about 100,000 people in prison with little prospect of an early trial and most of them are in the heavily populated northern states of Uttar Pradesh and Bihar.

In Bihar an inquiry discovered four boys who had spent almost half their lives chained up in a cell and officially forgotten. They were arrested when they were about ten years old and were confined for eight years and never tried. The supreme court judges, ordering their release, commented: 'This is one more instance of the callousness and indifference of our judicial system. People are easily forgotten and become mere ticketed numbers.' Such a prisoner was a woman who was in jail for nine years awaiting trial. She had been pregnant when arrested and her child, born in jail, knew no other environment.

A number of those who get lost in the prison system are the poor and illiterate who have no idea of their rights under the law. They do not know about bail and no-one tells them. Magistrates, who should advise defendants on their rights, frequently fail to do so. Many people are held for years because they are too poor to raise bail. Others are kept locked up, not because they are criminals but because they are witnesses and the authorities want to be certain they can produce them if ever a case comes to trial. A girl of 17 called Rina Kumari was kidnapped in 1976. Police eventually found her, and her captors, and kept her in custody to give evidence. She was still in a cell three years later.

Witnesses are often vulnerable to threats by the friends and family of accused men and many would flee in fear if they were not confined. In cases where witnesses are not available the police can draw on the services of professional or stock witnesses, who are part of the lubrication of the criminal law machinery. Such witnesses are usually small-time street traders, drink and food pedlars and the like, who pay bribes to policemen in order to ply their trade free of harassment. Some of them are persuaded to commit perjury as a sideline. They are often used to give evidence in drinking, gambling and theft cases, but from time to time swear to tell the truth in more serious cases. In 1980 the *Indian Express* exposed a man in Delhi who had been called as a witness 4,000 times (he had the witness summonses to prove it) and had even been fined twice for failing to appear in court to give his false evidence. The newspaper compiled a list of stock witnesses after one of them had forgotten his lines in court and the police were forced to admit he had testified often.

Considering the way justice works, and the conditions and traditions under which the police operate, it is not surprising that policemen should employ such methods. The reputation of the Indian police is low. They are feared rather than respected. In 1903 a police commission report said: 'The police force is generally regarded as corrupt and oppressive and it has failed to secure the confidence and co-operation of the people.' Little has changed. A deputy inspector-general of police in Gujarat said at a conference in 1977 that 'the police throughout India are at best tolerated with contempt, and, at worst, hated and condemned as a brutal force.'

The Indian police system is the most unfortunate of the British legacies, and democratic India has retained and strengthened it. It is rooted in the Indian Police Act of 1861 and has little in common with the tradition and practice of policing in Britain. They are not a people's police. They remain much as they were under British rule, essentially a repressive colonial force organized on military lines. They were not founded as a public service, but to keep order. They were meant to be the loyal instrument of the government and of the sub-governments run by the district magistrates or collectors. They became the intimidators of dissenters, the performers of the dirty work of the authorities, and never possessed any moral authority. Today they still use much force. Demonstrations are usually broken up with lathi (cane) charges or with gunfire. The number of police carrying arms has been greatly increased and the central reserve police, a force under government control, has also been strengthened.

As well as this there is now political control of the worst kind, with the police being an element, and a pawn, in the power struggles of politicians. Many policemen feel themselves the agents of the party in power, official bully-boys, their promotions and transfers being at the whim of their masters. And among the district bosses – the magistrates and the politicians – the policemen have a multitude of masters. Their functional independence is severely circumscribed. Their self-esteem is limited.

Considering the frequently-reported incidents of violence and high-handedness in which police are involved it is not surprising that there are few people speaking up for them. Yet the long-standing crisis in policing deserves understanding and those progressive police officers who ache for reforms deserve sympathy.

The task of the police in this huge, sometimes volatile, and complicated society is not easy and the police have a number of serious grievances against the government and local administrations. They are badly paid and poorly equipped. These grievances and the authorities failure to respond led to a police rebellion in Bombay in 1982, the breakdown of order, and the calling in of the army. Police chiefs have complained about the lack of such simple equipment as bicycles. The pay of constables is paltry, educational requirements low and the conditions in which many of them live scandalous. Training is poor. Inevitably the ordinary policemen do as many of their superior officers do: they intimidate and take money from the public. This is often done from avarice, but sometimes to achieve a merely decent standard of living.

In 1844 the great administrator and Thuggee-fighter, William Sleeman, wrote that people saw an incongruity in the government paying its revenue collectors well but not its policemen. 'Those who are to protect life and property, keep peace over the land and enable the industrious to work in security are left without any prospect of rising, and almost without any pay at all. There is really nothing in our rule in India which strikes the people so much as this glaring inconsistency, the evil effects of which are so great. The only way to remedy the evil is to give to the police security in office, a higher salary and a gradation of rank which shall afford a prospect of rising to those who discharge their duties ably and honestly.' A century and a half on, Sleeman's remedy remains exact and ignored.

Their pay and training inadequate, intellectual and material resources stretched, efficiency hampered by meddling politicians, public image poor, the police have obvious disadvantages in doing their work. The need for results drives them to illegal and brutal methods; and many have great faith in such measures. Confessions are often extracted with the aid of lathis, the most common police weapon, which are sticks four feet in length and an inch or so in diameter. A householder who reports a theft can be fairly sure the police will beat his servants as an opening to the investigation. The absence of genuine witnesses can be overcome by the employment of people blackmailed or otherwise pressured to give evidence. The killing of bandits in battles is justified, but sometimes other lesser troublemakers, and the sort of people described in India as 'bad characters', are eradicated by police guns and are branded, after the event, as dangerous criminals and outlaws.

Perhaps the police, like the civil service, suffer from a residual hostility stemming from the years of the freedom struggle. They were part of the ruling framework that the nationalist movement fought against. Inevitably, they get a bad press. There are frequent reports of shootings and beatings by police officers, of women being raped by them. There are complaints that policemen use their position to settle caste scores, that they are part of the power and weaponry in the class and caste struggles in the countryside, the allies of the rich in the suppression of the poor. In 1980 journalists revealed that policemen in the town of Bhagalpur in Bihar had systematically blinded thirty-one prisoners in their charge by puncturing their eyes with bicycle spokes and weaving needles, pouring acid into them and covering the eyes with acid soaked pads. There was some evidence that more men had been damaged in this fashion.

Naturally there was an uproar in newspapers and in parliament. 'What are we coming to in this country?' Mrs Gandhi asked, in some anguish, in the lower house of parliament. The *Indian Express* said: 'Every Indian must hang his head in shame, and not only in shame but for complicity as well. Many of us have prospered in a society in which we find such fiendish cruelty is possible in the name of authority. Not only possible but, as the perpetrators are bound to argue, even necessary to maintain that blood-spattered excuse for preserving the status quo: respect for law and order. We have been self-righteously quick to condemn other countries where women have been beheaded for adultery and hands severed for theft. These punishments for proven offenders were primitive, but they cannot compare with the casual cruelty practised in our own country.'

Fifteen policemen were suspended; but, curiously enough, people in Bhagalpur joined a procession in support of the police. They said the police had acted properly, meting out punishment to criminals who had richly deserved it. They were angry that the government had announced an award of £800, an enormous sum, to each of the blinded men. Someone wrote to a magazine that 'only after police have blinded some criminals have the roads become safe.' Police officers and politicians also said that the public supported such harsh measures.

It has to be admitted that people in many parts of India do not have much faith in the workings of justice. They want results and prefer to see criminals dealt with summarily. I once saw a thief thoroughly beaten by policemen with sticks to the evident satisfaction of a large crowd in Delhi's old city. Robbers and ne'er-do-wells are sometimes summarily punished by villagers themselves, beaten to death or hanged from trees or beheaded: justice in India can be rough.

Two months after the disclosures of the blindings journalists documented police brutalities in the city of Varanasi (formerly Benares), a holy place for Hindus to which pilgrims in their thousands go to wash away their sins in the Ganges. In the police stations here men were held down while booted policemen jumped repeatedly on their knees until the bones shattered. One man had a slab of stone dropped on his knee. He, and others, had to have legs amputated. Twelve cases were reported in the magazine *Sunday*, one of the modern breed of Indian magazines specializing in investigative journalism, which said there had been scores of similar brutalities in Varanasi. The *Indian Express* commented on the leg breakings: 'The known cases of atrocities by the keepers of law and order reveal only the tip of the iceberg, the bulk of which lies submerged in social apathy. Callous indifference makes our bloodthirsty police believe that they can get away with anything.'

A few months after this, *Sunday* exposed the treatment meted out to thirteen young men in Madhya Pradesh. They were hung by their ankles from a ceiling ring in a police station, beaten with staves and given electric shocks on their genitals.

Fear of, suspicion of, and contempt for the police is complete. Honest police officers with a sense of vocation are swamped. There is a widespread sense of helplessness. In other areas, too, the lack of official control and ease of circumvention undermine the Indian's sense of security. The police will not, or cannot, protect him; the other regulating agencies are ineffective or powerless.

Neither the authorities, nor the people themselves, seem particularly concerned about the regularity with which worn out and overloaded buses, driven by incompetents, fall off mountain roads and bridges and drive into canals and rivers. Bus crashes are a regular and routine form of death. Buses are ramshackle, poorly maintained, crowded and dirty. Owners are cynical and careless and drivers often unlicensed and untrained. They are also often drunk. Bribes take care of small details like driving tests and licences. The roads are lawless and the enforcement of regulations is made almost impossible because of the great need of ordinary people for bus services, even bad ones. The enforcement of even the simplest standards would cause severe dislocation and enrage the travelling public. People climb into their dreadful transport and trust to their gods, no doubt thinking that prayer is more reliable than the wild-eyed ruffian at the wheel.

Once, with a group of other travellers I rented a small bus to travel down a mountain road. It soon became clear that the steering, suspension and wheel alignment were bad. Several times the driver only just wrestled us back from the edge of a gorge. With great difficulty we ordered him back: it was difficult because his pride was hurt. We arranged another bus, this time with two drivers, one to take over when the other tired.

'Of course,' the owner said, bidding us farewell, 'the second driver cannot drive.'

'Can't drive?'

'No. The task of the second driver is to watch the first driver and to shake his shoulder when his eyes start to close. It is for your greater safety.'

The same disregard for safety in the pursuit of profit, and official incompetence and impotence, exists in the fields of drink, drugs and medical care. From time to time crowds of people are killed by moonshine liquor whose manufacture is a large and profitable business involving a network of thieves, suppliers of alcohol, liquor shop owners and smugglers. It flourishes with the connivance of policemen, excise officials and others who are bribed with the profits. In Bangalore in 1981 three hundred and twenty-five people died after drinking illicitly-made spirit which cost about three pence a glass. A few months earlier seventy people fell writhing and dying after drinking hooch in Haryana. In the autumn of 1982 sixty-two died after a celebration in Cochin. There are often reports of people being killed by the half dozen or dozen in this fashion, but it takes a large-scale disaster to make the authorities order a crackdown. The hooch is usually made with industrial alcohol and may be coloured by allowing some shoes to soak in it, or by adding metal polish.

The drinkers of such stuff are almost always the poor who cannot afford safe whiskey, gin, rum or vodka which costs about £2.50 a bottle. Even a bottle of beer at 40p is well beyond the means of people who earn only a few rupees a day. Safe liquor is kept out of their reach by the high prices charged by distillers and the duty levied by state governments. 'There can be no greater indictment of our society than the sickening regularity with which people are poisoned by laced alcohol,' the *Times of India* commented after the Bangalore incident. 'The victims are the poorest of the poor . . . their murderers are the traders and operators of stills able to buy protection for their criminal pursuits.'

The government of the ascetic Mr Morarji Desai (he was a teetotaller who believed in the benefits of drinking one's own urine) planned to move towards total prohibition. But India discovered, as many foresaw and as other countries knew from their own experience, that it was a hard policy to enforce. Prohibition increased smuggling and the manufacture of moonshine.

As with drink, so with drugs. In 1982 it was shown that,

according to reports of the Drug Controller of India, about a fifth of drugs on sale are fake, adulterated or sub-standard. At the same time police in Delhi found a backroom factory making millions of fake tablets to be passed off as well known brands of medicine. There is no real public concern about this sort of thing, and the policing is plainly inadequate. Another sort of quackery also flourishes: there are thousands of unqualified men who set themselves up in business as medical practitioners, trading on fear, superstitions and ignorance. There are all manner of sex advisers, abortionists, medicine drummers and sundry witch doctors, but worst of all are the untrained men who conduct operations with razor blades and rusty scissors. In mid-1982 the police arrested five young men who had been conducting peripatetic eye operation clinics in Rajasthan. (The arrests reflected no credit on the police who were well aware of what had been happening but had taken no action because 'no complaint was received'. They did not move until a doctor lodged a complaint.) The quacks had operated on more than 1,000 people by the time the police caught up with them and had blinded at least twenty-three of them with their razor blade surgery. They charged up to £30 for an operation. Elsewhere in Rajasthan police sought quacks who had performed abdominal surgery and others who treated headaches by making cuts in people's heads. The state health authorities did not seem to be unduly exercised about all this. Quacks flourish partly because medical services in the countryside are scanty. India has about one doctor to 3,000 people, but because medical services tend to concentrate in towns the ratio in rural areas is one to 12,000.

India has been justifiably proud of its record in medicine. Indian medical schools have always had the highest standards, and the Indian doctor is a familiar figure in the clinics and hospitals in other parts of the world. But in recent years apathy and cynicism have begun to gnaw at both traditions and standards. In 1982 the Medical Council of India withdrew recognition from nine medical schools in Bihar because of falling standards, this at a time when there were numerous reports of cheating and bribery in a number of universities and colleges. An inquiry started in Delhi into a racket in buying and selling medical college examination papers, and the reports of cheating and manipulation in the education system produced one of those episodes of critical self-analysis that punctuate Indian life.

It was not surprising to read at that time that university students in Delhi threw down their pens in an accountancy examination and staged a demonstration, blockading the principal in his office, on the grounds that the examination paper was too difficult. They protested for the same reason that thousands of students cheat their way through examinations. Indian society sets so much store by qualifications that failure cannot be countenanced. People believe they are born to follow a certain path, their dharma, and education and examinations are part of that process. A student is not on his own; he is, rather, a representative of his family and connected with the past and the future. Many educators and their students conspire to ensure that examinations are a door that can be opened, rather than a filter. Parents willingly pay bribes and fees to those who deal in leaked question papers because family pride is at stake.

Many educators and students, of course, are honest and the tradition of cheating embitters and confuses them. The honest are dismayed to see that degrees and diplomas can be had through manipulation and that they eventually lose their value. Students in some places have terrorized, or tried to terrorize, college authorities into permitting copying during examinations. In a college in Bihar students campaigned to win the right to cheat in examinations. Education in that state is in a considerable mess and it is no longer remarkable that students take their cribs and books into the examination halls. The students have argued that if everyone else cheats why should they be discriminated against?

From time to time, almost equinoctially it seems, there is a tide of soul searching and breastbeating among the educated and politically aware in India. Newspapers and journals sprout headlines like 'The roots of corruption', 'The tidal wave of corruption', and 'The gift of the grab'. The body politic is dissected, dirty linen is dhobied vigorously in public. In these bouts of self-criticism newspapers and conversation are suddenly full of the shame and anger and helplessness that many Indians feel about the corruption that poisons so much of Indian life, and also fuels it. Hands are wrung and those with a sense of politics and history ask anxiously: 'Where are we going, what will become of us?' And also: 'Who will lead us?'

Most of India's people do not feel this sense of shame or pricking conscience. Corruption, the need to find 'tea money', or 'speed money' or 'mahmool' has always been a part of their lives and they are quite resigned to it. They may feel hatred or contempt for the petty politicians, officials and police officers who extract money from them, or bend them in some way: but not a burning fury.

Corruption has been part of political and commercial dealing in India since ancient times and retains its place in a society with a considerable element of the feudal in its culture. Patronage and the using of office for profit and for granting favours have the sanction of long custom. Corruption exists in every society and in India is sustained for special reasons. Indians know well, as Orwell had it, that if all animals are created equal some are more equal than others. The caste system and rigid hierarchies have created a network of vested interests whose dealings with each other are carefully controlled for protection, profit and the maintenance of divisions. Some corruption arises from simple group loyalty, the pressures of which are very strong. Nepotism is hardly considered a crime. It is, rather, the proper discharge of an obligation. Family and caste come first and there is endless lobbying and string-pulling as people try to get their relatives into jobs, colleges and positions.

'Fixing' of routine necessities like licences, allowances, tickets and permissions is often done in response to family and group loyalties. These commitments are much more important than loyalty to some abstract ideology. 'Fixing' is also done for material gain, of course, and the receiving of money for such services is not condemned, for public office has always been regarded as a way towards the noble goals of enrichment, part of one's duty in life. Positions not only have status, they also have the envied 'over and above' that enables people to earn a more than average living.

A young businessman told me with a smile that 'All my friends want to be customs officers . . .'

An Indian wants little reminding of the need for material betterment. He can see and smell poverty everywhere. The gulf between poor and better-off is wide, and the sight and fear of poverty is another inducement for the 'haves' to have more, to strengthen the walls that will keep them safe from wretchedness.

So far as moral questions are concerned Hindus have a good idea of their obligations, and they also have a fairly easygoing and businesslike arrangement with their gods: they offer sacrifices and gifts to ask for favours, give substantial homage in gratitude if prayers are answered, and hurl abuse at the deities if things go wrong. When judged by other, particularly western, yardsticks, Indians may often appear hypocritical and dishonest, employing a number of standards for the conduct of their lives. An Indian looks in one mirror and sees a responsible man. He looks in another and sees an irresponsible one. Necessity, as Defoe said, makes an honest man a knave, and in India the forces of clan, caste and dharma contribute to necessity; although a quite naked avarice also plays its powerful part.

The spread of corruption in politics may be dismaying but should not be surprising. There is much anger and shame felt by those whose education, idealistic outlook and experience led them to hope for a certain rectitude in the public life of free India. There is, especially, disappointment among those who lived through the independence period and hoped that British principles of public service would remain pre-eminent. That there has been corrosion of such ideals is part of the pain of modern India. There is a feeling of betrayal and indignation. The British brought ideas of fairness, equality, impartiality and independence in such institutions as the judiciary and the press. Many of those who took part in the independence struggle, and later in the government of free India, were profoundly influenced by these ideas. In Nehru's time many Indians exulted in their democracy, parliament and courts. Standards in public life were good. Nehru inspired with such ringing phrases as: 'We have to build a noble mansion of free India where all her children may dwell.' Moreover, during the independence struggle thousands discovered the exhilaration of a cause in which they could see themselves as a great and united people, free of feudal constraints and pettiness, unchained. Today it may be easy to romanticize that period, but it was heady and noble, a reason for pride, and many look back on it now with great wistfulness, not least when fresh reports of graft and greed in public life are added to the pile.

'Those of us who grew up under the influence of the raj and the freedom struggle have gradually reconciled ourselves to certain departures from the ideals we once cherished', the *Times of India* said at the end of 1981. 'Jawaharlal Nehru tried to preserve and promote the best part of the British legacy, but it became clear towards the end of his life that he was fighting a losing battle. The reality of Indian life was too inhospitable to allow norms imported from Westminster to survive.'

Nehru, who died in 1964, never lived to be disillusioned. His daughter had no illusions. She knew much about the realities of power and the weaknesses of men and the nature of an ancient country in which democracy was newly arrived and would have to fight for its place.

Today corruption is omnipresent, an inescapable part of Indian political and administrative life. In a lecture in Madras at the end of 1981, Mr B.K. Nehru, governor of Jammu and Kashmir and a former ambassador in Washington and high commissioner in London, said he belonged to the age when India was honest and was unable to accept 'the canker of corruption eating into the vitals of our country.

'So inured have we become to it that instead of reacting to it as destructive of all morality and decency we accept it as a recognized way of life. Corruption is rampant in every sector of our society, private as much as public, but I speak today only of corruption within the governmental process for, given the dominant role that governments play in any country it is the values practised, rather than preached, by our masters that set the tone for society as a whole. Corruption has spread to every part of the governmental apparatus. We are powerless prisoners of the system within which we must operate. An uncomfortably large number of politicians and ministers are corrupt. Corruption is universal in the lower ranks of the public services, it has affected the middle ranks and is now affecting the apex which used at one time to be above suspicion.

'Why have we degenerated in one generation from being an honest society into a dishonest one? Part of the cause is the conversion of a static into a comparatively dynamic society. The change has upset old values but our exposure to wealth is so new that no new values have taken their place. But the principal reason we are corrupt is the political system we have adopted which cannot exist without large expenditure.'

Mr Nehru said the cost of fighting elections is enormous because constituencies are large, on average over 6,000 square kilometres with an average population of 1.25 million people. Apart from the cost of jeeps, posters, canvassers and the expenses of elections, there are the illegal costs of the private armies employed by many candidates to terrorize opponents and capture voting booths. It has been estimated that the cost of getting a man elected to one of the 542 parliamentary seats is between £30,000 and £120,000. To get a man into one of the 3,553 state assembly seats costs between £6,000 and £30,000. The costs to the parties and candidates are therefore colossal, and much of the money has to come from business, unions and other interest groups who will usually want some pay-off. 'The system has degenerated into a more direct relationship between money contributed and favour granted', Mr Nehru said.

Today, he said, only a small minority of politicians is interested in policy or lawmaking. New entrants are mostly interested in the pursuit of power and pelf. 'It is interesting, as an index to the kind of person who now wields power, that in one state no less than 30 per cent of the legislators are involved in criminal cases.' Chief ministers of states keep their supporters happy by giving ministerships to as many as possible. 'They enjoy the salaries and perquisites of office and are free to indulge in less palatable activities . . . Political corruption, which leads to a disregard of the rule of law, completely demoralizes the administration. Why should the civil servant bother about rules if a telephone call to the minister can upset his decision? Why should he stand up against the local politician if all that it earns him is the disruption caused by a transfer, and why, if his superiors are taking money should he not also share in the loot? The temptation to corruption is enormous, for the salaries of public servants have become ludicrous through the combined effects of inflation and taxation, with the consequence that those who by virtue of the power placed in their hands should never be in economic difficulty are always in acute physical want.'

Jawaharlal Nehru half-jestingly called himself the first English prime minister of India. In his day many politicians were like him, drawn from the westernized stratum. Today the majority of members of parliament come from rural areas. The country has come to town and brought with it some of the ruthlessness and toughness of a more feudal way of life: and country life in India is no idyll. This is an inevitable part of the development of Indian democracy. The new men have, in a way, been freed from old constraints and find themselves in a new and uncertain milieu where the standards are not enforced. Loyal to themselves and their families, they betray only the people of India.

The state of Bihar in northern India has always been a feudal, backward, incorrigible place, plagued by violence, difficult to manage . . . as the British found. Authority's hold has always been tenuous. By the early 1980s Bihar had become a symbol of waywardness and dashed hopes. Corruption, gangsterism, intimidation and the rusting of standards in public life had combined to give it a nightmarish quality. It was a world turned upside down. That students should take their cribs and books into examinations, having agitated for the right to cheat, became a matter of no remark. Education, like so much else in Bihar, had become a mess and the state a kind of sewer.

'Hardly anyone here talks of morality, honesty, or example', a university professor said to me in the state capital of Patna. 'In Bihar today honesty simply means a lack of opportunity to make money corruptly. There has been a collapse of standards. This is a place of criminals and tyrannies. You know that there is corruption in many parts of the world, but in Bihar everything is worse. There are many honest people here and their lives are marked by the shame they feel.'

Bihar is not blessed climatically: it suffers the worst of the cold and the worst of the heat, and considerable flooding, too. It has 70 million people, being the second most populous state, and is rich in resources, including two-fifths of the country's mineral wealth. But it is badly managed and thirty-eight of its forty public undertakings are chronically in the red. The great majority of people work as marginal farmers and landless labourers. They are in the thrall of landlords and their caste allies who have much of the police force on their side. The ruling élite has contempt for the law and pays well below the minimum legal wage. The labourers, many of them untouchables, are serfs in a feudal system, cowed, effectively disfranchised by a ruling class determined to maintain the upper hand. Much of Bihar's bloodshed and brutality springs from the efforts of high caste masters to keep the lower caste helots beneath the hatches. Tension has grown because the poor have demanded their rights.

I went to a low-caste village called Pirhi, forty miles west of Patna. There was no road to it and it took about an hour to walk there from the main road along a dusty footpath through fields and hamlets of rough mud houses. As always in villages there was much courtesy and kindness. Chairs were fetched and dusted, tea and fresh milk brought, and a curious crowd gathered, small boys watching intently as I wrote notes. A little earlier some of the people had shown courage by demonstrating for better wages. Some of them were getting only threequarters or half the legal minimum of twenty-five pence a day. In retribution for the demonstration the police visited the village and arrested 128 people. When the villagers protested the police opened fire and killed two. A boy of 17 showed me his arm. He had been hit by a police bullet and the wound had turned gangrenous. A doctor asked for £118 to amputate and to save their son's life the boy's parents sold more than half their patch of land to raise the money.

The people were bitter. They talked of organizing to fight the oppression of their landowner bosses, and the molestation of their women by police and the landlords' goondas, or toughs. But they were hopelessly ill-equipped to carry on any kind of struggle, too beaten down to be in prerevolutionary turmoil. I asked them if they had ever voted. They said no. They made their fingers into the shape of pistols and said they were kept away from polling booths by goondas' guns. They were angry about this, for they knew they were being deprived of something important, but they also knew they were utterly helpless.

In Patna that night I met a magistrate and we talked about Bihar's progressive legislation guaranteeing minimum wages and instituting land reform. 'When I was serving in north Bihar I tried to enforce the minimum wage laws, but the landlords got at me. I was called a communist and was transferred to Patna and put out of the way.'

In 1981 the state government introduced pensions for people over 60 of thirty rupees, £1.80, a month. An old woman explained, in an interview with the *Indian Express*, what happened. 'First, the local clerk has to recommend your name to the block office and the bribe he demands is 50 rupees, plus a regular commission on the quarterly payments. The block office sahib charges 40 rupees for signing the application and he also receives his cut every quarter. In the 18 months since the scheme started I have been entitled to 540 rupees, but I have received only 90. I am lucky. My name is on the register, so I get something.'

In 1980 Jagannath Mishra, a member of a rich Brahmin landed family, became the state's chief minister for the second time. More than anything else this man and this state came to represent the rhinocification of India. His regime was characterized by cynicism, dishonesty and inefficiency. Even the members of his own party took a memorandum to the prime minister saying his name was synonymous with corruption and nepotism and that he had made money the basis of Bihar politics. People were reminded that in a case in Patna high court in 1978 a judge had said that 'if the chief minister (Mr Mishra) can take a bribe, why should not other members of the services?' Mr Mishra laughed it all off with a wave of his heavily beringed fingers. As a politician he was a creature of Mrs Gandhi and an enduring insult to her judgment. 'God up there, Mrs Gandhi down here,' he once said in an interview. And in another: 'I enjoy the confidence of the electorate so long as I enjoy the confidence of Mrs Gandhi.'

Mr Mishra was a religious man, frequently seen praying and offering homage. His domain, his area of darkness, was, when I saw it, a defeated place with a pervading moral drabness. Those who cared about their home state wore an air of weary resignation. Anarchy was complete. The police had become, by and large, the people's enemies. A former chief minister wrote that Mr Mishra had 'acquired the knack of selecting corrupt officers to run his departments, so that we are saddled with a corrupt ministry, a corrupt administration and a corrupt people.' Part of the network of corruption run by politicians and public servants was the trade in job postings, with bureaucrats, engineers, policemen, educators, doctors and others paying thousands of pounds for 'wet' postings, that is jobs where bribes are handsome. 'Dry' posts were occupied by men who could not afford to buy lucrative ones . . . or by honest men. Some government-employed doctors pay up to £10,000 for a posting to urban areas where they can also run private clinics. During a general strike in Bihar doctors looted government hospitals, carrying off equipment to their private clinics.

The workings of justice were manipulated by court clerks who, for a fee, changed the court lists to suit lawyers and their clients. The courts recognized the abuse by insisting that the clerks paid for some of the court stationery out of their bribes.

Almost every week the newspapers carried a fresh crop of horrors.

'Welcome to hell', a newspaper editor said when I called on him. His newspaper was under pressure from the state government for publishing critical reports, and the Congress party was complaining that newspapers were 'spoiling the image of the government and the prestige of party men.' In the summer of 1982 Mr Mishra hurried a bill through the assembly intended to intimidate the press. There was nothing subtle about it. It was an open act of aggression against the democratic structure. Under Mrs Gandhi's aegis Mr Mishra felt safe to do as he liked. Newpapermen who criticized the Mishra regime would simply go to jail. When the journalists of Bihar marched in peaceful procession to present a letter of protest to the state governor they were attacked by police wielding lathis. I read that the editor who had bid me 'Welcome to hell' was beaten unconscious.

Bihar is not an island, of course. What happens here happens in some form in many parts of India. The struggles between castes, the rule of hosts of petty tyrants, the repression of the weak, the fight for a meagre existence and the intimate knowledge of poverty, are the enduring lot of most people, and this has not changed much in many hundreds of years. India seems to many who visit it to be hard and uncaring, long on ruthlessness and short on pity, a society better known for its elbowing than its embracing.

I cannot say whether India is more callous than it was 50, 100 or 500 years ago. The tyranny of the land and rulers and invaders have produced in this ancient civilization a willingness to bend reed-like before oppression and evil: the people's obeisance to power, their readiness to compromise, their resistance to change, their suspicion of those not their kin, are elements in the survival of the Hindus. They have bent and, like their religion, have accommodated.

They have frenzies from time to time, and dreadful and bloody ones at that; but they have no decent long lasting rage, an anger that could be channelled into reform. Their bursts of outrage at injustice are honest and sincere enough. Their hurt is evident. But a fine anger does not root: it evaporates, as if shrivelled by the sun and blown by the wind. India's soil is too thin for revolution. It is not a place for mass movements and a determined common purpose (with one or two notable exceptions), and in its history its people have not often linked arms. India is a land of communities and clans and hierarchies, and therefore of wariness and mistrust in personal dealings. It is a land of small shops and family firms, not department stores. Its political parties are riven by cavilling and backbiting, and splinter readily. In keeping their distances from each other and upholding their myriad demarcations, in concentrating on their immediate circles and on themselves, Indians have learnt to disregard others, to keep care and compassion on a tight rein. Perhaps, too, the simple realities of life and its awesome paradoxes, the wretchedness side by side with wealth, the struggles, the crowds, the climate, force people to harden their hearts. To consider the poor might be unendurable for many. The idea of consideration is, in any case, not strong.

So it is that when a new building is erected its staircases are soon covered with red pan spittle, the paint peels and the cement crumbles and no-one ever cleans or mends. But homes are neat and clean. The gap between private cleanliness and public squalor is one of the notable paradoxes of India. Men empty their nostrils and throats in front of you. Buses run you off the road. Electricity junction boxes lie broken open in a tangle of fuses and scrap wire. Farmers pay labourers in poisonous lentils, which lead to paralysis and crippling, just as they have done for centuries. Bodies lie for hours on railway lines or roads, a public spectacle, before someone makes a decision to move them. People flee after road accidents, rather than help the injured, for fear of becoming involved. Concern, altruism and a fire for reform are not the attributes of the new politicians. The low-caste man bows his head: he has deserved his lot, and perhaps, after this expiation, his next life will be better.

There are no better critics of Indian callousness than Indians themselves. They have a very sharp critical faculty and they are certainly more scathing about their national shortcomings than any foreigner could be. Indians know how to heap contumely. There are journalists, politicians, social scientists, academics and any number of ordinary people who deplore the evils they see. When one considers the vastness of India they are very small in number; but they are beacons.

Those aspects of life that so many Indians find disagreeable and worthy of their contempt, or anger, are of course much more public than they ever were. Freedom may not be unbounded, but this is a country in which abuses can be revealed in the newspapers, debated in parliament and made the subject of marches and meetings, and explored in the cinema. Indians today know much more about their country and the conditions of their countrymen. But that has not made them angrier. The cultural and historical disposition to indifference is not easily modified by exposure. Mahatma Gandhi, Nehru and many others offered

Dacoit Malkhan Singh surrenders in June 1982 at Bhind: it says much about the status of bandits like Malkhan that his surrender was received at an astonishing public ceremony

Rickshaw loaded with paper, Delhi: Indians have learned to cram . . . to sit on one buttock, to stretch the seams of their streets, houses and vehicles

India an alternative: their movement was to remove a foreign management that had stayed quite long enough, to restore and build Indian self-respect along with the founding of a nation. They proposed something astonishing, a polity rooted in self-lessness, sympathy, a broad encompassing unity. It was one of the wonders of the world and even today it is possible to be touched by its distant excitement. It remains for some a genuine inspiration, and, at the same time, the basis of their feeling of betrayal: that perhaps, after all, what happened in the march to independence was a noble aberration; that India, like the beer-brown Ganges, rolls on, sweeping all before it.

7

The mirrors of India

Films and the press

Wicked! Immoral! Devilishly Atrocious! A Hot Box of Sins!
NEWSPAPER CINEMA ADVERTISEMENT

THERE WAS a large crowd outside the cinema and a seething scrum of young men in flared trousers at the ticket office.
A bulky Sikh used his paunch to clear a way to the front and he
thrust his muscular arm and rupee-stuffed fist into the guichet,
demanding thirty-four tickets for his family and friends. Seeing
that Indians believe in positive queueing I shed my western
diffidence, wrestled my own wrist through the thicket of hands
and bought a five rupee balcony ticket. I was just in time. A couple
of security men pushed a steel grille closed, fighting off some
squirming bodies trying to wriggle through, and posted a House
Full sign. The ticketless waited hopelessly for a while, their hands
groping like prisoners', faces pleading, until at last they drifted
away.

The cinema was fairly typical, a great hangar like the British
provincial Regals of old. The air was clean because smoking and
eating are forbidden. There was no smell of hotdog onions as
there is in the west, and no gluey popcorn underfoot. The pre-
liminaries to the main film were some advertising slides – a slide
showing a drawing of a girl in her modest underwear provoked a
full-throated Punjabi roar of approval from the young men in the
two-rupee seats below – and a government documentary. The
showing of these documentaries is compulsory, which is rather a
good idea. The cinemas have to contribute a little of their income
towards them and this money finances a large documentary
industry which is a breeding ground for writers, directors and
technicians.

One of the documentaries I saw held a mirror up to the citizens
of India and asked them to behave better. Indians, like most other

people, do not much like foreign criticism and love, perhaps too much, foreign praise; but in print, conversation and on film they can be stern critics of themselves. This particular film was devoted to Indians' bad habits: it showed them clearing their throats and spitting, vigorously scratching their genitals and being in other ways unmannerly and careless of the sensibilities of their fellow men.

The main features, the popular films, meet a profound need for romance, drama, colour and escapism, and are made to an aggressive and repetitive formula. A typical film is very long, between three and four hours, because filmgoers like to feel they are getting value for money. In general, films have a love story woven into a battle between good and evil, much action, a little slapstick comedy and, almost always, four or five sudden breaks in the plot in which the leading actors break into song. A film usually has at least two sad songs and two happy ones, so that almost every film is a musical. As in the days of white hats and black hats in old Hollywood, the difference between good and bad is plain. The bad are always defeated and the rich are made to suffer in some way. The good girl gets the hero and the vamp does not. The bad policeman and domineering mother-in-law are stock characters, while the heroes' mothers are good ladies often seen praying for their sons. A happy, or at least a positive, ending is mandatory. India is a country where people aim to survive and they want their films to give them ideas of survival. They do not want unresolved dilemmas, to be sent out into the night puzzling.

Social themes are popular and the story has to be strong. People see enough of poverty and various kinds of wretchedness in their ordinary lives not to want film makers to dwell on these things. But all social issues, dowry, the oppression of women, the ruthlessness of landlords, the brutality of the police, are explored in films. Indeed, films are an important popular medium for ventilating such matters.

Films are often historical epics or have references to Hindu mythology so that, as in pantomine, the audience addresses itself to a well-known theme. Film heroes tend to be almost excessively handsome, chocolate-faced as they are called in India, and many of them look rather well-fed, their belts and tight shirts under considerable pressure. Most films have fight scenes to enable the hero to demonstrate his masculinity. Battered and bloodied, he wins through. He is usually an uncomplicated character and few directors allow their heroes to have human weaknesses. Although some of the violence is stylized much of it is gratuitously brutal and sadistic.

Villains are identified by scowls, cruel moustaches and their adoption of western customs and technology. The first cigar seen on an Indian screen was smoked by a baddie; and the first helicopter was flown by the forces of evil.

Heroines, too, are cast in a mould. They tend to be luscious and ripe, sometimes a shade over-ripe, catering to the Indian male preference for big bosoms and haunches: ideas of female beauty have changed little in centuries, as you can see from temple sculptures. The epic poems celebrate these characteristics and also the admired three folds of skin at the waist. The 2,200-year-old *Mahabharata*, for example, talks of 'the broad-hipped one . . . her breasts dark-nippled, rubbed with heaven's sandalwood, were shaken up and down. Through the upborne burden of her breasts, and the sharp movements of them she was bowed down at every step, with the surpassing splendour of the centre of her body gloriously girdled around by three folds.'

The cinema is an important outlet for young men, the one place where, for a few rupees, they can look uninhibitedly at lovely women. In a society where there is little dating and courtship, and boy does not meet girl, the cinema fills the gap. As in the west, films show girls' figures to advantage. A director may be lucky and wriggle a bare thigh past the censor. The camera may linger on a bejewelled and undulating bodice, a scapula may briefly thrill. The heroine will perform a chaste dance. The bad girl, the villain's moll, will be more decadent. She smokes and drinks and wears a low cut blouse and a slit skirt, so that you know she is going to come to a bad end.

The marketing of films has a strong sexual emphasis. The hoardings are full of garishly painted pneumatic ladies. The newspaper advertisements promise 'Hot Sexy Drama!' 'Wild Sex Games!' 'Titillating Hot Stuff!' 'Seventh Thundering Week! Voyeuristic Glimpses Into The Sensual Erotic World of High Fashion!' None of the films actually provides anything of the kind. There is nothing in Indian cinema remotely resembling the frank portrayal of sex common in other parts of the world. Censorship in India is strict. Indian film makers usually censor themselves because they know what the censor and the public will stand for. Western imports are invariably cut heavily and unskilfully. In its dealing with the erotic the Indian cinema inevitably has a keyhole quality.

Foreign films are reputed to be sexy and film festivals in India are therefore well attended. An international cinema festival in Delhi developed into a bear garden because of heightened expectations about what was showing. Police wielding lathis dispersed angry audiences, shows were broken up by furious spectators, actresses were in tears, government ministers were accused of wangling free tickets. 'Audience Turns Violent', said the headlines, 'Bedlam At Festival', and 'Stampede For Hot Film'.

Much of the trouble was caused by rumours that certain films were more revealing than they actually turned out to be. A capacity audience waited excitedly for a risqué European film to begin, having half-exhausted themselves in the rituals of begging and fixing tickets. The film, however, was black and white, Spanish, serious and quite sexless. The audience grew restive. Men stood on their seats and held their hands and handkerchiefs in the projection beam. There was a sudden rush for the doors and people besieged the ticket office demanding their money back. A frustrated man smashed a glass door with a mighty kick. Seats were torn in frenzy. Some of those who left early were clever enough to sell their tickets to people who had been unable to get in, promising that the film was hot, and these late entrants added their dismay to the uproar inside.

'Film festivals in India provide an opportunity for the well-heeled and well-connected to engage in titillation', the *Hindustan Times* commented. 'If there is no nude scene the film is bound to be a flop. If there is the slightest exposure of the female form people will beg, borrow and steal and consider the effort worth the humiliation. On the surface it is all in the interests of art. But the mass of skin is the message. It could not be anything else for a people so sexually frustrated as the Indians.'

Indian films do not show nudity or explicit love scenes. An endlessly worked topic in film magazines is: to kiss or not to kiss? Actresses are interviewed and say they would kiss if this formed an honest part of an honest film. Others say they would never do on screen what they keep private in their off-screen lives. Thus physical contact is mostly a matter of suggestion. The hero's cousinly peck on the heroine's forehead carries a considerable emotional charge because of what it hints at. Songs sometimes carry lines of *double entendre*. The camera can linger on a hip or a navel. A glimpse of a sari being re-tied signals that hankypanky has occurred.

Everything is relative, of course, and there is a continuous criticism of the increasing sexual overtones and violence of Indian cinema. Popular films are the despair of the critics. A Bombay film magazine editor said to me: 'In the past year or two the quality of films has gone down from dismal to very bad. There is no reason for producers and directors to do better. People like the trash they serve up.'

The serious filmgoer and the critic deplore the Indian cinema's straying from its roots. India was excited by the possibilities of film ever since the first was shown at Watson's Hotel in Bombay in 1896. Early film making was rooted in mythology, historical drama and rural folk theatre and the Indian cinema enjoyed a golden age of integrity and maturity during the 1930s and 1940s. After independence, however, Bombay began increasingly to ape Hollywood, complete with a star system and big-money investors demanding quick profits from mediocre and formula films. The film industry is an important conduit for black money – income not declared to the tax authorities. Cinema developed with the phenomenal growth of the cities and towns, cinema-going being primarily an urban pursuit. The critics wish there could be a wider appreciation of the work of directors like Satyajit Ray and Mrinal Sen, whose films are internationally known for their originality and strength.

In south India, the Madras studios, which turn out films in a dozen languages, have been involved since independence in politics, and, in particular, in the rivalry between the Congress party and the DMK, the southern party fuelled by resistance to the domination of northern India and the superiority of the Brahmins. Congress was routed in Tamil Nadu in 1967 and 1971 partly because of the DMK's campaigning through films written and directed and acted by DMK supporters. The introduction of political points into films, both subtly and blatantly, became something of a sub-art. Southern politics have been dominated by film stars and film writers. The present chief minister of Tamil Nadu, M.G. Ramachandran, an extraordinary figure in dark glasses and a fur cap, is a star who has drawn millions to his long, mushy, exciting, noisy films, and is worshipped by his fans. He stands for the pride and independence of an ancient people.

Nothing demonstrated the hold that film stars have on the lives of ordinary people better than the illness, in 1982, of the Bombay actor Amitabh Bachchan. He was injured during the shooting of a fight scene and for some weeks lay at death's door with severe abdominal injuries. His struggle for life gripped the country. Crowds kept vigil outside the Bombay hospital where he lay, pierced by tubes and fed by drips. Public prayer meetings were called and people gathered in their thousands to plead for him. Advertising hoardings were rented to carry messages urging the hero to survive. The prime minister and her son visited his bedside. Hospital bulletins on his condition were front-page news every day and newspapers and magazines carried large articles. In the robust way of Indian publications they spared no details and all India knew of the state of the star's lungs, stomach, intestines, throat, liver, blood, faecal matter and much else.

Mr Bachchan, who was 40 at the time, was a mixture of Superman, Valentino, Clark Gable, James Dean and the better sort of pop star. He was a heart-throb and tough guy. In an industry notorious for its sulky, overpaid and insufferable stars he was a paragon, an actor who always arrived on the set on time and never displayed temperament. He was the most famous, most adored, most handsome star in the land. He could earn £200,000 a film, making him the highest paid actor in Indian film history, and his popularity made him an important part of the industry's financial foundations. His name on a contract guaranteed a film's success. Nowhere were the hospital bulletins read more assiduously than in the offices of the producers. For Bombay's moghuls he was a human fruit machine stuck permanently on jackpot. As the star lay between life and death his films played to packed houses. For weeks in Bombay a 30 pence ticket for an Amitabh film could only be had on the black market, for £3, with a two-week waiting list.

There was a happy ending to the story. The prayers were answered and people gave thanks to their gods. Banners were hung in the streets expressing gratitude. Advertising hoardings proclaimed with joy:

GOD IS GREAT

AMITABH LIVES

Interviews with film stars, excerpts from old films and, above all, the Sunday film, are the most popular features of Indian television. Indeed, old stock from the studios of Bombay and Madras is the very backbone of the nation's television service, not just in viewing terms but financially, too: there is heavy competition for advertising slots at the times the films are shown. And film music is an important part of radio output.

Both radio and television are strictly controlled by the government and are, in the main, drab and unimaginative. It is not surprising that those viewers who live on India's edges often tune in to more enjoyable programmes, including western films, broadcast from Pakistan, Bangladesh and Sri Lanka. A man wrote to All India Radio in 1982 threatening to place a bomb in his local radio station because the programmes were so boring: many people knew the feeling.

The development of broadcasting in India has been stunted. Its possibilities as a way of spreading education, information and entertainment have remained largely unexplored. Broadcasting journalism is a small and undeveloped craft of little importance. Radio and television have barely any role to play in the democratic process. Jawaharlal Nehru once said that broadcasting should approximate as far as possible to the British model, but his and subsequent administrations have been afraid to allow broadcasting to develop: this particular box is securely nailed down and Pandora is kept well away. The government's strongly-held opinion is that radio and television should not have autonomy, that their function is to project government policy and government versions of events. In the dissemination of news they are totally at the government's service and are the official voice. Critics complain frequently that broadcast news is rather like that in totalitarian countries. It has a flat official tone, is read in a portentous fashion, is woodenly scripted and presented. Controversial matters are played down or left out. The official imprint, and the omissions, undermine its credibility.

The government's case is that radio and television are meant to educate and enlighten a developing society and should not be a forum for political controversy or the cause of spreading trouble when feelings are running high. Public order is a central consideration in India, a country where there is social tinder not found in more homogenous societies, and the government feels that the contemporaneous (and, inevitably, dramatic) reporting on radio and television of, say, a bloody clash between Muslims and Hindus would trigger off rioting elsewhere. There is a firm view that India is 'not ready' for unrestricted radio and television reporting. Apart from that, ministers are often irritated by newspaper reporting and believe that official control of broadcasting is an effective way of balancing it. 'You are not giving correct picture', is a complaint often made to journalists by those in power in India: and radio's job is therefore to give correct picture. Mr Vasant Sathe, a former broadcasting minister, once said that 'news from All India Radio is the most acceptable form of news.'

Broadcasting is run as a government department, by civil servants rather than by broadcasters and professional managers. The whole operation is hallmarked by timidity and not a little sycophancy. There is little encouragement for writers and artists, the financial rewards are poor and production facilities old-fashioned and bad. The grip of the government and its bureaucracy throttles imagination and innovation. Indian talent never gets a chance.

All India Radio has a strongly regional character and broadcasts in many of India's languages and dialects. News forms a quarter of its output and it can reach nine-tenths of the people. Television has grown more important in recent years, thanks largely to popular soap operas. Those who can afford them buy video machines and watch pirated films and copies of western television dramas. The bulk of the people stay loyal to the cinema which, for two or three rupees, gives them the stuff of dreams.

In the few years since the emergency of 1975-77 the press in India has been experiencing a remarkable and exciting development. It is an irony that the suppression of democracy and the choking of press freedom should have been the prelude to the invigoration and modernizing of one of democracy's pillars.

The emergency itself, however, was a bleak episode for journalism, for most of the press acceded to the regime of censorship with barely a whimper. 'Not even a dog has barked', Mrs Gandhi is said to have remarked drily. An opposition politician rebuked the press, saying: 'You were asked to bend but you began to crawl.' The *Indian Express* offered an exceptional defiance, but, overall, resistance was never likely to be strong because the proprietors were afraid and most journalists naturally did not want to lose their jobs or go to jail (although some were imprisoned).

By suppressing the news the emergency created an appetite for it. Just as the people came to value democracy more, because the emergency thrust the question of democracy's survival in front of them, so they came to esteem a free press more highly. The ending of the emergency led to an outpouring of information. The new government, in a spirit of openness, made access to official information easier. There was a binge of discussion and writing. People enjoyed reading about the emergency, its aftermath and the Janata government's doings. A new journalism began, particularly in new magazines, with an emphasis on brighter writing and research. Investigative reporting entered the Indian press, turned over some stones and found ugliness beneath.

Traditionally, most of India's newspapers, especially the mass circulation national dailies, have had a solidness of appearance, much like British newspapers of the 1930s. They are broadsheet and heavily loaded with seriously written politics and economics, the statements of government. Until the post-emergency period Indian journalism had little tradition of investigation. The press was a recorder. It received and registered – statements, speeches, proclamations – rather than found out and explained. The government span but the reporters did not delve. In the news pages there was little inquiry into the condition of the people, little attempt to tell them what they were entitled to know. To a large extent the newspapers ignored greater India.

The leader columns, editorial pages and the cartoonists of some newspapers, however, had the virtue of casting light and colour on matters of moment. It was this part of the press that affronted Mrs Gandhi and her advisers, and which was the target of her censorship. And it was this narrow stream of explanation, comment and critical analysis in Indian journalism that was broadened and developed dramatically and with great effect by the current affairs magazines which sprang up in profusion in the late 1970s and early 1980s. Some of these soared and fell, but others have survived to become staples of current affairs reading. The best of the weeklies, fortnightlies and monthlies set high standards in reporting, photography, design and production. There is now a wide range of magazines on every news stand. Never before has India been so well revealed to its people. Moreover, the new journalism has done much to raise the standing of the journalists' trade, as well as its quality. Except at its higher levels, pre-emergency journalism was not well-regarded and many of its practitioners had low pay to match their status. Today an increasing number of well-educated young men and women are making a career in journalism.

All this needs to be put into perspective. Major newspapers, like the *Times of India*, the *Hindustan Times*, the *Statesman*, the *Hindu*, the *Tribune*, the *Indian Express*, *Amrita Bazar Patrika*; gadflies like *Blitz*, sundry big-type-and-hot-air sensation sheets; and magazines like *India Today*, *Sunday* and the *Illustrated Weekly*, serve a market confined to the two or three per cent of the people who speak English. This is the middle-class, educated class, the administrators, bureaucrats, politicians, academics, business-men, industrialists and others who run India. English is the working language of the managing élite. With the expansion of education the number of people literate in English, and the potential market for newspapers, is growing.

At the same time more papers are being published, like the *Sunday Observer* in Bombay and the *Telegraph* in Calcutta. It is very much a growth industry. The circulation of newspapers is more than 40 million, more than it has ever been. The vernacular press is in some regions growing faster than the English press. The sales of Hindi newspapers, for example, are increasing remarkably. In accentuating the positive the Indian government naturally likes to draw attention to the growth of literacy; and the book shops and news stands and the crowds of browsers around pavement book vendors bear witness to this. Publishing is enjoy-ing a boom; so, too, is pirate publishing which meets the demand for very cheap textbooks and paperbacks. India is now self-reliant in pirated books, once imported from Singapore. As one would expect, India is the third largest publisher of English titles after the United States and Britain. The number of comics being published has grown suddenly and there is a new demand for Indian heroes and stories to take their place alongside James Bond and Superman.

The growth of publishing in general is, as I have said, an indicator of spreading literacy. At the same time the increasing robustness of the newspaper press is naturally seen by many Indians as evidence of the strength of the democratic idea and of the public appetite for information and discussion. Certainly, Indians who can read are better informed now than they have ever been, and the working and actions of government, law enforcers and others with power have come under closer scrutiny, sometimes to their discomfort. There is pride in India's possession of a free press. But, as in most democracies, press and government do not always see eye to eye. There are those who believe that, in a developing country, the press should have a 'positive and constructive' role, with the 'national good' at heart. They argue that too much criticism of government, too many exposés of bungles and scandals and criminal officials, is bad for morale. They call some newspapers 'anti-national'. I have heard it argued that India is 'not ready' for a completely free press, just as in Pakistan and Bangladesh, the rulers say the people are 'not ready' for democracy.

Mrs Gandhi was sensitive to press comment, exhibiting a lack of robustness in this respect remarkable in a leader of her experience. In 1982 she said that 'the press functions as the opposition'. It was meant as a complaint but it was a backhanded compliment. Mrs Gandhi justified her curbing of the press in the emergency by saying: 'Once there were no newspapers there was no agitation. The agitation was in the pages of the newspapers.'

Politicians, journalists and readers agree, from differing standpoints, that the press has its failings. Politicians and administrators wince as the editorial punches hit home, but many journalists grumble that there is not enough critical journalism, that the press stands essentially for the establishment, the middle classes, as it always has; that 'the common man' is unrepresented in the press and in politics. Large parts of the press are stodgy in appearance and approach and the new Indian journalism has by no means swept all before it. The average Indian newspaper reader still has a heavy diet of politics, and the newspapers which provide it thrive. Most of the press is conservative, and certainly most proprietors, with their considerable business interests and preference for the status quo, do not wish to fall foul of the government.

One cannot be sure that press freedom in India is secure. Among those in power are people who find an active press tiresome, and the statements of some who would claim, in all other respects, to be democrats, reveal a wish to see the press hogtied. In 1982 the autocratic chief minister of Bihar sought to enact a law securing imprisonment for journalists writing material he and his tame magistrates considered scurrilous. He was forced to back down after protests. Elsewhere, fingers were wagged threateningly. Newspapers are reminded that there is government control of the import, price and distribution of newsprint. The press, one of India's strengths, remains vulnerable.

8

A Tale of Three Cities

Delhi, Bombay, Calcutta

Life in the crowded conditions of cities has many unattractive
features, but in the long run these may be overcome, not so much
by altering them, but simply by changing the human race into
liking them.

CHARLES DARWIN

THE FLEETING, savoured spring of the plains of northern
India has almost passed and we shall soon be in the furnace,
meek subjects of the sun. Along Delhi's broad boulevards the
trees have suddenly greened and spread into parasols. The first of
the season's water carts are being wheeled on the cracked and
betel-stained pavements, the nation's cuspidor. A glass of chilled
water is less than a halfpenny. In the old part of the city, where
pungent spicy smells linger in the narrow secret streets, the
traditional water sellers hump leaking goatskin bags on their
backs and squirt water into little tin cups. Customers swill and
toss coins into the sellers' marsupial pouches. There will soon be
times when I shall envy the ice men: they strap large blocks of ice
beneath their bicycle saddles with hairy string and know the
pleasure of cool buttocks on roasting days.

The garden is bright with snapdragons, roses, dahlias, daisies,
hibiscus and bougainvillea, flamboyant as a matador's cape.
Bulbuls, with jaunty Robin Hood caps, red cheeks and red underwear are contesting the lime tree with sparrows. Mynahs have
bursts of communal violence, or stride self-importantly up and
down, shrieking like politicians in parliament. On the wall doves
gaze into each other's eyes. Lizards are out scouting, signallers of
summer. A little way off, an elephant proceeds on his lawful
occasions with stately stride, the bell swinging beneath his middle
donging like the call to evensong heard across a meadow.

Outside there is a dusty road, its edges swept by women forever
bent over their stiff brushes in the attitude of Millet's gleaners.

Cooks bicycle by with their shopping baskets, flitting bee-like from market to market, from meat to fish to fruit to cheese to vegetables, ordering chickens off to instant execution. Shopping can be a complex operation. There are no supermarkets; nor, one imagines, will there ever be, for they would be so much against the Indian grain of small and intimate family businesses and little shoulder-rubbing shops grouped together in like trades. Across the road is a maidan, the village green of this neighbourhood, surrounded on three sides by houses and tall trees. Some boys are playing cricket on it, and it is a serious affair, with the batsmen looking pukka in pads. I ought to move inside to avoid being brained by a six. There is an evocative smell of newly cut grass, which for me always means cricket. The maidan was cut this morning by a mower drawn by an ox, and now the beast is grazing up in one corner while the mower-wallah dozes under a tree.

There must be a dozen men in white dhotis slumbering in patches of shade, and out in the sun a group of women in red and green saris, servants and the wives of servants, sit in a circle with their small children, talking and laughing.

Strolling schoolgirls in white dresses, their shiny hair in thick plaits, lick ice cream cornets bought at the shop around the corner. That place is a magnet: every evening the little piazza in front of it is crowded with men, women and children sucking ice cream and popping sweet and sticky things into their mouths with dripping fingers. It is a carefree congregation, lapping at the evening waterhole of sugary indulgence. Indians love sweets and the price of sugar is politically sensitive. The children have white mouths and splashed shirts, the women have desired rolls of waistline fat which wobble as they chatter like jolly parrots. Fastened to their waists, and jingling in concert with the wobbling, are the keys to their houses, refrigerators, jewellery boxes, money drawers and whiskey cupboards. The men stand with their ice cream or plates of sweetmeats, talking about cricket or absent in reverie. They are oblivious to the confusion and jam they have caused in the road by their inconsiderate parking. Indians do not park: they arrive and stop – and what happens around them is someone else's problem. In the road there is rage, gesticulation and scratched bodywork, but in the piazza of sugary peace and closed ears it is of no concern as tongues lovingly carve ice cream cones into periwinkles.

There is a group of men lolling on the maidan grass, wearing white uniform jackets, blue trousers, black boots and red caps, and around them lie drums, trumpets, horns, a sousaphone and bells. Crisp they are not: they are a wedding band and soon they will start up the tremendous blaring and crashing that accompanies a Hindu bridegroom as he processes to the meeting with his bride at the sacred fire. The groom's transport, a white horse with a red velvet saddle, is nearby, nibbling at the grass the ox mowed. In the road is the gaudy mobile bandstand, equipped with loudspeakers, which will be pushed along by sweating minions.

Some boys are flying kites and the upperworks of the trees are full of crashed ones. There are also forktailed kites of the feathered kind swinging in circles overhead. At their altitude they can see one of their food sources, the swimming pool at the large hotel down the road. Many an air stewardess, glistening at the poolside, has been astonished to see her club sandwich lifted from its plate by one of these insolent thieves, right under her Ambre Solaire'd nose.

Just up the road, in a shady patch beneath some trees, is a shamiana, a bright awning raised on four bamboo poles, under which, on a platform rather like a bier, lies a man in loose white shirt and trousers. There are placards around him, in English and Hindi, announcing that he is fasting unto death in pursuance of a campaign for teachers' pay and rights. He has been there for some days now, or perhaps two or three weeks, employing one of a number of techniques for bringing pressure to bear on employers and authorities. (Another popular method is gheraoing, in which a factory, college or police station is surrounded by the aggrieved and no-one is allowed in or out.) Fasting is, however, vested with a kind of sacredness, because Mahatma Gandhi used it. Relay fasting is another and rather more comfortable way of making a point, a modern development. In this, a large number of people fast, not unto death, but unto dinner time; and when they go off duty their place is taken by another shift of fasters. It may not seem much sacrifice, but Indians love snacks and eating between meals, and relay fasters can suffer quite gratifying pangs.

The thinning starver has become part of Delhi's mosaic: when he was won or lost he will be replaced by another, in some other shamiana. He is as much a part of the pattern as the occasional ash-covered holy man asleep on the edge of the road, his nakedness unnoticed; or the dancing bears; or the office workers dismounting from their motor scooters and solemnly aiming their

Dabbawallahs with lunches, Bombay: the 'Union of Tiffin Box Suppliers'
taking home-cooked lunches to office workers

Juggernaut festival, Puri: by tradition 4200 men pull each wagon . . .
struggling and shoving for the honour of dragging the gods

Rajasthani women

Fruit seller, Bombay: there are no supermarkets . . . they would be too much
against the Indian grain

Brick kiln worker, aged six, recently rescued with his family from bonded
labour

pellucid arcs against walls, clutching briefcases in their free hands; the city has few pissoirs.

Sir Edwin Landseer Lutyens, of course, did not draw pissoirs. The British legacy of urinals in India, magnificent temples of bladder worship, are to be found and admired in the splendid clubs like the Gymkhana in Delhi, the Willingdon in Bombay, the Bengal and Calcutta in Calcutta, and at Ootacamund. Sir Edwin's board was occupied by the grand sweep of his imperial celebration, the eighth Delhi, built in a district littered with the stones, tombs, domes, ruined walls and gardens of former capitals, the historic grand crossroads and battleground of India. Among these remnants is the majestic finger of the Qutb Minar, built in the 13th century and, at 234 feet, the tallest free-standing stone tower in the world. In 1981 its winding staircase was the deathplace of forty-five people, crushed in a panic that was started, it was said, by some boys taking advantage of the gloom to molest some girls.

Lutyens's Delhi was built to the south of what is now called the old city, or the walled city, the seventh Delhi, Shahjahanabad, built by the 17th-century Moghul emperor Shahjahan. This is a place of quite different flavours, and of endless movement in its squares and little lanes chequered with shadow and hard sunlight. The red and white Jama Masjid mosque, the largest in India, imposes a Moghul imprint and around it commerce proceeds with vigour. Pavement vendors have piles of substantial brassieres, drawers, trousers, watch straps, gear wheels, car wings, hammers, saws, spanners and petrol engines. 'You want to buy shop observers, sahib?' 'Shop observers . . .? Ah, shock absorbers!' 'Yes, sahib, shop observers. You buy?'

Delivery lorries piled high with fish from the Bombay ice-trains are unloaded by porters bent under the weight of baskets filled by the fish shovellers. Stink of fish and pong of dung wafts with the smell of tea and spices. A charity food stall dishes out rice and lentils to the poor on fresh leaves. Sugar cane is crushed on a barrow and juice sold by the glass for a few paise. Outside the police post a ragged man writhes on the ground while a constable beats him with a stick, kicks his shoulders, rolls him over and hits his legs. The crowd around this spectacle seems to approve: the man is a thief. After a while someone calls a rickshaw and he is dumped into it. In the mosque, where the quadrangle is half the size of a football pitch, there is a torpid air. The side galleries are filled with sleepers, women suckling and girls plaiting each other's hair. In the alleys nearby tailors squat with their sewing machines in alcoves just big enough for one crosslegged man and his work. Metalworkers carry on their old crafts. Apprentice boys chisel wood and stone in shadowy workshops. In a glittering alley tinsel, wire, paint and paper are made into gaudy decorations. Doctors in their cubby holes listen to the chests of wide-eyed little boys. In the paper bazaar merchants sit in alcoves with telephones, and tea boys slop and spill and skitter through the minefield of cow dung and pan spit. Ear cleaners ply their trade, wiggling their probes into their customers' waxy recesses, and pavement barbers lather and scrape.

No greater contrast than the intimacy and rhythms of the old city, and Lutyens's new, could be imagined; and when Lutyens drew it they were quite separate. The foundation stones were laid by King George and Queen Mary to the north of the old city in 1911, but it was decided that the site was a bad one and the stones were exhumed one night and carted to the new place. Lutyens's Delhi, the old city and the modern expansions which might be termed the ninth Delhi, are now meshed in one built-up sprawl on the burnt, pitted, red, Martian plain. It is curious that many of these new buildings are somehow pre-aged: their paintwork rapidly becomes grimed and their stairways and passages blooded with pan juice. New Delhi is simply one part of a large settlement with ancient foundations, and the 'new' is superfluous.

Lutyens and his collaborator, Sir Herbert Baker, with whom he quarrelled often, made an emphatic statement of the grandeur and permanence of empire. It was inaugurated in 1931 and the British quit only sixteen years later. It used to be fashionable to criticise the architecture as too imperial, too grandiose. Today there is a tendency to make virtues of these same qualities. The centrepiece of the work, the pink presidential palace and the secretariat buildings, have a certain nobility. I find them grand, but somehow aloof and curiously stranded. At weekends especially they have the deserted feeling of the abandoned city of Fatehpur Sikri, 140 miles to the south. They seem almost eerie, cut off from India's essential vitality and clamour. The palace is remote and rather secret, and the president seems shut away behind his wrought iron and beautiful parterres, like a difficult old relative.

The secretariat blocks nearby are magisterial, housing the

turbines of government, the bureaucrats turning papers in count-less rooms on endless corridors. Messengers and tea men scurry, and large monkeys may be seen walking in the corridors, serious and preoccupied as if on their way to difficult meetings. Recently a British diplomat on his way through the secretariat corridors, in search of a government official, encountered a monkey drinking a cup of tea and inquired of a messenger how it was that the beast was refreshing itself in that manner.

'The monkey is sick, sahib,' the messenger said, 'so we are giving it tea to help it get better.'

The main business of Delhi is government. It is a city of administrators, politicians, clerks, communicators and diplomats; the last possessing most of the foreign cars you see in India. Every day the planes carry in fresh batches of politicians, wheed-lers and hangers-on to dabble in the pool of power. There is a smell of sycophancy in the air. The international flights bring in envoys and deputations from all over the world, almost always in the small hours. The capital is unhappily situated in the world's flight schedules so that many airliners arrive and leave when life and hope are at their lowest ebb.

Here, where refreshment, comfort and information are meagre, tempers may grow raw. Here I have witnessed terrible outbursts of emotion and group apoplexy.

'Bloody hell,' a passenger roared to an official in a melee. 'I shall report you. Give me your name at once!'

'My name is Bloody Hell,' the official shouted back.

No country should be judged by its airports and airport officials.

Much administrative and political action goes on below the acropolis, in the circular colonnaded Parliament building, poli-tical headquarters, government blocks, and, not least, at the home of the prime minister in one of the many tree-lined avenues which are Delhi's most agreeable physical feature. Many trees were planted as soon as roads were marked on the plans, and they endow the city with blessed shade and a sense of maturity. In the spring people camp under the silk cotton trees and collect the cotton-like fibre which falls from them during that time, and they sell it as stuffing for cushions. They also camp under the jamun trees and wait for the olive-like fruit to fall.

These people, too, are part of Delhi's rhythm, just like the indefatigable female coolies digging trenches, humping sand, breaking stones like convicts in a quarry, hauling bricks and bearing concrete, side by side with their men in the equality of weariness, helping to build Delhi with their bare hands. The work is hard and unrelenting and on hot days it is punishing; their suffering shows in faces which do not stay young or pretty for long.

On the site of a new bridge, a woman drops out of a line of skinny labourers who are carrying mounds of wet concrete in baskets on their heads. She seeks and retrieves her scrap of a baby from the ragged children with matted hair babyminding in the dust. She squats in some sand near the clanking concrete mixer and draws the child to her breast. After he has fed she wipes his face and backside, hands him back to the small minder and returns to the rhythm of the line. She picks up her basket, has it filled at the concrete mixer, fixes it on a pad on her head and walks in the file of people up a crude plank ramp to dump the load, descending another ramp to fill the basket once again. It is building by the teaspoonful. There are cranes, bulldozers, pile-drivers and other machines, but Delhi, and indeed much of India, is developed in this ant-like fashion.

When the day's work is finished the drooping men and women hoist their babies, pickaxes and mattocks to their shoulders and return to rough huts and torn tents made of sacking, scraps of plastic sheeting and twigs, set up under trees near the building sites. During 1982, when the stadiums, hotels and roads were being built for the Asian Games in Delhi there were more than 100,000 labourers at work on the city's greatest building operation since Lutyens's Delhi was grafted to the ancient city. They were silhouetted on bamboo scaffolding, shuffling in perpetual motion on flimsy gangplanks, like the casts of thousands in Cecil B. de Mille epics, or perspiring coffles on their way to the Pyramids. They are the descendants in sweat of the coolies who gave shape to Lutyens's drawings between 1912 and 1931, the labourers from Rajasthan and Punjab, the stone workers whose ancestors had fashioned the Moghul emperors' cities and tombs. Most of today's building workers, like their forerunners, are migrants drawn from the countryside by the prospect of a long spell of work. After giving some of their pay to the overseers who recruit and bring them to the city they may get £3 a week – more than they would get in the fields. But many get less than that and have poor water and medical facilities. They all live in their hovels, luckless and unconsidered, vulnerable to disease, sworn at by overseers, while the contractors break safety and labour laws with impunity.

The women cook rice and lentils on fires of twigs or dung cake while their babies mew and crawl, and men rest. From the road-side patches the children have an extraordinary worm's eye view of life. Their nostrils are filled with dust and the stink of exhausts and the odour of excreta. Delhi roars and rumbles by, a swirling Corryvreckan of traffic.

According to statistics Delhi is the most dangerous city in the world for road users. Traffic is anarchic and rules are readily broken. In practice the roads of India are lawless. Drivers plunge into roundabouts and change lanes without slowing or looking to right, to left, or in their mirrors. They stare fixedly ahead, taking no interest in what is happening on their beam, their quarters or in their wake. At night their vehicles are usually unlit. Passengers and drivers stick their arms out of the windows making flapping, desperate, pleading signals, so that from behind a car often seems like some monstrous flightless bird trying to get airborne.

Bicycles and scooters are often ridden against the flow of traffic. Scooter rickshaws, not much bigger than a royal prince's pram, appear head-on in your lane. When hit they roll and bounce like misshapen balls, passengers falling out like laundry. Ice cream carts are hauled the wrong way round roundabouts, and on the broad avenues drivers make a third or fourth lane while overtaking, keeping the horn ring firmly depressed. In India a man with a broken klaxon considers himself a form of eunuch.

Indian women are intrepid. They perch sidesaddle on the pillions of scooters and motorcycles, a babe or two in their arms, their saris waving in the warm slipstream, unconcernedly taking the risk of being throttled like Isadora Duncan.

Buses and lorries race at high speed, with compressed air horns screaming, as if they were fire engines on their way to a disaster. The lorries are overloaded and sway dangerously. The suspen-sion of the buses has broken under the weight of passengers so that when negotiating a roundabout they lean drunkenly and the bodywork makes a shower of sparks as it scrapes the road.

These vehicles often crash. Many are badly maintained and overloaded, owned by cynical men and driven by picaroons and callous oafs, sometimes drunk, often unlicensed and untrained. They have fatalistic ideas of risk and rely on bullying and bulk to get their way.

Bus and lorry crashes are a routine form of death in India. The buses fall into ravines and canals, carrying people by the twenty, thirty or fifty to a now unremarkable death. No-one draws lessons from these crashes. They are regarded as acts of God and almost everyone using the roads does so in an indifferent and fatalistic spirit. It is as if road danger were a western concept. But how can all those beautiful girls with such intelligent faces walk unconcernedly into seething traffic without glancing about them? The astonishing thing about road accidents in India is not that there are so many, but, given the behaviour of the people, that there are so few.

In the pecking order of Indian traffic, my apple-green Ambassador car ranks third. I give way to anything larger, to the top-heavy lorries and the capsizing buses to which external passengers cling like wasps to marmalade. Lower forms of life, the lower castes, like rickshaws, cyclists and pedestrians stop or scatter from my path. That is the law of the jungle. But all of us detour around the inanely wandering cows and aldermanic elephants.

We have to find our way through a bobbing flotsam. There are creaking carts drawn by bullocks, black buffaloes, horses and camels, the last a reminder of how close the capital is to the desert. There are two-wheeled carts laden with furniture, filing cabinets, boxes and smuggled video machines, pushed and pulled by two or three men. Cycle rickshaws, often heartlessly overloaded with people or loads of paper, or armchairs, or steel rods, are propelled by men with knotty calves.

Black and yellow taxis, well up in the hierarchy, shoulder aside rickshaws and wobbling bicycles, and riding in one often seems like taking part in a stock car race.

Taxis in Delhi live in small herds under the shelter of roadside trees, and their nonchalant drivers, many of them Punjabis, rig up an awning, set up their charpoys, light a fire and build a hut for the telephone. They live like the front line fighter pilots they seek to emulate, in and around their machines, tinkering and dozing, waiting to scramble. Some of these encampments have a tap under which the drivers soap and bathe themselves and comb and pile up their hair and rewind their turbans. The telephone rings and a taxi lurches like a crocodile from the kerb, into the stream of traffic, its driver, intent on his prey, looking neither left, right or behind, leaving his safety in the hands of supernatural forces. His insurance policy, a postcard picture of a god, is taped to the dashboard.

In winter the drivers sleep on the back seats, parcelled in blankets, and if you call a taxi in the night it arrives with the seat pre-warmed and the slightly hircine odour of a stale sleeper. The driver sits hunched at the wheel in his blanket, looking like some desperado.

More often than not the taxi is an Ambassador, the backbone of Indian private transport, the pre-eminent Indian-built car. It is basically a 1954 Morris Oxford, strong and solid, good in a crash, an excellent developer of forearm muscle, but a glugger of petrol, which costs as much as it does in Britain. Indians have a love-hate relationship with the Ambassador. Its strength and high chassis fit it well for rugged Indian conditions and it can be repaired almost anywhere by any mechanic or even blacksmith. It is not a dream car although some young men try, rather pathetically, to romanticize it by painting Toyota or Datsun in large letters along the side. I have seen one whose owner had painted Rolls Royce on the sides; presumably a Brahmin. With constant attention the car is a robust runner, and some Indians extol it as an almost noble beast. It is built from the original dies and sometimes, it seems, the pieces do not fit as well as they might. A distributor in Delhi admitted with grim pride that he had never had a satisfied customer. They are expensive cars by any standard, costing 80,000 rupees (£4,850) in 1982, well beyond the means of the great majority of the people. Mrs Gandhi, and every government official, is driven around in one, for the Ambassador, and the other Indian built car, a version of a 1960s Fiat, represent Indian emphasis on indigenous production. But they also represent a lack of innovation. The Fiat, being smaller, nippier and more modern is coveted. The official waiting list is twenty years, though a bribe or a word with uncle puts you higher in the queue.

The Punjabi taxi drivers of Delhi are part of the wave of strong men of the north who thronged to the city after the division of India and Pakistan, when millions of people changed sides and restarted their lives. Today they form a large part of the city's character. When people in Bombay, Calcutta and south India criticise the manners and customs of Delhiwallahs they mean the manners and customs of Punjabis. To many Indians Punjabis –

and Sikhs are also Punjabis – seem to be brawn not brain, ostentatious, all money and no culture, a physically big, vulgar, noisy people, their women over-jewelled. Like many caricatures, it is unfair and exaggerated; but it has done nothing to undermine Punjabi pride.

Delhi was a small, genteel, conservative place with a considerable Urdu culture. The arrival of the Punjabis helped to change all that. They even Punjabized the sound of Urdu. They brought their go-ahead, uninhibited ways, their loud talk and laughter, their love of meat eating, their tandoor ovens and naan bread, their earthier speech and lusty jokes. Their women shocked with their lower necklines. They grew powerful in transport, business, journalism, the army and air force (and began to dominate the film world in Bombay). They proved themselves as farmers, moving into the jungles of Uttar Pradesh and turning them into productive land. Punjabis pride themselves on being hard-working pioneers, and challenge you to find a Punjabi beggar.

You can see their swagger on Republic Day, January 26, when India displays its martial might along the dramatic sweep of Rajpath, Lutyens's grand avenue. Bobbing vermilion lancers are followed by perfectly matched sets of marching Punjabis, Madrasis, Grenadiers, Rajputs, Assamese, Dogras and deadly glittering Gurkhas. They are part of the organization which is, perhaps, the most British of all the legacies: the cantonments are the smartest settlements in the land, with white painted kerbs, neat roads, buildings and brass. Trouser creases are blades, haircuts a delight to any sergeant major. Boots and brasses are heliographs and uniform moustaches seem to have been drawn from the stores. Officers' messes are as they always were, down to the exquisite manners, old-boy accents, slapped thighs, jaunty pipes and concern for form. There is a strong idea of regiment, of loyalty, tradition and smartness. There is very strong competition to get into the army. The money is good and there are queues at recruiting offices. Men pull strings to get a place in the ranks. Some criminals made money in 1982 by setting up fake recruiting offices and taking money from would-be soldiers.

Inevitably the pageantry and oompah of the Republic Day parade is followed by a display of military machismo, a tedious series of tanks, missiles and rockets. Gandhi, of course, would have hated it all; that is one reason why there is no statue of him at the end of Rajpath. Just beyond the pink arc de triomphe of India Gate is an elegant stone pavilion topped by a dome. George V stood in it for some years, but was extracted by the authorities after some affronted patriots chipped the nose. It was always thought that the cavity would be filled by a statue of Gandhi, but people could not agree on whether the statue should be standing or sitting. Apart from that many of the Mahatma's followers felt that a statue of him could not occupy the cupola because the Republic Day parade would pass beneath his steel-rimmed gaze, a ludicrous and painful contradiction, an insult to Gandhi's memory.

There is a considerable matutinal traffic across the grass and up the garden path. There is the morning paper boy, of course, and then the smiling postman on his bicycle, bringing my mail as if every day were my birthday. The stick-thin mali, the gardener who works in several houses around here, makes the first of a number of appearances – he darts like a bee from garden to garden and after lunch draws up his dhoti'd legs embryonically and sleeps in the shade beneath my lime tree. Soon comes the procession of fruit and vegetable sellers, each with a distinctive yodel, one of them standing at the gate and bleating like a sheep on a Welsh hillside. On two days a week the washerman arrives, takes over a bathroom, throws laundry in the bath and jumps in himself, splashing like a courting walrus.

Occasionally the parrot vendor calls at the house, his bicycle laden with little cane cages occupied by green parakeets. More frequently the monkey man attracts attention at the gate by banging a drum with his fingers. A small knot of children and adults gathers, a rupee or two is offered and to the sound of the drum the bored monkey performs its tricks, jumping and prancing.

Something of a performer, also, is the basket man. His bicycle is piled high with laundry baskets, cane chairs, tables and flower stands, and he alights from it with a smile and a wave. He advances across the lawn bearing a small cane table. 'So you don't think this is strong?' he asks, by way of introduction. I say nothing. He sets the table down, retreats a few paces and then suddenly sprints and leaps upon it, striking a dramatic Nureyev pose. He jumps up and down. 'So now you think it is strong?'

There are gem sellers, silver merchants, cloth vendors and carpet men. There are occasional mendicants. This morning a young man strides through the open door into my study and says: 'I am from Goa. Give me money please.' He surprisingly takes no for an answer and strides off. Fortune tellers and fake holy men may be more persistent. Two bearded men in saffron robes, with ash on their faces, approach me as I read a newspaper in the garden and say they will chant prayers for me in exchange for money. They do not budge when I tell them to go, stand their ground and fix me with their gaze, while I raise the newspaper like a crucifix to Dracula. About ten minutes later, when my arms are aching, they finally admit defeat and shuffle away.

I often contribute a few rupees to a man who calls with a large ledger, claiming to represent a society which is apparently devoted to the retrieval and decent disposal of dead bodies found in drains.

Telephone engineers call on their missions of mercy. The telephone is a factor in the national blood pressure. Many thousands are employed to spend their working lives with their fingers in the dial, turning it relentlessly to find a way through the jungle of crossed and unresponsive lines. Monsoon rains deaden hundreds of thousands of lines, and engineers shrug hopelessly. They are among the professions, like postmen, telegram men and electrical repairers, whose representatives call at public holidays, touch their forelocks, wish you a happy Christmas, Easter, Holi, Diwali, and present a note explaining that they deliver and repair day and night, dutifully and tirelessly, and hope to do the same next year. Some telephone men called one holiday eve and presented me with their petition for baksheesh which began: 'We are four telegram men who serve you through the year . . .'

'But I've already paid the telegram men.'

'They were inland telegram men, Sahib. We are international telegram men.'

From time to time there is the buzz of a motorcycle engine and the toot of the horn announcing the arrival of Mr Jiwan Singh. He advances with stately weariness. In old age his beard has turned cream. As always, he has something to say about butter. I must eat more of it, he tells me gravely, or I shall grow thin; and it is not good for men to be thin. He himself has always eaten plenty of butter; and look. His hands spread and indicate his abdomen as if he were a merchant demonstrating the qualities of a carpet. The stomach is arrested in its final avalanche fall by a wide leather belt. Mr Singh's appearance is not a good advertisement for the craft he practises, which is tailoring. His baggy green trousers are ruched like a gunny sack and his bursting shirt has breast pockets like litter bins, crammed and overflowing with pens, spectacles, papers, tape measures and his order book.

His conversation varies hardly at all. 'In British days I had a shop in Rawalpindi. All the officers and gentlemen came to me. Bush shirts, pants, blazers, riding pants, everything British style . . .'

He suggests a more generous waistline for my trousers than the tape measure indicates is necessary. 'In British days I always gave slightly bigger pant. In India British gentlemen grow bigger round the waist.' I tell him I will have the trousers made to my size and he regards me with worn patience. 'Very well, but when you start eating the butter you will be calling me and saying: "Mr Singh, my pant is too tight".'

I choose from his samples and he names a price. I suggest a lower one. A great sigh escapes Mr Singh. His shoulders droop, his eyes turn to me like those of a condemned spaniel. 'In British days, sir, the gentlemen accepted my prices as fair. When I first made clothes for you you accepted the prices as fair. Now you have been in India some time you try to get me to reduce my prices; and my costs are so high.' He sighs again, we agree a price and Mr Singh retreats to the motorcycle. 'Please do one thing', he says. 'When you next go to London buy me one blood pressure testing machine. These days I am having high blood pressure and I am needing English machine to see how high.' I say I will see what I can do. Mr Singh departs with a sigh.

The afternoon is wearing on and the sunlight is taking on a ruddy colour in the dusty atmosphere, thickened by woodsmoke and dung fires. In the embassies the waiters are fixing their starched white cockscomb pugrees, smoothing their whites, polishing the salvers and readying the drinks for the evening receptions. Soon the limousines will deliver diplomats and their ladies who will take up with each other where they left off the night before, and the day's new rumours will be discussed. Delhi is nothing if not a city of rumour in a land where rumour is prevalent and feared for its great power. There was a terrible rumour once that one of the embassies was watering its whisky and it took several conscientious tastings to nail the lie. Receptions, dinners and home gatherings are one form of entertainment in a city where theatre and foreign cinema are thin and television is too bleak, controlled and unimaginative to be worth having. Consequently conversation flourishes.

The embassies, of course, are small splinters off the home block. The Americans have an imposing modern place with an indoor lake, a big polished Marine with a revolver at the front desk, nice ladies saying 'hi', coffee in paper cups, a genial atmosphere and very long cars parked outside. The Pakistanis have blue mosque domes, the Russians have a rather solid building with a red neon star, heavy furnishings, a portrait of Lenin and, of course, excellent vodka and comradely smiles. The British have what looks like an advance factory built to relieve unemployment in Wales, photographs of gear wheels and pump assemblies, an extraordinary large number of pictures of the Queen, as if in readiness for a snap check by loyalty police, a Rolls Royce at the front door and a grubby copy of the *Sun* in the front office.

Dinner tends to be late in India. It is the last event of the evening: guests consume it and leave at once, a custom at first disconcerting to westerners not used to eating at the tail of the evening, and with whose digestions it plays considerable mischief. Restaurants may be nearly empty at 8.30, full at 10.30 and often noisy with the sound of small children, for they are commonly kept up late, a part of the family, untroubled by the western idea of bedtime. At night in the hot weather many families go to the open spaces around India Gate, buy balloons for the children and sit until after midnight licking ice-cream bought from lamp-lit barrows.

The chowkidar, the nightwatchman, has arrived. During the night he whistles to other chowkidars in the neighbourhood and hears their distant whistles in answer, a network of comfort. He taps his bamboo stick on the gate and the other chowkidars do the same in answer. Sometimes these modern linkboys can be heard singing softly, the equivalent of 'three o'clock and all's well'.

An idiot is marching up and down by the sea wall near the Gateway of India. He holds an umbrella and jerks his fist at the turbulent, dirty milk-chocolate sea, shouting imprecations. Every few minutes the sea, as if in irritation, buckets a dollop of its dishwater over the wall and drenches him; but he only shakes his fist and his umbrella all the more. Farther along there are some pavement entertainers, a young man and a girl, soaked by sea and rain, turning somersaults and walking on their hands. They have a bored brown dog who reluctantly perches on a stack of old paint tins and jumps through a hoop pierced with dagger blades as the man beats a roll on a drum. The girl looks around, smiling beseechingly, and a passerby tosses her a coin. Around the corner there is the rasp of sawing and the thud of axes: a tall tree was blown down in the night and it crushed half a dozen roadside stalls selling lamps, shirts, cloth, pictures, beads, walking sticks and other tourist necessities. Nobody was hurt, although a score of pavement sleepers had a narrow escape, and the tree is now being butchered by a swarm of men wet with sweat and drizzle as if it were the carcase of a dinosaur. Every twig will be utilized. At the quayside nearby are tethered heavy wooden brightly-painted boats, bucking like nervous horses in the swell, waiting to take intrepid passengers to the caves and cave paintings of Elephanta Island. Around the arches of the Gateway of India are some tourists and knots of local people staring pensively into the mist at the rusting ships in the roadstead, or watching the sea bulling at the Gateway wall. The Gateway is an inelegant lump looking uncomfortably out of place and pretending to be older than it is. It was built in 1924 to celebrate brilliant imperial arrivals, but, like Lutyens's Delhi, it was erected too late for its purpose and became noted as a point of departure, India's sally-port, the wicket-gate of empire.

The warm rain seems ceaseless and Bombay's shine and its enthralling seaside vistas are lost in the grey clammy pall. The stained and crumbling buildings in their array of styles – gothic, colonial, art-deco – so shabbily picturesque in sunshine and shadow, present a forlorn appearance in the rain. The tall white and cream towers of commerce and luxurious living are stained and glowering. Everything is sodden. Day in, day out, crowds splash to work under black umbrellas, shuffling patiently like a Roman testudo against the hosing monsoon storms. Hardly anyone wears a raincoat, except the policemen directing traffic. The people hoist trousers and saris with one hand and hold gamps aloft with the other, but they nevertheless arrive at work with wet clothing, and girls have mascara running down their cheeks. Inside buildings there is a smell of warm damp cloth overlaying a danker, mouldier smell. At the art gallery café, popular with young people, there are a couple of inches of water on the floor and customers sit with their feet in it, wet but smart. Only the Arabs, who have made Bombay their holiday resort since Beirut's charm faded, are enjoying what for them is a rare treat of rain, and they leave their quarters in expensive hotels to saunter in the drizzle by the brown Arabian Sea.

The spreading slums and pavement hovels which house millions of Bombay's workforce are drenched and double-drenched. Sacking, plastic sheets and bamboo are unequal to the task. In the monsoon months the slum dwellers are as wet and uncomfortable as soldiers in trenches. Little faces peer out, mirrored in stinking puddles.

The wretchedness of these people, and their presence in such large and increasing numbers, are a major part of the city's modern crisis. Bombay today is in a mess and has no clear idea of how to get out of it: a blow to its self-esteem because it always thought of itself as the Big B, a city which got things done and made things work. It took pride in its robust cupidity and acumen, ruefully paying a third of the country's income tax and doing today what the rest of India would do tomorrow. But its swagger is no longer what it was. The journalism of the apocalypse grows more insistent. 'Death throes of a city', a headline in the *Times of India* said in 1982. 'The edge of chaos', said another.

Reports of Bombay's death may be exaggerated but the crisis is plain to see. The city has become a victim of its own success and now pays the price for its greed, foolish planning and lack of foresight.

Bombay has been a great trading city with strong European connections for more than three centuries. It was formed from seven islands and the reclaimed land around them. Hindu cremation ghats, once on the edge of the sea, are now inland because of reclamation. The city is now a peninsula drooping into the Arabian Sea, but greater Bombay extends eastward and northward on the mainland, a spreading, tapering, linear city. The heart, though, is the peninsula, the commercial arena. Here, as in Hong Kong and Manhattan, there has been a tremendous pressure on a naturally confined space. Here are the gothic piles of the Victorian city. Some of these are outrageous and pompous, some hilariously eccentric, some imposing and handsome; but Bombay had the sense to keep nearly all of them. Here too are the soaring office towers, hotels and blocks of preposterously expensive flats, all sticking up like arrows crowded into a bullseye.

On kind and sunny days it can all look grand: the riviera sweep, the opal ocean and the palms. And in the healing night the city's suit of lights and neon badges can look satisfyingly romantic. 'There, sir', a taxi driver said, his outstretched arm indicating the glittering sweep of Back Bay and the eyries of the film stars on Malabar Hill, 'doesn't it look like Paris?'

People have always believed that Bombay, like New York, has gold specks on its pavements. It has always seemed a good place to start, to work, to climb. It has, after all, been devoted to the accretion of wealth and its favourite god is Ganesh, the plump, baby-limbed elephant-headed little fellow with four arms and a gold-belted bathing suit, the god of material advancement. During the past twenty years, however, the flow of people from the countryside has become a flood.

The city's buttons are popping, but 300 families still arrive every day. The textile mills, on which much of Bombay's prosperity was built in the 19th century, and from which about a third of India's cloth comes, remain a magnet although they are noisy, dusty, hot and unhealthy places with a bad record of tuberculosis. The millworkers inhabit the overcrowded chawls, gaunt and gloomy buildings where men live packed in cells. In January 1982 the quarter of a million textile workers began a protracted struggle against their employers, one of the great battles of Indian industrial history. Average pay was not bad by Indian standards, about £30 a month, but the millhands felt the owners could afford more. They resented their living and working conditions, their lack of security, and the fact that the owners could choose from a great pool of job-hungry submissive labour. The great textile strike was led by the extraordinary Datta Samant, a doctor turned trade union leader, who, from the late 1960s became a hero to the working class. He was a freelance union organizer (or mercenary, as his detractors called him) who offered himself as a pay negotiator to groups of workers, and was thus outside the normal union system. He defied both employers and the conventional union leaders and within a decade earned the allegiance of 1.5 million workers in various trades. His popularity rested on his results: he called hundreds of strikes and won large pay rises. The battle in the textile industry was his largest. After several months, tens of thousands of striking workers had to retreat to the countryside to scratch a living and others found themselves in the hands of moneylenders, their family ornaments and jewelry sold long before.

The pressures on Bombay make the prices of even the rudest dwellings a fearsome burden. A two-roomed slum hut can cost £2,000. At the other end of the market an unremarkable three-bedroomed flat may cost £150,000; and rather more distinguished properties can cost £250,000. The property boom of 1981 tested even Bombay's sangfroid; and the subsequent fall in prices was from the outrageous to the merely amazing.

Peeking over their Scotch at the troubles below, the wealthy and the middle classes became increasingly perturbed in the early 1980s. Bombay was clearly coagulating. Facilities adequate for two or three million were shared by more than ten million (the population will be sixteen million by the year 2000). About half of the people live in more than 500 slums: one of them, Dharari, has a population of more than 500,000. A hut here can house ten or twelve or more, whole families growing up, sleeping, cooking, eating, listening to the transistor radio, in the sort of space an Englishman would regard as adequate for his garden tools. The people who live here are choking. Air and water are polluted, and sanitation is very poor. 'The stink of shit brought vomit to my throat', Khushwant Singh, then editor of the *Hindustan Times* wrote starkly of a visit to Bombay in 1982.

The rapid colonization of pavements in the late 1970s and early 1980s frightened both the authorities and those many citizens who feared their 'Queen of Indian cities' would become as hopelessly congested and nightmarish as Calcutta. Seeing the pavement colonies as breeding grounds for disease and crime, the authorities began to clear them. Thousands of shacks made of bamboo, cardboard and sacking crumpled under the bulldozers. Their occupants were simply meant to return to the countryside. The authorities saw these clearances as tough but necessary, the excision of malignant growths. To the tens of thousands of pavement dwellers the demolitions were brutal. They went to the courts to argue their right to live on the streets, however squalid their conditions, and in mid-1982 won a temporary stay in what is likely to be a protracted struggle. Some of these people are government and municipal workers who can find nowhere else to live.

People come to Bombay to 'make it', not to idle. Consequently there are thousands in marginal occupations, filling in the crevices by hawking sweets and pan, ballpoint pens and flowers, cleaning shoes, mending, stitching, running messages for the Shady Motor Car Co. and other, more happily named, business houses. There are beggars, of course, ragged platoons at traffic lights. People here say that begging in Bombay is more rewarding than anywhere else in India.

The pressure of human flesh in Bombay is seen most starkly at railway stations. Desperately hard-pressed trains carry more than twice their designed capacity. Passengers cling to the outsides of carriages – youths hang on like stuntmen – and several fall to their deaths every day. Others are run down as they attempt to cross the tracks. There is a perpetual dispute among the authorities over whose job it is to retrieve the bodies.

It costs £2 to get into the discotheque. One of the glossy magazines says it is the best in town, a haunt for those social bats who like to flit in such places until the small hours. Drinks are painfully expensive and even a sixpenny soft drink costs £1. Some men from the Gulf, whose eyelids droop with the weight of whisky, are hungrily watching girls dancing. The girls, pretty in that sullen, spoilt, pouting way of so many of their class in India, wear western fashions. Many Bombay girls of a certain milieu consider themselves answerable only to New York, Paris and London. Of all young Indian women they are the exceptions, up to date with the slippery shifting fashions, music and trivia of the west. 'Bombay women', I was told many times, 'have class.'

A certain self-confidence and fashionableness have for years given Bombay women a chic; and matrons in other cities have long had lemon-sucking mouths when discussing them (at least, that is what Bombay girls delight in saying).

Mohammed Ali Jinnah, the founder of Pakistan, married a Bombay girl, by all accounts beautiful, adorable and irrepressible. Once, at a dinner with Lord Willingdon, the Viceroy, she dared in her vivacious way to wear a low-cut dress, very Bombay, and Lady Willingdon asked an aide to bring a shawl for Mrs Jinnah in case she felt cold. Mr Jinnah, the stern ascetic who yet was bewitched by his wife, made one of his best squashing speeches and told Lady Willingdon that when Mrs Jinnah felt cold she would ask for a shawl herself. One wonders how different

Pakistan would have been had both Mr and Mrs Jinnah lived to see the 1960s.

Bombaywallahs, like many second-city people, define themselves and their city partly in terms of the capital.

'Delhi, you see, is an overgrown village, Punjabi dominated, and we are well aware it looks down its nose at us', said Shobha Kilachand, editress of a magazine for Bombay's elite. 'It thinks Bombay is the tinny vulgar film city, the worst of Beverly Hills, and, of course, in one respect that's right. Part of Bombay is superficial, a veneer. This is where the best parties are, and the in-crowd. But the high life hides unhappiness. Look at those rich women with empty eyes in empty faces. They have everything but they have nothing.

'Still, Bombay is more fun than Delhi. It has class. You can't deny it has an almost electric charge, a feeling of vitality you don't have in Delhi. Bombay is a painted-up hustler, a city of opportunity, and a place for adventurers, where you can claw your way to the top. Life can be terrible here, but it is still a city of hope. Why else do people come in such numbers? They believe they can make good. Their energies give Bombay its character. It is a cauldron, with millions of rootless people. It is more mature, too.

'Women are treated better here than anywhere in India. Those crass Delhi men don't know how to treat women. They ogle and pinch bottoms. Eve-teasing is a Delhi phenomenon; you don't find it here. They think foreign women are an easy lay. But in Bombay a girl can sit at a bar without raising eyebrows, she can walk home alone from the disco without fear and travel in a train or bus and not be molested. She doesn't do those things in Delhi. Bombay men are accustomed to career women, working alongside them, treating them naturally, mixing with them socially. Have you been to those north Indian parties – the men at one end of the room, the women at the other, never meeting? As you know there's no dating in India, except in Bombay. There is greater mobility between the sexes. Virginity is not so prized; and anyway you can always get a certificate of virginity if someone is a bit stuffy about it. But don't be deceived: those lovely Bombay girls in the wealthy middle classes are not kicking over the traces all that much. They still respect their daddies. They date and disco and keep pace with Manhattan and London and they stick to their class. They never date beneath them. They keep to the magic circle and they marry for money. In Bombay people are franker about adultery. In Delhi, they're so awfully mealy-mouthed about it.'

Of all the people who have 'made it' in Bombay none has done so more notably than the Parsis, whose ancestors fled Persia and the religious persecution of Muslim conquerors, and made their way across the Arabian Sea to India. Most live in and around Bombay and are uniquely bound up with its history, having done for it what Scottish businessmen did for Calcutta. The Parsis are an eminently sensible people, and great survivors, giving their allegiance to whoever has been in charge. Their ability to prosper is famous, and the Parsi family Tata is India's most successful business clan, with interests in steel, chemicals, engineering and vehicles. The Tata T on the front of lorries is one of India's best known symbols. In numerical strength, however, the Parsis are dwindling; and the reason for this is their high living standard. They are being eroded by their own success. They have needed no convincing of the benefits of small families, and Parsis have seen to it that their progeny are, in general, well off, well-educated and relatively few in number. There are now about 90,000 of them, their numbers falling by one per cent a year since the Second World War. Since 1970 more than twice as many have been taken to the five towers of silence on Malabar Hill, to have their bones picked clean by vultures, as have been born. Many young Parsis have settled in Europe and North America and about two fifths now marry outside the faith. Apart from their numerical decline there has been a large falling off in their interest in their own religion, history and traditions. Few men now enter the priesthood and not even a hundred men now know the rituals concerning temple fires. (What is happening is similar to what happened to the Jews of Cochin, now so small in number that they have to send to Bombay for a mohel to perform circumcisions.) The traditional Parsi hat, an intricate turban-like affair, is not worn much now, and the last hat maker died in 1981. Even burial and cremation are now being considered by some Parsis as reasonable alternatives to the open bowls of the towers of silence. Parsis are not fire worshippers, and are angered when described as such; rather, as followers of the prophet Zoroaster they venerate fire, water and earth and avoid polluting them: hence the birds of prey wheeling over the pleasant gardens on Malabar Hill.

Like the Parsis, the dabbawallahs of Bombay, or, to give them their full title, the members of the Union of Tiffin Box Suppliers, have also made enterprise their watchword. Their business is lunch and they are a unique Bombay institution, ensuring that every day up to 100,000 office workers in Bombay eat a lunch prepared by the loving hands of their own wives. The idea is simplicity, the practice is complex and requires careful timing and organization. Every morning at a particular time, the 2,300 city dabbawallahs knock on suburban doors and collect lunches from wives. The lunch is in the four compartments of a standard pail, or dabba, the size of a two-pint paint tin. Typically, a dabbawallah will round up thirty or forty dabbas, fix them to his bicycle, and pedal rapidly to the nearest station. Here he meets other dabba-wallahs and as their train heads for Bombay they work like postmen sorting out the dabbas into districts. Each dabba is painted with symbols and numbers to ensure that the right rice, lentils, chapattis and curds reach the right husband. The grand meeting of dabbawallahs in Bombay, as trains disgorge hundreds of lunch carriers and thousands of lunches, is a remarkable spectacle. Working at great speed they sort the dabbas until they are ready for the last stage. The tiffin pails are piled onto trays and borne off on the heads of the dabbawallahs. They run into government offices, commercial offices and dish out the lunches. Thus are thousands of Bombay men linked each lunchtime with their caring wives. The dabbawallahs pride themselves on getting the right lunch to each man at the same time every day. After the food has been consumed the dabbawallahs return, round up the empty pails, and, reversing the whole process, return them to the wives for washing up.

The dabbawallahs are partly a by-product of Bombay's over-crowding. There was a time when many men could get home to lunch, but those more comfortable days ended as the city grew. But the conservatism of married men being well known, they still wanted home-made lunch. An Indian loves his lunch as much as anybody, and feels that only his wife can guarantee the quality and the quantity he requires, that restaurant food is expensive, of poorer quality and is served in meagre portions. A Bombay wife can make lunch for one or two rupees and the dabbawallah service costs her about 20 rupees (£1.30) a month. A restaurant lunch would cost 7 or 8 rupees a day so the dabbawallah service makes good economic sense. Dependability, of course, is all, and there can be few services in the world to equal the reliability of the Bombay Union of Tiffin Box Suppliers.

As it is lunchtime there are crowds of pretty popinjay girls in the smart shopping arcades looking at the jeans and blouses. The music-to-buy-to is western disco. It is a small shock to go outside to endure the monsoon rain again. I call a taxi and it heads off like an amphibious war vehicle into the flood. On the way we have only one (small) crash, and the driver says the stars are against him today. Somewhere in the swirling water and traffic I see a man I have seen before. He is crippled, his legs hopelessly twisted and wasted. He sits on a small wooden tray mounted on little wheels and propels himself with his strong hands. What he does I do not know. Perhaps he sells pencils, or cleans shoes or begs. He can be glimpsed as he paddles through the storm of splashing traffic and rain, drenched and wild-looking like a sailor on a raft, almost overwhelmed, but surviving.

One day I took the city and slum tour suggested by the Calcutta authorities. Mr Bhattarjea, my guide, was waiting for me in the hotel lobby and we wrestled our way through the sticky crowd of touts, shouting taxi men and flapping beggars on the pavement. We entered our car and nosed into the teeming maelstrom. It was a humid day and the black exhaust from the scarred, roaring and leaning buses hung in the air, reluctant to disperse. There was that strong smell of urban India, a compound of vegetables, drain water, perspiration, fish, bidis, petrol, damp pavements, sacking, dungcakes, urine and rot. Boys and men squatted in their pants and vests in the gutters and sluiced water from hydrants and standpipes around their loins and rubbed soap into their hair. They laughed and threw soap and revelled in their pleasure. Barefoot pavement women, clad in rags, bent over iron pots heating on little fires, stirring gummy messes with sticks. Flies crept over the lips and runny noses of their grimy match-limbed children asleep in embryonic posture on the roadside. Thin, mangy, desperate cats with mad eyes prowled about them. Some skinny cattle, ungainly as pantomine cows, were picking their way through the sleepers and around an old man, dozing or dead, who lay beside a black puddle through which rickshaws splashed.

We passed a large hoarding saying 'Calcutta is forever'. Mr Bhattarjea, leaning back in his seat, pointed out a succession of particularly bad places where traffic jammed. Vehicles just stopped and coagulated as if they had run into pools of syrup. He showed how, with flyovers and other works, the authorities were trying to bring relief to the people.

'Of course', he observed, 'even with all our improvements the traffic demands will never be satisfied. We run faster and faster to stay in the same place. If you like you can write in your notebook that our traffic remains abominable.'

We passed slowly by a bus queue. Resignation was etched in the people's faces and Mr Bhattarjea drew attention to them.

'If you like you can say that getting to work in Calcutta is horrible. Public transport is 100 per cent overcrowded. Not enough buses and much traffic jam means lateness. Three days' lateness means one day knocked off holiday. That is why the people in the queue look like that. You have noticed their faces? They do not want to be late. It is not their habit. Sometimes they get mad and demonstrate. You have probably heard that Calcutta is famous for its demonstrations. People set fire to trams and turn cars over. You have heard of these demonstrations. You have seen the pictures, I expect. But there are not too many of them because there is also very much of perseverance in Calcutta.'

Perseverance and a certain robustness have always been important qualities for Calcutta's citizens, for it is a demanding city. Job Charnock, its merchant founder, set up a factory in this unhealthy silty place in 1692-94 and there gradually arose what was once called 'a city of palaces' devoted to trade in jute, tea, indigo, cotton, silk and minerals. It became, for 139 years from 1773 to 1912, the British capital of India and a monument to the Scottish entrepreneurial spirit. Calcutta's loss of capital status to Delhi still hurts. As can still be imagined, its architecture gave it grandeur in its heyday. The maidan is a necessary and welcome Hyde Park of a lung and some of the commercial and administrative buildings are handsomely imposing. The white Victoria Memorial is rather matronly and overbearing: a blancmange, but an enjoyable, handsome blancmange, bespeaking its epoch. The decaying classical villas still have stained and crumbling dignity.

The grandeur today is somewhat dog-eared and a little wormy; and it always was a veneer on Calcutta's incorrigible callousness and naked devotion to money. The other side of the city's coin is, as ever, the spreading encampment of a vast, mired and sunken proletariat living in brutish squalor. For much of Calcutta is a midden. A third of its people inhabit the slums which spread through 97 of 100 municipal districts.

One of those books, so popular in India, of pre-written letters to cover every occasion, has the following in its complaints section: 'This is to inform you that during the last few days a slum has sprung up on the pavements in our neighbourhood.'

The sharp stink, excreta, slums, pavement colonies, knotted traffic, the daily electricity blackouts, flooding, disease and hope-lessness make it seem a version of hell. It is not long before the newcomer's sensibilities are affronted and tested by a gruesome thrusting stump, a nightmarishly eroded face, pleading streaming eyes, beggar children clinging like burrs, and streets of human piggeries. It all inspires anger, hatred, revulsion and pity.

For the burnt-out cases, the desperately poor and hungry, the foundlings and other flotsam, there are Mother Teresa's remark-able establishments. The city's hospitals, of course, are over-crowded. Mother Teresa's homes for dying people, trawled from the streets, provide simple beds, a little comfort, the sound of human voices and the touch of hands, rather than any great medical skill. They are shelters, places to die in some cleanliness and dignity, the alternative to the gutter. There are a number of westerners, mostly young, moving among the beds of the hollow-eyed, skinny and groaning human embers. They have dropped in to help the nuns for a while. Few of them have knowledge, but they can clean floors, mop brows, hold hands and cover corpses for a few days or weeks before returning home. They have journeyed a long way to skivvy in Mother Teresa's famous sanc-tuaries, and Mother Teresa provides something for them too, in a way. Many Indians are proud of Mother Teresa, herself an Indian by adoption. Her compassion and practical channelling of it have made her known throughout the world. She is the Calcutta equivalent, relatively speaking, of those organizations, like the Salvation Army, which pick up the bits of society that do not fit or have failed for one reason or another. By being there at longstop she is not only saintly; she relieves the pressure on consciences.

As the second city of empire after London, Calcutta was never anything for the British to be proud of, and history's subsequent unhappy deals made it worse. It has known any number of shocked spectators who down the years have groped for the superlatives of shame and degradation. It was Kipling's 'city of dreadful night . . . the packed and pestilential town.' The young Winston Churchill wrote to his mother that he was pleased he had seen it because he would not have to see it again. A hundred years ago a visitor, reflecting on its marshy location and stinking stews, wrote: 'Its situation is so bad by nature that there is little that man could do to make it worse, but that little has been faithfully and assiduously done.' The *Statesman* newspaper, founded in Calcutta in 1818, commented recently that 'the city known and feared for its volatile temper continues to show a resigned acceptance of unending misery.'

Yet this same Calcutta has many citizens who love it with fierce loyalty. There is a perverse and desperate pride in which epithets and condemnations, like 'hell hole', 'burnt out case' and 'disaster area' are treasured like encomiums.

However awful it is, many people have a natural affection for their home and root. Others feel the sort of gratitude they would for a lifebelt: and that is exactly how many new Calcuttans feel about the place. Two-fifths of greater Calcutta's 12 million people arrived in the upheaval of partition. Rather romantically, it was suggested to me, Calcutta is an accommodating foster mother.

It is pre-eminently the city of the Bengalis, and Bengalis will tell you they are the brightest and most inventive and most interesting of India's people. 'We are a special people, a mix of Aryans, Muslims, Mongols and Huns. When the Aryan blood comes to the top you see our intellectual side. But when the Mongol blood gets to the top we might assassinate and demonstrate violently', a Calcuttan said. 'There is a fierce pride here – people say "My city, right or wrong". This is an intellectually satisfying place. That is why Bengalis stay here. Satyajit Ray could make his films anywhere in the world, but he stays in Calcutta. It is a big city in many ways.'

Calcutta has been in its time a spring of Hindu nationalism, a centre of Hindu culture and of literary renaissance, and its citizens take much pride in this. Among the clogged streets, the rotting colonial buildings and the dark flat-topped office blocks, some jerry-built and leaning, there bubbles a lively intellectual and creative stream. This is cultured Calcutta, with its café society, Bohemian airs, political argument and love of gossip, a city au fait with the latest political trends and tracts of the west. Calcutta is India's Left Bank.

There are many thousands of people here engaged in writing, versing, talking and pamphleteering. There are hundreds of drama groups and art galleries, but the city's art world today worries about the fall in numbers of the middle class gentry who have traditionally supported local artists.

Calcutta's intellectuals (and intellectuals regard themselves as a class or tribe) take pride not only in the city's culture but also in its against-the-grain politics. West Bengal was, in 1982, one of the two Indian states with a communist government. It was popular in the countryside for its agrarian reform and liked by the business community in the city for being relatively free of corruption and for ensuring that unions kept to their bargains. It offered some sort of stability as a pragmatic and not a revolutionary government. The left front government fitted in with the city's determinedly independent outlook: it is said of other places, but it is certainly true of Calcutta, that if you go out into the streets and shout 'Yes', Calcutta will shout back 'No'. That was one of the problems with the old city council: it was blathering and useless, addressed itself primarily to argument rather than action, and had to be replaced by the Calcutta Metropolitan Development Authority which was charged with getting something done. Calcutta is one place in India where Mahatma Gandhi is by no means universally venerated. The city does have a statue of Gandhi, and it has had to be protected by the police in its time. It also has a statue of Lenin and of Subhas Chandra Bose, a local hero, a pompous would-be dictator who hoped that Hitler would help free India and who died in a wartime plane crash. Bose is loved because he raised a fist. He talked, but also acted. Calcuttans not long ago renamed Clive Street after Bose; and during the Vietnam war they took pleasure in renaming the street where the American consulate is located after Ho Chi Minh.

The intellectual, creative and political strands, along with commerce and industry, help to charge the city with a vigour which is sharpened rather than depressed by the environment. Augean, dislocated, shocking, Calcutta yet represents a crude triumph of human survival in monstrous circumstances. It is for many of its citizens a vital and fascinating place. People die in the gutter, but fastidious citizens somehow manage to keep their clothing white as they pick their way through chaos. Schoolchildren, combed and neat in smart uniforms, trot through the slums to schools which have to operate two or three shifts a day to meet the demand for education.

In spite of appearances a huge and gallant effort is being made to improve Calcutta. The challenge is formidable, if not insuperable, but somehow the Metropolitan Development Authority has already made life better for many people. It has spent more than £200 million on digging poor Calcutta from its own ruins. Instead of building soaring towers and other civic vanities the authority has been tackling the basic job of shifting ordure, laying on water, improving more than 300 slums and trying to do something about the traffic. It is a kind of rescue work. It is impossible to clear the slums and rehouse the four million people living in them. They are, after all, communities with their traditions and networks of neighbours, families, shops and services. Instead, the slums are being improved while the dwellings stay intact and the people remain. 'For better quality of life, for fuller growth, slum life should be made more noble, more meaningful and more hopeful', the authority says.

The first step is to pave the streets and light them. The water taps are installed at the rate of one for each 100 people. One lavatory is built for every 25 people and the authority has a plan to convert more than 150,000 privies into sanitary units connected to sewers or to septic tanks. In this work it has the help of the Easy Toilet Society of Patna, a pioneer in this branch of public health, founded in 1970 by a Bihari sociology student. The society is based on Gandhian ideas of liberating a group of untouchables, the scavengers and sweepers, who traditionally have cleaned primitive lavatories and carted away night soil; it also seeks to improve public health, a difficult task in a country where defecating is largely an open air activity and there is a belief that ordure is best dried by the sun and rendered into dust. Nevertheless the society has designed and made tens of thousands of cheap flush latrines and has been called in to help make Calcutta cleaner.

The city's water supply has also been doubled in recent years, according to the Development Authority. Calcutta is no longer the cholera capital of the world as it was in the 1950s and 1960s when the disease killed 1,000 people a year. But Calcutta will continue to be flooded during the monsoon, as it always has been. It would cost too much to prevent water-logging during the worst time, 'and dry feet would be simply a luxury'.

Much money is being spent on new slums on the city outskirts for what is termed the EWS, or economically weaker section. These people would not be able to afford housing even if the authorities could afford to build it. Instead the city is building units which consist of hard standing, one brick room, a lavatory, water supply, access to power and some land on which a family can build as it wishes with thatch, corrugated iron, plastic and sacking. A unit like this costs £400 and a family has 20 years to pay for it. It is what the authorities call an improved slum. To satisfy political feelings one of these slums, a 60-acre plot, has just been built in a middle class housing development as a reminder to the comfortably off that the poor are always with them. 'In Calcutta', it was explained to me, 'you can't have people living in an ivory tower. The rich should see the poor.'

Calcutta's development has been in keeping with an important change in India in recent years, the growth of the cities. Since 1971 the major centres have swollen by 40 per cent, and there are now twelve cities with a population of a million or more. The urbanization of India increases as more people look to the towns for opportunities unavailable in the countryside. Twenty-three per cent of Indians now live in towns and the way they have to mix helps to break down the barriers of caste and class. You cannot ask a man his caste in a jammed commuter bus. Many people make their move to the cities by following in the footsteps of a relative or fellow villager who can provide a helping hand. A large number of the labourers in Delhi come from Rajasthan, for example. The newspaper sellers have migrated from a small part of Tamil Nadu, while people from a part of Andhra Pradesh monopolize the bicycle rickshaw business. The large-scale migration to the cities creates its own appalling problems, of overcrowding, squalor and unemployment. At the same time, the cities are breakers of moulds and broadeners of attitudes.

9

The lie of the land

Wildlife, forests, the green revolution

Richly-watered, richly-fruited, cool with the wind of the south,
dark with the crop of the harvests.

INDIA'S NATIONAL SONG

REVEALED in the glare of the car's headlights, my tiger
bounded across the track in majestically lazy parentheses and
slid into the blackness of the jungle, leaving in the memory a
bright burning image.

Like all the best quests the search for a tiger offers the prospect
of a glimpse of a creature legendary, beautiful and rare; and only a
small chance of success. But success can be thrilling. To hear a
tiger's threatening bronchial growl from the tall dry grass is to
have all the senses sharpened.

The beast is no longer on the edge of extinction as it was until
the mid-1970s. India fortunately applied the brakes just in time.
It was a close thing. In 1969 a wildlife conference in Delhi
declared the tiger an endangered species and the government
banned tiger shooting the following year. The ban was incor-
porated into a protection law of 1972, the year in which an
all-India tiger count revealed there were only 1,827 tigers left.

It has been estimated that at the beginning of this century there
were between 30,000 and 40,000 tigers. They were hunted on a
large scale. The sprawled striped corpse and its topeed bare-
kneed killer became a cliché of the Raj. Photographs of mounds
of dead animals and birds are a commonplace in the old books
about India. Tiger shooting was conducted on such a careless
scale that it might now be seen as a form of aristocratic hooli-
ganism. The official report of the visit of King George V to India
in 1911 notes that: 'On this day Lord Durham, Lord Charles
Fitzmaurice, Sir Derek Keppel and Sir Henry McMahon killed
between them seven tigers and a bear, making a total bag of ten
tigers, a bear and a rhinoceros; a wonderful day's sport . . . on the

28th the King killed his twenty-first tiger. The total bag for the ten days was thirty-nine tigers, eighteen rhinoceros, of which the King killed eight, and four bears, of which the King killed one.' The account noted that after a few days' heavy slaughter 'the sport of the previous days by this time had begun to tell on the quantity of game still afoot . . .'

Half a century later Colonel Kesri Singh, a leading tiger hunter, wrote in his book *Hints on Tiger Shooting* that when he arranged a tiger shoot for the Queen and Prince Philip in Rajasthan in 1960 there were protests in England. 'I used to laugh at the ignorance of those agitators . . . There was nothing wrong in the Queen's accepting to shoot a tiger when the world knows that offering a tiger-shoot to a distinguished guest is traditionally a part of Indian hospitality.' He also wrote, however: 'I observe with much regret that wildlife in India is diminishing every year. Unless steps are taken quickly to preserve it, the country will lose her varied and valuable fauna.'

He blamed poaching and deforestation for much of the trouble, but did not include tigers in his list of threatened species, although he must have known what was happening. He remarked only that: 'It should be borne in mind that tigers help India to earn foreign exchange. It is the only place in the world where exciting tiger shooting can be arranged very conveniently.' Yet when the Colonel helped Prince Philip to become the last member of the British royal family to fell a tiger there were fewer than 3,000 of the animals left; so it needed some stage management to get one in front of the royal gunsight.

Although western and Indian aristocrats killed many tigers they were not the worst offenders in bringing them to the edge of extinction. Poachers caused much destruction and were encouraged by dealers responding to the strong western desire for tiger skins. The forests where tigers roamed were steadily cut down for industrial and agricultural purposes, and the fleeing and diminishing tiger families were ruthlessly sought out by the proprietors of hunting companies which organized package holidays with kills almost guaranteed. Along with everything else working against the tiger, the western hunter, justified in some Indian minds by the handful of dollars he brought in, added an intolerable pressure. For country people, the scarcity of tiger added to the value of the bits and pieces of the animal traditionally held to have medicinal or magical properties. Tiger droppings, for example, are thought to cure piles; the brain is recommended for pimples, the flesh as a guard against snake bite. It is believed that the gall bladder, if pressed to the eyeballs, stops the eyes watering and makes them stronger. The application of tiger kidney fat to the appropriate organ is said to make a man tigerish in bed.

In 1973, Project Tiger, financed by the government and the World Wildlife Fund, was launched to create strongholds for the tiger and arrest his decline. There are now eleven of these throughout the country, each with a core area of 120 square miles, this core being the exclusive domain of the tiger and his prey, ranging from deer to fish. About thirty villages and 5,000 people have been moved from these areas, resettled and compensated. Farmers living around the reserves are paid compensation for any cattle the tigers kill. In 1982 the reserves provided a home for nearly 800 tigers, but more than threequarters of the total tiger population of more than 3,000 still lives outside the reserves. Eight years after Project Tiger was started the population had increased by a third. 'In my view,' Mr Koppiker, then a director of the project, said to me, 'the danger of extinction has passed. In the reserves we develop a complete environment for tigers, ensuring that there is enough forest cover and water and a large enough population of other animals for the tigers to prey on; and these animals in their turn need grass and other vegetation. The development of water resources in a reserve can also benefit people in the surrounding district. Forest rangers and radio communications have gone a long way to protecting tigers from poachers, and there are now very few instances of disabled tigers turning maneater. When the tiger has enough food man is never on the menu. He is, after all, a great gentleman.'

Nevertheless, as the tiger population grows the number of cattle killed on the fringes of reserves is increasing. The tiger is looking for more living room, and to prevent congestion and trouble some tiger families will have to be taken to areas where there are few tigers or none.

A tiger census is conducted by rangers and foresters who divide sections of forest between them and search for spoor. Tiger pug marks are as distinctive as fingerprints and experienced rangers know the marks of the tigers in their sections. On finding the prints they make a tracing of them on glass and transfer them to paper. Thus a record is made of each tiger's print which can readily be compared with others during the two-day period of a census: this prevents double counting and ensures a good degree of accuracy. But outside the reserves the tiger population is a matter of estimate, based on local knowledge and experience.

One of the reserves is Corbett Park, on the edge of the Himalayas, 140 miles north-east of Delhi. It takes its name from Jim Corbett, a genuine *Boy's Own Paper* Jungle Jim, who hunted man-eating tigers and leopards in these parts from 1907 to 1939 and whose stirring tales, like *Man-eaters of Kumaon*, are the essence of the adventure and manners of a vanished era.

Corbett Park's wilderness has crocodiles, elephants, deer and birdlife in plenty. But it is the slight chance of seeing a tiger that adds spice to a stay in one of the forest lodges. As it happened, I was driving at dusk down a jungle track to dine with Brijendra Singh, a tiger expert, when I saw my first tiger. It leapt across the road, paused briefly to glare into the headlights, and was gone. Presumably he was going out to dinner, too.

Next morning we mounted elephants, putting our legs around the corner posts of the howdah, and made off through tall grass into the jungle. The elephant has all the qualities of the toughest four wheel drive vehicle and bulldozer, and much else besides. We plunged through the cool greenery of the jungle, the elephants shouldering and trunking aside branches and saplings. We eventually came upon a place where a tiger had killed during the night: a scrabble of pug marks and blood stains, and the drag mark of a dead deer. We followed the drag mark to a river. Otters scuttled into the water and a jackal mooched off, looking guiltily over his shoulder. The elephants were urged into the river and hosed water into their mouths as they forded. On the far bank we picked up the blood spots and mounted a ridge to re-enter the jungle. About a hundred yards in we found the hooves and gnawed skull of a deer in a patch of tall whispering grass beneath some trees. The elephants froze. We suddenly became very quiet. From the grass there came a low and menacing growl, a chesty ticking sound. It was a tigress. Had she been alone she might have broken cover. But, close by her, was a cub, still and silent at mother's order. Its face was just visible through the grass, but the tigress was better hidden. I could only hear her and not see her, but what I heard was warning enough. It was unwise to irritate her. The elephants backed away and we moved off. The growl was unforgettable.

Later that day we stopped for tea beside a blue lake. Water, a handful of tea, some milk and generous measures of sugar were boiled up together in a pan. As we drank, we heard five gun shots from a spit of land across the lake. Shooting is forbidden in the park and Brijendra Singh took three of us to investigate. After half a mile, we encountered a group of men. They were big game: a divisional commissioner, two magistrates, a police superinten- dent in mufti and a police inspector in uniform, complete with revolver and bandolier. One of the group had a shotgun. About a hundred yards off, on the fringe of the jungle, we found the fresh bright blood of a wounded deer dripping from leaves in the undergrowth and a trail of blood leading into the trees. The shooting party were persuaded to explain it all to park officials who arrived with rifle-toting forest rangers. It was a small illus- tration of the way things so often are in India. Many officials, not least those appointed to uphold justice and order, consider them- selves above the law. Had these men been challenged by a forest ranger they would have used their superior rank to tell him to clear off and keep his mouth shut. Now they sat on stones, by the light of a camp fire, writing out statements for the park officials saying that one of their companions had fired the shotgun acci- dentally. The moon rose above the lake and, quite close by, a tiger started roaring. In the distance some elephants bellowed. The pens of the upholders of the law squeaked. Somewhere out in the jungle a wounded deer was bleeding.

At dawn next day, some rangers went in search of it. They picked up the blood trail and traced it until they found the deer's remains, the skull and ribs gnawed clean by a tiger.

From time to time there is criticism of the 'sentimentalists' who have devoted their energies to saving the tiger. Tigers, it is pointed out, still eat people and occasionally terrorize rural com- munities: they are therefore pests which should be destroyed; and tiger lands should be thrown open for development by the people. A conservationist robustly put another view, that 'you can always replace people, but you can't replace tigers', adding, less jocu- larly, that saving the tiger and his habitat has a direct and benefi- cial bearing on the welfare of people and that the small incidence of man-eating is a price worth paying. The tiger is a piece in a jigsaw. He is worth saving for himself, and the requirements for his survival are also part of the requirements of the people who, directly and indirectly, share his patch. Interest in the tiger has helped to focus interest on the forests.

India, and parts of Pakistan and Nepal, have reached an ecological crisis through the widespread and indiscriminate destruction of forests and the resulting increase in floods and landslides. Vast tracts of the Himalaya and other regions have been laid waste, and much of the damage has been done by contractors who bribe officials whose job it is to protect the forests. The government of India has admitted that the country is heading for 'ecological disaster' as felling goes on unabated.

In thirty years, according to official estimates, India has lost more than 17,000 square miles of forest, an area larger than Holland. The actual loss may be greater than this.

A recent estimate put India's forest cover at 135,000 square miles, about a tenth of the country. It makes a mockery of the 1952 forest policy which set out to raise the forest cover from a fifth to a third of the land area. 'We have', says Mrs Gandhi, 'squandered our assets.'

Almost all of the great forest areas have suffered, but the damage has been most serious in the north. In the Himalayan belt, from Kashmir to Assam, once covered with majestic forests, the slopes have been denuded below 6,000 feet. In Kashmir a number of famous forests have been obliterated. In the neighbouring mountain state of Himachal Pradesh the tree cover, which was two fifths in the early 1960s, has since been halved. The ransacking of the woods is even worse in some parts of Uttar Pradesh. Without tree cover the topsoil is being washed away, leaving large stretches of land barren. Substantial areas have become saline or alkaline. Rivers and reservoirs are increasingly silted with topsoil and the flooding potential of these arteries of the northern plains is being enhanced. Water supplies once retained by the sponge effect of forests have dried up and there have been many more landslides.

The rapidly growing population makes severe demands on forest areas. There is a shortage of timber and firewood, the most important cooking fuel. About three-quarters of the people need wood for most of their cooking and heating. The increasing need for timber is being met by contractors whose devastations have not been made good by the government. The emphasis is on profit and replanting has been neglected. Only 5 per cent of forests consist of government-planted trees. Forests designated as virgin, meant to be untouched, are being pillaged. Roadbuilding in mountainous regions, which makes life more agreeable for the inhabitants, enables the tree fellers to reach forests more easily. Contractors not only bribe forest officials; they are also important contributors to political funds. Nevertheless, the state government in Himachal Pradesh has put a ban on contract felling, a step considered brave in view of the importance of the contractors' lobby.

What is happening in Nepal provides a terrible lesson: the people there are steadily tearing their country to pieces. As the forests recede the women have to walk farther for firewood, up to ten or twelve miles a day in some areas, and many communities have been forced by the scarcity of fuel to cook only once a day.

Country people in India see, with increasing dismay, that the unscrupulous plundering of the land is making their existence harder. The beautiful neem trees, for example, have been ripped down in their thousands. Villagers' concern has led them to join a resistance movement, known as Chipko, the Hindi word for hug. In poignant defiance of the contractors they hug trees when the fellers arrive with axes and chainsaws. By wrapping their bodies around trees they help to draw attention to what is going on; but the movement is too small to make a really effective impact on one of the great threats to the land of India.

Much wooded land has been cleared, of course, to make room for agriculture, India's mighty ballast. The story of agriculture in the past twenty years has been one of considerable achievement, but the benefits are not spread evenly and for many millions of people the national self-congratulation seems to be premature.

In a country determined to be self-reliant agriculture has to be a priority. As a predominantly agricultural country, whose national song extols the bounty of water, fruit and the lush greenery of growing plants, India was embarrassed by its image of poverty and starvation and its need to import large quantities of food. Agricultural production was neglected: between 1900 and 1950 the annual growth rate was less than one third of one per cent. The turning point came in the middle of the 1960s through the 'green revolution' in the growing of wheat. The heart of the revolution was Punjab where varieties of Mexican wheat were introduced with great success. High yield seeds, better irrigation techniques, mechanization and, above all, the greater use of fertilizers, shortened the time between planting and harvesting and gave crops two or three times larger than those of traditional varieties. Punjab soil is fairly fertile and the people are hard-working, go-ahead and receptive to new ideas. The state has a strong tradition of agricultural education, agriculture-oriented banks, land consolidation and skilful marketing. There was a setback in the early 1970s when disease damaged the crops, but scientists quickly developed resistant strains and production soared again. The concurrent development of roads and power enabled farmers to forge ahead. Punjab is, pre-eminently, the state of the tractor, and of electrification, and is the richest state in the union, India's bread basket, growing more than two thirds of the country's wheat. Parts of Haryana and of western Uttar Pradesh are also strong in the revolution, but the technology has not spread to any important extent in other states. Poor management, ignorance and a certain shiftlessness make these huge areas lag behind. Technological advances are mired by caste customs, conservation and lack of education. The uses of irrigation and fertilizers are best understood by an élite. Punjab and Co. are far ahead, and exceptions: one part of the imbalance of Indian agricultural production and distribution.

In short, although the green revolution is admirable, the very phrase is misunderstood and misleading: it implies that India's difficulties have been settled, as if by a magic wand. This is not true. The food problems have not been resolved. Food stocks still have to be augmented by imports. Monsoon behaviour is, eternally, the central factor; and drought, population growth and the need to maintain large buffer stocks of wheat are important considerations. As Mrs Gandhi said in 1980: 'Our food production has gone up two and a half times. No longer are we subjected to the taunt that we, an agricultural country, have to seek food from outside. But the battle is far from won. Hunger is far from vanquished. Many old problems persist.'

The green revolution primarily involves wheat, partly rice and, to a lesser extent, maize. It is centred on a small, well-irrigated and prosperous state. Outside Punjab the bulk of the land, about seven tenths, remains unirrigated and the work being done to improve matters has fallen behind schedule. Meanwhile, between two-fifths and a half of the people live below the poverty line and cannot afford to buy the food they need. In any case, distribution failures mean that food is not reaching many areas that need it. 'Although India has achieved comparative self-sufficiency in food, malnutrition is still prevalent,' Mrs Gandhi said. 'Not because of lack of food in the market, but because many people have no money in their pockets to buy it.'

But India remains confident that it will be able to feed its rapidly swelling population, that technology which has, hitherto, benefited the better-off farmer, will eventually reach the poorer people. Wheat is being introduced where it has not been grown much before, in east Bihar, west Bengal, Assam and Orissa. There remains a need for a green revolution in rice, and agricultural technologists are producing better varieties.

About three quarters of India's people earn their living from the land. There are thousands of wealthy farmers; but many millions eke out a living on scraps of land, utterly at the mercy of the weather, with nothing to fall back on. There are others, perhaps 150 million, who have no land at all and who depend on landlords for paltry wages. Country life can seem, and no doubt can be for those with a reasonable holding and income, rhythmic and satisfying. But for millions of Indians village life may be brutal and anxious and violent, with its strong emphasis on caste, its poverty, frustrated hopes and the ill treatment of the weak by the strong. There are, therefore, the conditions for revolution; but the poor have never shown any interest in revolt. The passivity of country people is part of India's easygoing massiveness: religious belief, the conditions of life, the prod of the police lathi, dampen volatility. Fatalism yokes men uncomplainingly to their ploughs, their lot in life being what they earned in their last existence, their hope in this life being for enough to eat. Mahatma Gandhi reflected that those without enough food see God in the form of bread.

India can be a place of sudden and terrifying violence. Caste and communal strains create an explosive vapour. But India is like the ocean. The waves clash on the surface when storms blow, but the great body of deep water moves on relentlessly.

There are, however, currents of change among the people. More of them are having their horizons broadened by education, technology and contact with the towns. Perceptions and resentments are being gradually sharpened, and conflicts inevitably follow as rights to land and wages are claimed and rejected. The beheadings, beatings, burning and raping of the untouchables and peasantry are part of a struggle on the land as an old order is challenged and defended and here and there begins a slow and agonising change. Pressure on the land is growing steadily more serious. The landless want a stake. Those with tiny farms want larger ones. The politically powerful landowners resist. Land reform, redistribution, which might have been possible at independence, seems politically unachievable but grows more urgent. The need for rural industries is desperate.

A few miles outside Delhi, in a small settlement of huts made from twigs, straw and sacking, I met a man called Wasal and his wife and children. They had just been freed from a version of slavery. Poor, ignorant and pliant, they had allowed themselves to be cheated and intimidated by the owner of a brick kiln in Punjab, and had become his property. Wasal, who was skinny and knotty and said he thought he was 60, was not at all bitter. He said, matter-of-factly: 'I had nothing to start with. I was just a poor farmer with about five acres. I thought I could do better by taking my family to the kilns. I was told there was good money and I was promised a commission if I could recruit others. I did it for money. I persuaded eighty people to leave the land, including twenty-five of my relatives. There was nothing for us in farming. But I was tricked. The master said that he had given me 6,000 rupees and I would have to work until I paid it all back. Of course, he had given me nothing. It was just his story.

'For the first seven years we were paid nothing. We were given our food, but sometimes it was not enough and we went hungry. As you can see, we are not fat. I often worked sixteen hours a day, every day of the week, making bricks. It was four years before I was allowed to visit my home village and the master kept some of my family as hostages to make sure I came back to the kiln. After that he allowed me to go home every two years, and I worked for him for eleven years. I was beaten up three or four times, but rough treatment is normal.'

Wasal heard about a Hindu religious teacher who had started a group to rescue bonded labourers. He escaped from the kiln and rode a train to Delhi, without paying. Eventually he found his way to the swami and told his tale. The swami and his men set off in a lorry to rescue Wasal's family, his wife, five children and three grandchildren, and brought them back to a kiln near Delhi. Here, although the work was hard, they were paid and were free to leave.

'Rescuing bonded labourers does not solve the problem', the swami admitted, 'because it is too deeply rooted. Rescuing them is simply a way of drawing attention to an abuse.'

The employment of bonded labour is illegal, but the Gandhi Peace Foundation, which specializes in social research, estimates that there are more than two million such labourers in ten states. The bondage system will be hard to reduce because there is a need for cheap labour in industries like farming, quarrying, construction and brick making. There will always be people who drift into this form of slavery because of their desperate need for work and food, however bad the conditions. Poor people are recruited by middlemen who promise attractive wages. They are paid in advance and are then committed to paying it back. But the employer charges interest so high that there is never any hope of the workers settling the debt. They are trapped.

The group formed to rescue slave labourers is one of a growing number of voluntary organizations springing up in the Indian countryside to improve the conditions of the poor. Many of these activists are educated middle class people who have decided to forgo orthodox careers to work with untouchables, landless and tribal peoples. Some of the groups have a religious or communist inspiration, but many are non-political. They meet a need for rural leadership, filling a gap left by the corruption, decay and centralizing of political parties. They organize credit for poor farmers, run co-operative dairies and clinics, and take up local issues. As educators, eye-openers, aids to dignity and self-assurance they have become a part of the dynamic of change.

10

Neighbours

Big fish and little fish in the subcontinent

I earnestly hope that this severance may not endure, that the two
new dominions we now propose to set up may come together again
to form one great member state of the Commonwealth.

CLEMENT ATTLEE

INDIA'S population is three and a half times greater than the
sum of the peoples of all its subcontinental neighbours. Its
territory is three times larger than that of the others added
together. It predominates in every respect and its paramountcy is
the obvious and most important fact of regional relationships. It
has the giant's share of resources. Its industrial might is far
greater, its technology more advanced. Its political system is more
free, more stable, more responsive, more mature, more emanci-
pating than that of any other country of the subcontinent, except
Sri Lanka, and is more free and representative than in any other
part of the broad region. It has one of the largest armies in the
world, growing steadily stronger. It is under no threat of invasion
and is, in any case, unconquerable. There is no question of
equality in cousinly subcontinental dealings; and India, which is
stern and not generous in this respect, believes that in the relationship between the neighbours there should be recognition of
the realpolitik created by geography, population and sheer bulk;
and of the realities of south Asia's place in global politics.

In the years since the British left, the political shape of the
subcontinent they unified politically has been adjusted, usually by
war, and, here and there, by an acceptance of the stark facts of
might. For the time being this shape is settled, accepted by realists
as probably permanent, and disputed mainly as a matter of political and romantic ritual and humbug.

Kashmir joined India in 1947: the two wars of possession, of
1947-48 and 1965, have left India holding the larger and better

pieces of it, not least the sublime vale of Kashmir. The French left their Indian enclaves with a dignified adieu in 1954. The Portuguese had to be pushed out of theirs by force in 1961, leaving behind churches, portraits of po-faced governers, saints' bones and a blood mix which happily makes pretty girls. Tiny Sikkim was taken over in 1975 so that, under Indian management, it would cease to be a source of security anxiety on the sensitive Himalayan frontier with China. The small neighbouring kingdom of Bhutan, whose national sport is archery, walks to heel, its foreign affairs guided by India; and the kingdom of Nepal knows its place. China secured what it wanted from the 1962 border conflict which was Nehru's greatest foreign policy failure and a humiliating blunder. The Chinese put their fences around a large and remote chunk of land, Aksai Chin, where Kashmir and China meet, and where the frontier was vague and disputed. India will never get it back. The Chinese also called India's bluff by marching over India's north-eastern frontier and then withdrawing, leaving unresolved the question of the border demarcation in that region. Pakistan inevitably split into two and Bangladesh was born in blood and lives in woe. These halves of Jinnah's Pakistan have failed to be democracies and are governed by vulnerable military élites. The Russians' expansion into Afghanistan, the securing of what they regard as their sphere of interest, will not be reversed and its reverberations have made more uncomfortable the relationship between India and Pakistan. Existing rawness has been salted by Pakistan's reinforcement of its military strength, with American help, against what is perceived as a threat of Russian oozing; and by India's consequent suspicion that the new bullets are more likely to fly at Hindus than communists.

The partition of the subcontinent left a legacy of disaster. It led to violence, genocide as Hindu and Muslim groups tore each other apart, increased rivalry and suspicion, and an immense and wasteful expenditure of energy, resources and lives. It left seeds of war which readily flowered. It was made all the more bitter for being an estrangement, a family matter, a divorce complete with a futile squabble for custody of a child, Kashmir. India and Pakistan continue an ancient quarrel, steeped in the mean and dreadful prejudices of tribe and faith. They store and treasure the slights of history, willing only to believe the worst of each other, taking offence on a grand and histrionic scale at the smallest insult, real or imagined. They relish petty cruelties, putting obstacles in the way of citizens wishing to travel to the neighbour, making communications difficult between themselves. There is no direct air link between the two capitals; and it is not easy to telephone. Yet, quite apart from defence and politics, they retain an intense curiosity about each other. Anyone who travels often between Pakistan and India finds himself being asked: 'What's it like over there? What are they saying and thinking? What do they say about us?' One sometimes feels like a go-between cross-examined by two related people not on speaking terms. There is very little journalistic interchange and occasionally an Indian journalist comes back from the other side and writes as if he has been to a strange land far away.

After three wars the forces of India and Pakistan are permanently toed to the scratch. Pakistan has two-thirds of its army along the Indian frontier; and this is perhaps the clearest illustration of how the two countries feel about each other. There is a pervasive and corroding mistrust, a constant questioning of motive, a wary circling. Pakistan makes its defence assessments primarily in relation to India. The prospect of Soviet encroachment is not as important as the presence of the Hindu multitudes. There is an idea, fostered by Pakistan's leaders, that there is a longing in India to settle scores, to conquer. India, too, finds it useful to remind its people that there is a potentially threatening and perfidious neighbour with a criminal record. For its part India makes its defence dispositions mainly with Pakistan in mind, and, to some extent, with an eye to China. (But apart from that, India also wants to be militarily powerful so that it can be much more in the reckoning on the world stage; and it criticizes what it sees as Pakistani attempts to achieve defence parity on the basis that this intensifies the arms race.)

There is a sense in which Pakistan needs India as part of its effort to define itself. It is an invented country, still wrestling with its identity, still stuck in 1947, trying to decide what it should be. It has not evolved as its founders would have wished: indeed, it would be a profound disappointment to them.

Pakistan was created by people who wanted to escape religious, political and economic discrimination. They wanted a place where they could earn their living as well as be their Muslim selves in an atmosphere free of oppression. Democracy did not root, for Pakistan was not, like independent India, the product of a political movement imbued with a democratic idea and with a long history of struggle and broad intellectual commitment. Pakistan was a by-product of British abdication, a relatively hurried concoction. It owed its existence to the steely and intractable Mr Jinnah. He was backed not by a large and broad people's movement, but essentially by landowners and zamindars and the élite class, who went for separatism because they felt they would lose out in India. They had no real commitment to democracy and with Jinnah's early death the keystone was pulled out of the structure. The country came under military rule in 1958. Pakistan was not best served by its most notable elected leader, the brilliant and monstrous Zulfikar Ali Bhutto, who met a sordid death under the military regime which took power in 1977. Alive, he would always have been a threat; dead, his name exerts the same awful fascination as Peron's in Argentina, haunting and tantalizing Pakistan down the years.

General Zia ul-Haq, the army chief who became ruler in 1977, having told Bhutto he would not permit Pakistani soldiers to turn their guns on Pakistani citizens demonstrating against the government, was seen at first as just another cardboard cut-out general. With his dark, hooded eyes and moustache he looked like a silent pictures villain who tied girls to railway tracks. Indian cartoonists made him look cruel; and also, for some reason, fat, which he is not. Being a soldier, he was unpopular with the people and his wife thought this unfair, saying he was really doing his best for everyone.

Although indecisive at first, he learned management quickly and tightened his grasp, shrewdly and ruthlessly squashing political parties and dissent by imprisoning, exiling and intimidating political leaders and party workers. He strove diligently to keep their powder wet and made sure that possible threats from his peers were dampened. He ran Pakistan like a barracks. The Russian occupation of Afghanistan strengthened him by focusing attention on an external disturbance and causing the Americans to name Pakistan as a 'frontline state', giving it economic aid and arms, which pleased the military. He was also aided by good harvests and remittances from legions of Pakistani expatriate workers. He was affable to visitors and his good manners became the marvel of the subcontinent, so that there was a danger of his giving dictatorship a good name. He was far from being in the top league of tyrants.

Relatively secure in power he was able to address himself to the central question of Pakistan's existence: what it should be. Jinnah had talked of a secular state, but the devout President Zia reasoned that that was wrong, that Pakistan was created in the name of Islam, that it had to be Islamic or nothing. Just as Israel had been established as the homeland for Jews, so Pakistan was the homeland for subcontinental Muslims. As he saw it Pakistan had lost its way. How could there be any place for democracy? There was an inherent contradiction between Islam and democracy; and, to his mind, it seemed that Muslims needed an authoritarian environment. In any case, democracy had been tried and the politicians had caused confusion and disorder. Certainly they had strayed from the Islamic way.

He ordered that the country should become thoroughly Islamic, in the functioning of the courts, the economy, in education, in the way in which it comported itself. Drinking became a serious, flogging, offence. 'Do you have whisky?' is the first question Pakistani customs officials ask when you enter the country. Female hockey players were banned from playing in front of male spectators. An Islamic system of banking, obedient to the Koranic injunction against usury, was introduced. Greater emphasis was placed on Muslim festivals. The Ramadan fast was strictly enforced and hotels were ordered to cover their restaurants with brown paper so that foreigners could lunch without causing offence to local people during the fasting period. The punishments of stoning and hand amputation were introduced (although so far none has been carried out). I recall talking about the penal code to a religious leader in Islamabad, the beautiful and dull capital, and he was postively excited at the prospect of hands being chopped. 'It will have to be on television for the maximum effect. It is all allowed for in the Koran', he said.

There is no general enthusiasm for all this. There is anger at the emphasis on Islam's penal aspect rather than on its practical and compassionate side. Many Pakistanis feel they are already good Muslims and resent having a military representative of the middle class telling them what to do. Their faith is evidently strong and Zia is not responsible for this. Islamization offers the prospect of offending minorities, like Shia Muslims, who have differing practices and beliefs.

The president was not the first leader to turn to Islam for help in securing his position and there was a suspicion that he exploited it, not as a means of developing society, but as a disciplinary framework, the tool of his authoritarianism. As Islamization proceeded, the militarization of the administration went on apace, too. Army officers were moved into posts in all the key areas. The press, of course, was strictly controlled. After years in the saddle Zia looked confident and as permanent as any soldier who has taken power. He could say with some pride that he had given his country years of stability after years of confusion and was trying to bring it closer to God.

Hopes of democracy still flickered, and Zia talked teasingly of elections, but the prospects for it withered away. Pakistan is, in many respects, a sad and disillusioned country, still unsure of its identity, casting its eye down a history of failures, its people having sought freedom and found confinement. A vignette of Pakistan can be seen on its national day when General Zia, wearing two sashes, takes the salute in Rawalpindi, as the regiments march past. Far, far away in the distance, watching from behind strong fences, are the people of Pakistan.

Islam and Pakistanization are applied like paint in the redecoration of a house. The image of Jinnah, the father of the nation, is being changed. His secularism is not referred to; certainly not his liking for Scotch. His portraits, which adorn every public building, are being changed to show him in the clothing of the country rather than the western suits he habitually wore. Civil servants were ordered, by presidential edict, out of western suits and into shalwar kameez.

National self-respect and identity cannot, however, be achieved through the imposition of loose trousers. Islam may not be enough. It was not enough to keep old Pakistan together, not enough to stop Muslim genocide in Bangladesh. Because Islam is an unreliable glue, the threat of India, and evidence of its beastliness to Muslims, are still an important unifier. Reports of communal rioting and murder in India are featured prominently in Pakistan newspapers, a reminder of what Muslims fled from and why there is a country called Pakistan.

Pakistan and India glare across their border. They roar about 'cartographic aggression' when they see maps, for no-one can delineate Kashmir in a way that pleases both. General Zia once sent Mrs Gandhi some mangoes, and she sent him some lychees; but worthwhile political fruits are unlikely to be harvested in this generation, imbued as it is by bitterness and suspicion. Young Pakistanis and Indians look forward to a better relationship, and the passage of time, the scabbing of wounds and educational and economic improvements may make this possible. An Indian told me how taken aback he was when his son asked him: 'Daddy, why was there partition?'

Bangladesh, the other segment of the partitioned subcontinent, is watery, grossly overpopulated, cyclone-prone. It was not destined, after wrenching from Pakistan, to enjoy much political stability. Its brief and turbulent history has been of coup and counter coup, assassinations, rivalry between civilians and the military, army mutinies and the assertion by the soldiers that since they fought for Bangladesh's independence they should play a large part in running the country. As in Pakistan there is a soldiers' belief that politicians are corrupt and incompetent, that civilians need discipline. Inevitably the president elected in 1981, following the murder of the previous president by soldiers, was removed by the army in 1982 because he said the military should stay in barracks. Bangladesh does not have the same sort of identity problem as Pakistan: it fought for freedom as the nation of the Bengalis.

The emergence of Bangladesh – the defeat of Pakistan in 1971, 'Pakistan cut to size' as it was put with some relish – made India feel more secure. Meanwhile the military balance in the Himalaya improved and the sensitivity of the border question diminished as China and India began to talk again, though with no short term prospect of an agreement. On a broader front India pursued its bedrock foreign policy of non-alignment; foreign affairs remained firmly in Mrs Gandhi's grasp, just as they had stayed in her father's. In 1982 she visited the United States after eleven years to improve a relationship that had gone sour through neglect and sometimes wilful misunderstanding. The Americans had seen India as being too close to Russia as well as irritatingly self-righteous, and had left India out of their deliberations, a considerable foreign policy lapse. Mrs Gandhi said with justification that the Russians had helped India when others had not; but that India was not under Soviet influence. She made a good impression on the Americans and went to Moscow after that to tell the Russians she had not been seduced by the Americans. But the nature of her visits to the Americans and Russians indicated that India, like Indira, preferred to be independent, and wanted nobody's arm round its shoulder.

11

Pudding

British footprints in the Indian sand

What good has England got by India? Little more, short-sighted cynics will be apt to say, than gorged livers, grass-widows, chudders, chutney and curry.

PUNCH, 1897

THE OXFORD Dictionary lists the word snooker as being of unknown origin. But there is a room in India where the game had its nativity. It has a handsome table over which, if you are fortunate, you may be permitted to lean and sight your cue almost as a kind of obeisance. The room's furnishings are redolent of leisured snookery evenings, joshing and cigar smoke, as the balls click, spin and glide across the faded baize. On the wall near the cue rack there are framed accounts and letters testifying to the origin of the game and its curious name.

The room is in the Ootacamund Club – the Ooty Club for short – almost a mile high above the broiling lowlands of southern India. Ooty is set sublimely in the blue-green Nilgiri Hills, likened by expatriates dreaming fondly of home to those of Devonshire or south Wales. It can be reached by a picturesque railway, or by a serpentine road on which signs warn that 'Sleeping While Driving Is Strictly Prohibited'. Up here in the club the ghosts of Ooty and their prey have inherited impressive silence. Mounted heads of jackals and tigers snarl across the empty polished floor at the sepia photographs of the men who hunted them long ago in a vanished age: the Capts, Cols, Brigs and Gens who created this extraordinary setting for respite from the rigours of running an empire.

What these men set store by was standards, a code of mannerly behaviour incorporating British ideas of discipline, breeding, ritual and seemliness. Standards are what the club maintains uncompromisingly today. There are fewer than 300 members now, Indian and European, and the club is frequently as deserted as a church, the servants padding about its spacious rooms with no-one to serve. In the village the few Britons who stayed on call it The Morgue. But the place is kept as it always was, polished like regimental silver. The flayed tigers and glum stags are dusted often. The gong in the grand portico shines, and brasswork and woodwork gleam, as if inspected daily by a sharp-eyed sergeant; and the air has the sniff of polish.

The club is a continuing memorial to the officers, planters and other pukka sahibs who made Ooty a stronghold for their caste. There are still no concessions to informality. A note in the complaints book, answering a member's grumble, says: 'Action has been taken to see that the butler shaves daily'. It is as if the men in the photographs on the walls, defiant, proud and some-times pop-eyed in their unsuitable throttling collars, keep an unrelenting eye on what goes on.

Thus it was that, when I arrived at the club and signed the register, a servant in crisp white rig gave a discreet Jeevesian cough and inserted into my view a printed card reminding gentle-men that under by-law 13 they could not dine in the dining room unless accoutred in jacket and tie: standards.

This presented a difficulty. Such clothing is not normally in my bag when I travel in India, other things being more practical and comfortable. Also I was in the club unintentionally. Two col-leagues and I had booked to stay in the Savoy Hotel in Ooty, and had had our bookings confirmed, but as is sometimes the way of things in India, this meant nothing. The rooms had been taken and the hotel was full. The manager shrugged and suggested we might try the club, and so we did. The secretary, a retired Indian colonel, was a model of courtesy. We were each given quarters with a bedroom, sitting room and a bathroom with empire plumbing large enough to kick off riding boots in. There was an allowance of firewood.

The question of dining in proper clothing was resolved by returning to the Savoy Hotel and persuading the manager that the least he could do was to lend us jackets and ties. The jacket sleeves ended a little below the elbow and the ties tended to the garish, but we nevertheless passed muster in the dining room that evening, and sat at a round table, the only inhabited island in the large wainscotted room. We consumed an excellent dinner of celery soup, baked fish, roast chicken and lemon tart, served on crested crockery by an immaculate and inscrutable servant.

It was such a decent meal that I could scarcely believe the note penned some years before in the complaints book: 'The peas contained live worms. This completely upset the appetite of the table.' And another irritable entry: 'No cheese again for lunch . . .'

After dinner there was a choice. There was the Men's Bar and the Mixed Bar, which once rang to the slap of thigh and the roar of laughter, and there was a third bar, Colonel Jago's Room, which has Colonel 'Bob' Jago's hunting crop mounted in a glass case, in the manner of a stuffed tench.

'Can't something be done about the fire in the Mixed Bar?' someone had grumbled in the complaints book. 'In windy weather the fire erupts clouds of smoke, covering members in a carpet of ash.'

There was also the magnificent main room, full of plump armchairs and sofas, and a display of British magazines like the *Field, Illustrated London News, Punch, Vogue* and *Blackwoods*; and, incongruously, a four-month-old copy of the *News of the World*, with its images of British prurience and dreariness. Another fine room is the reading room, a colonial treasure with a tiger skin, a carpet of character and the smell of old books. It has a large picture of Queen Victoria, Imp Ind, in her diamond jubilee year, and throne-like dark leather chairs split and honed by a century's trousers. It has a 19th-century *Encyclopaedia Britannica*, volumes from the Colonial and Home Library, ranks of bound periodicals like *Vanity Fair, Baily's Magazine* and the *Calcutta Review*; and books on the Afghan wars and similar campaigns.

In the Ooty club, of all places, a game of snooker is the proper *digestif*, for this is the source, the temple. The room itself is entered through a door properly fitted with a peephole, marked 'Wait for Stroke', so that you do not in ungentlemanly fashion cause distress at the table. The room has ceiling beams and white walls hung with the skulls and heads of nineteen beasts and with large pictures of the Defence of Rorke's Drift, the Retreat from Moscow, the Battle of Tel el-Kebir and the Charge of the Light Brigade. There are a number of wicker-backed chairs for spectators and a sturdy chair presented by Captain Winterbotham of the Madras Miners and Sappers, in 1875. There is a single table under a green fringed light.

According to the history and letters mounted on the wall, the game of snooker was thought up in the officers' mess at Jubbulpore, in central India, by a subaltern in the Devonshire Regiment called Neville, later Sir Neville, Chamberlain. During the long afternoons of the rainy season in 1875 he added variety to the game of black pool by experimenting with additional coloured balls. Six years later, after fighting the Afghans and being holed in action, he joined the staff of the Commander-in-Chief Madras, repairing in the hot weather to the cool Nilgiris and the pleasures of the club.

If snooker was conceived in Jubbulpore, it was born in Ooty. Here it was that the game was perfected by Neville Chamberlain and fellow officers and on these walls the rules were first posted. How the game got its name was related by Sir Neville himself in 1939. He recalled that while a game was in progress he was chatting with another officer about the Royal Military Academy at Woolwich and the fact that the first year cadets were known as snookers, apparently a corruption of the original soubriquet, neux. Sir Neville went on: 'One of our party failed to hole a coloured ball close to a corner pocket and I called out to him "Why, you're a regular snooker". I had to explain the definition of the word and to soothe the feelings of the culprit I added that we were all, so to speak, snookers at the game, so it would be very appropriate to call the game snooker. The assertion was adopted with enthusiasm. While it is correct to say that the game was first played at Jubbulpore in 1875 it never really made progress until played by members of the Ootacamund Club.'

The servant who materialized like a genie to frame the reds and mark the board, perhaps wincing at my shots, said rather sadly that the snooker room was little used now. For much of the year, and particularly outside the March-April season, the Ooty Club echoes to footfalls and is itself an echo. The Ootacamund Hunt, founded in 1847, and one of the most famous in all of British India, now only exists in a much reduced form. Pictures of its masters line the club walls. Fat scrapbooks evoke innumerable grand mornings on the rolling downs, and the library has the breeding records of the hounds. The hunt generally chased after jackals, vulpine enough for good sport.

The British built homes in Ootacamund with names like Harrow-on-the-Hill, Woodbriar, Lupin Cottage, Runnymede, Bideford and Sydenham, and they called the town centre Charing Cross, and one of the highest hills Snowdon. In St Stephen's churchyard are numerous graves of infants and young men and women, with their poignantly inscribed stones: something it has in common with other British churchyards in India.

Few British people have stayed on here. 'I suppose there are only a dozen of us left in Ooty now', Mrs Kathleen Carter said. 'I am an old lady and there is no point in going back. I belong here. I first came to India and Ceylon in 1920 and lived on tea plantations and had a grand life. Such fun we had in the old days up at the club, balls and parties and the place full of life. Tea parties and lunch parties, lectures and dancing, riding and golf. It's all gone now, and the club's heyday has passed. But Ooty is still lovely, and with the British gone the deer and the porcupine are coming back to the hills.'

Most of India's hill stations have an alien, transplanted quality. Just as London Bridge was transported brick by numbered brick to Arizona, so it seems, bits of Godalming and Weybridge had been taken to the hills above the dusty plains. Today they still have that artificial quality, and seem like film sets, so that one half expects ladies and subalterns to appear arm in arm, singing in some imperial musical for the cameras. In the cold weather they can be as bleak as an English seaside town in November, and have a mouldy air. The bed linen seems to have been taken off the line too soon, and aged retainers, not a day under eighty by the look of them, stumble across your room bearing a shovelful of blazing coals to start the fire. In the billiard rooms where broken cues lie in the racks, the balls are as cratered as the moon, and the charge for repairing a rip in the mildewed balding baize is 35 rupees a half inch.

Simla, the hot weather capital, government out of a suitcase, is today a dismal place (I admit I have seen it only in rain), a pain to itself, secured as it is to cliffs and hillsides, its houses joined by a tangle of steep, congested roads. It is a vista of corrugated iron roofs, like a town of church halls and scout huts. The deplorable reality of Simla is plain at first glance: it lived on the backs of pack animals and coolies who carried every last bottle of gin up the steep mountainsides. It is hard to imagine now that it was once a place of romance and delicious furtiveness as the grass-widowed Mrs Robinsons, whose husbands were sweating it out on the plains, put young officers through their social and terpsichorean paces.

As well as their Himalayan re-creation of mock-Tudor England, the British also left a small gastronomic legacy which may be sampled still, especially in the old hotels. It is, reduced to its bare bones (which it sometimes is), brown soup of indeterminate flavour, roast chicken which was on its feet shortly beforehand and cream caramel like an ice hockey puck. The saving grace of this cuisine, apart from the breakfast porridge, is the pudding. There are still many cooks in India, working in embassies and private homes, who carry in their heads the great pudding recipes of a bygone age. They learnt them from their fathers and grandfathers and their puddings are a direct link with the regimental mess tables, houses and nurseries of Victorian times. The volume and richness of these puddings make them more suitable for the cooler weather in northern India, so that the pulses of men who enjoy a proper pudding quicken a little as November approaches. India is, perhaps, the last refuge of the freshly made British pudding: in its land of origin it has been largely displaced by ready-made desserts from supermarkets and the cruel demands of dieting. In India belts may still be freed a notch for spotted dick, plum duff, jam rolypoly, upside down pudding, bread and butter pudding, treacle tart, apple crumble, fruit pudding, suet pudding and others, all accompanied by thick custard.

Such devastating desserts will become rarer, one imagines, as the line of handed-down knowledge grows more tenuous. (Indians, in any case, prefer ice cream, sugary titbits and sticky, highly-coloured concoctions.) The cannonball Christmas pudding may be fading away. Cooks will no longer pipe the words Merry Grimmus on Christmas cakes whose memorized ingredients are a link with Mrs Beeton.

There is some innocent enjoyment to be had from seeing English at work in India, just as there is in reading English menus in foreign restaurants. In common with many people using the putty language Indians roll and squeeze it to suit their needs and add some ingredients of their own. Indian English is much like the Queen's in content, but has a distinctive and piquant flavour of its own, a matter of words and phrases as well as accent, which, incidentally is nothing like any of the accents of Wales. I have already mentioned the Shady Motor Car Company in Bombay. I have also seen a Useless Engineering Company and, here and there, Ladies and Giants Tailors. Hindi phrase books are pleasurable sources of a certain English as well as being guides to a vanished age. My own Hindi book offers *Your breastplate is dirty*, *the lock of your musket is trusty*, and *A sepoy shot himself*. Evidently the book would have been more use to Clive, Curzon and Kipling. *Dig a mine, wash the barrel, show me the cock*, it instructs. *Undress me, Are your bowels regular?* and *I had four motions*. And also, a reminder that the British were keen hangers, *He will be hanged tomorrow*. The word for executioner appears in a list of professions which also includes beggar, king, jester, slave, tyrant and mace-bearer.

The books of ready-made letters-for-all-occasions, for which there is much demand, are also enjoyable and instructive, covering almost every predicament.

'I am very much sorry for the abusive language used by my son who has become a bit rustic on my negligence', goes an apology; and: 'I did not ignore you in the street on purpose. Perhaps you are aware that my eyesight is not as good as it should be.'

A suggested off-the-peg letter to a soldier reads: 'How do you face death-warranting situations during different campaigns? Is the feeling of death meaningful to you? May your spirits be always high and make you strong to strike hard whenever there is any infiltration over the border.' A letter to a newly-married girl says: 'You must have adjusted yourself in the family of your in-laws. Always give good impression and impact to them by your every action.' To which the girl might reply: 'They treat me just like their daughter. Really they are affectionate and fondling.' Lovers are advised to write: 'In spite of suffering pangs of love, we should commit our love daringly before our parents. How long can we hide true love from elders?' Slightly desperate swains are urged to copy out the words: 'I am waiting to have a rap in your sweet bosom.'

Some Indian English has a period flavour. The bereaved are always condoled and the prime minister is always felicitated on her birthday. Boxing fans are described as followers of the roped square, and criminals, unless identified as dacoits, are called miscreants. Hooligans and the like are called anti-social elements. They are never caught by the police, always nabbed; just as political parties always bag seats in elections. Criminals still carry swag and detectives are called sleuths. Women take, not lovers, but paramours and may be referred to as socialites. Eve-teasers are young men who annoy girls; hence the frequent headline Cops Nab Eve-teasers. Criminals do not flee. They abscond. Accounts of bus crashes often conclude with the words 'The driver is absconding'. This, incidentally, is unusually prudent, for a guilty driver in rural India runs the risk of being thrashed by survivors to within an inch of his death.

Canvas shoes, which the British call plimsolls and the Americans sneakers, are known as fleetfoots. And a man puts on wearunders before putting on his trousers. He calls his rupees bucks or chips and when he talks of the ordinary people, the public, he speaks of the common man. If he is a government minister he does not fly – he airdashes.

In finding one's way about cities and buildings it is important to know frontside from backside, partly because taxi drivers are often unfamiliar with the area they work in, and one directs them by saying: 'Turn rightside, now leftside, here's backside.'

As well as their language, the only linguistic common ground in a country which has fifteen official languages, the British left a delight in cricket, a form of theatre whose rituals exert a strong appeal, a liking for golf, a love of bureaucracy, majestic lavatories, bagpipe music, a fondness for good whisky, a military tradition and pleasure in soldierly things, clubs, bridge, ladies' lunch parties, democratic ideas, puddings, some magnificent colonial buildings, churches, crumbling gravestones and progeny.

There remains, too, a love-hate relationship between the British and Indians. The obverse of a certain admiration is a residual sensitivity and bitterness which emerges in occasional recitations of colonial wrongs and reminders of the long struggle to throw off the yoke.

The *Hindustan Times* exemplified some of this feeling in an editorial, headlined 'British Intolerance', which said tartly: 'Perhaps without an empire and far-flung outposts to lord over, the British have reverted to what they basically are – a small, little people with small, little minds, inhabiting a small, little island in the Atlantic.'

The reason for this particular jab was a report that an Indian theatre group had been badly treated by customs officers at London airport. Reports of such incidents are always featured prominently in Indian newspapers, and Indians are enraged by them. In any other country Indians endure the entry procedures with equanimity. But Britain is expected to be different. Some

Indian parliamentarians whose briefcases were searched, as everyone else's are, in the Palace of Westminster, complained to the Indian press that they had been thus humiliated, and the press gave prominence to their complaints. The short-lived, isolated and foolish British procedure of checking the virginity of certain immigrant girls caused an uproar in India, combining as it did the potent ingredients of colonial echoes, race, oppression and sex.

'One is led to wonder', the *Hindustan Times* continued, 'whether the United Kingdom government and its agencies have not discarded even the pretence of fair play that was once the hallmark of the British. The race phobia that was once believed to be the preserve of pressure groups seems more and more to represent the thinking of Britons as a whole in which Whitehall willy-nilly acquiesces. It must be galling to the British that their colonial impulse to civilize the heathen world has ended up with the benighted heathens in their midst – the Indian and Pakistani immigrants – best exemplifying the qualities of thrift, hard work and the never-say-die attitude in the face of adversity that the British made famous in their colonial exploits.'

The small, little Briton, the colonial overlord, the rapacious exploiter of India's wealth, the civilized chap, the fairminded administrator and lawgiver, are all elements in the tangle of emotions Indians feel about a people and a culture that, with some reservations and exceptions, they admire. It still matters deeply to Indians how they are written about and represented in Britain. They are angered when their scandals and warts, which they stridently criticize at home, are exposed abroad. There is an almost desperate concern for image, for these are people who take themselves seriously and stand on their dignity. There is a post-colonial sensitivity, fierce pride, assertive independence, an insistence on the due their size, importance and achievements demand.

Perhaps the passage of time will lead to a cutaneous thickening, but the fact remains that Indians expect the British to behave better than any other people in the world . . . including Indians themselves. The idealized Brit is decent, a man of his word, above all the inventor and guardian of the idea of fair play. These, after all, were the qualities that the shrewd Mahatma Gandhi perceived in the British and which he exploited in persuading them to quit a land that was not theirs.

Other nationalities are expected to be beastly. But if the British conduct themselves in anything less than a gentlemanly and pukka fashion Indians feel slighted and wounded. In spite of – and because of – all that passed between them in the 150-odd years that they lived together, Indians believe that manners makyth British man; and this is part of an enduring belief in a special relationship. It would be surprising if there were not one between these two peoples, considering their many shared interests, their close understanding of subtle matters like caste, class and deference; and the length of their extraordinary, mutually rewarding and fascinating cohabitation.

Index